EUROPEAN EVOLUTIONS
AND
INTERNATIONAL LAW

Dr. Ion Diaconu

EUROPEAN EVOLUTIONS

AND

INTERNATIONAL LAW

Quo Vadis, Europe?

Dr. Ion Diaconu

Table of Contents

FORWARD .... - 6 -

CHAPTER I - JUS COGENS - as REFLECTED by the EUROPEAN PRACTICE .... - 9 -

   Abstract .... - 9 -

   Introduction 10

   SECTION I - Evolution of opinions and practice before the 1969 Convention on the law of treaties. .... - 12 -

   SECTION II - Evolution of practice and concepts after the Vienna Convention .... - 19 -

   SECTION III - International and internal judicial practice concerning mainly Europe .... - 30 -

CHAPTER II - AGAIN ABOUT the NON-USE OF FORCE and OF THE THREAT TO USE FORCE .... - 45 -

   Abstract .... - 45 -

   SECTION I – Legal Framework in Force .... - 46 -

   SECTION II – Consideration of Recent Cases of Armed Intervention on the Territory of other States .... - 53 -

CHAPTER III - EUROPEAN UNION and INTERNATIONAL LAW .... - 72 -

   Abstract .... - 73 -

   Introduction .... - 74 -

SECTION I - European Union and norms on human rights and freedoms .... - 77 -

SECTION II - Concerns for human rights in a situation of economic and financial crisis. .... - 81 -

SECTION III - European Union and the crisis of illegal migration. .... - 89 -

SECTION IV – European Union and European agreements in the field of environment. .... - 96 -

SECTION V - Position with regard to international law in general. .... - 101 -

CHAPTER IV - FREEDOM of EXPRESSION and OPINION-EVOLUTIONS and CONCERNS at the EUROPEAN LEVEL ..... - 108 -

Abstract .... - 108 -

SECTION I - International and regional regulations .... - 109 -

SECTION II - Exclusion *de plano* by the European Court of Human Rights of the Protection, for Abuse of the Freedom of Expression. .... - 118 -

SECTION III - Protection of the freedom of expression and of information according to the decisions of the ECHR-general aspects. .... - 125 -

SECTION IV - Protection related to specific professions or public functions. .... - 130 -

CHAPTER V - ECONOMIC, SOCIAL and CULTURAL RIGHTS on the agenda of EUROPEAN and INTERNATIONAL JURISDICTIONS .... - 160 -

Abstract .... - 160 -

Introduction ....- 161 -

SECTION I - Regional courts ....- 168 -

   European Court of Human Rights (ECHR). ....- 168 -

   European Court of Justice of the European Union (ECJ).- 174 -

   Inter-American and African courts on human rights. ..... - 178 -

   SECTION II - Opinions of quasi-jurisdictional bodies concerning economic, social and cultural rights. ....- 179 -

   SECTION III - Additional Protocol to the Covenant on economic, social and cultural rights ....- 188 -

CHAPTER VI - EUROPE, MIGRATION and the RIGHT to ASYLUM ....- 202 -

   Abstract ....- 202 -

   Introduction ....- 203 -

   SECTION I -The Court of Justice of EU ....- 213 -

   SECTION II -The European Court of Human Rights. .... - 232 -

CHAPTER VII – JURISDICTIONAL IMMUNITY of STATES before EUROPEAN JURISDICTIONS ....- 271 -

   Abstract ....- 271 -

   Introduction ....- 272 -

   SECTION I – Applicable law ....- 274 -

   SECTION II - Immunity of jurisdiction for acts committed in connection with the Second World War.............................- 277 -

   SECTION III - Other cases ....- 288 -

CONCLUSIONS ....- 299 -

FORWARD

This book is about Europe, about its place in the world from the point of view of the rule of law. Not because I would think or believe that international law is less known or respected in Europe than on other continents, nor that I would think that norms concerning the protection of human rights or of the environment are less observed than elsewhere.

On the contrary; everybody knows that Europe adopted norms and created institutions that are more advanced than those of the general international law, again in the fields of the protection of human rights, of the protection of environment and of social and humanitarian issues as a whole.

But this does not prevent an analyst to see what the loopholes and deficiencies are. Because I want to see that norms of international law, to the adoption of which Europe and the Europeans took the initiative and substantially contributed, are fully applied in Europe, and that respect of these norms prevails over power or other interests.

Therefore, the chapters of this book try to reveal the evolutions of positions in Europe, mainly in the judiciary, with regard to events and situations from the point of view of principles and norms of international law. The analysis is focused mainly on the decisions of the judiciary in Europe taken by the two regional courts-the European Court of Human Rights (ECHR) and the Court of Justice of the European Union, as well as by the national courts of European States, considering that they are indicative of the extent to which Europe places itself with regard to these principles and norms.

In some fields, the existence of two regional courts and two systems of norms and institutions, one within the Council of Europe, the other one within the European Union (namely the EU norms and the related jurisprudence with regard to human rights, with their implications in other fields), offers not only different solutions of similar cases, but also different approaches, which leads to uncertainties and misunderstandings. There is also a difference in the systems, as ECHR receives individual petitions from persons under the jurisdiction of States parties to the 1950 Convention (including the (still) 28 member States of the EU) alleging violations of the rights enunciated in this Convention, while CJEU examines such allegations only under prejudicial questions submitted to it by national courts of member States.

Of course, there are mostly common elements in the evolutions and approaches in Europe, as well as between evolutions in Europe and in other parts of the world with regard to institutions and norms of international law. They have the same basic sources-from Illuminists, to the democratic revolutions in Europe in the XIX-th century and the movements of liberation and independence in all parts of the world, then to the Charter of the United Nations, the Universal Declaration of Human Rights and the two Covenants on human rights, to which all European States and most other States are parties.

The book reflects both the common and different approaches and solutions, as well as efforts and trends to bring them closer and to ensure legal certainty.

To summarize, there is no uniformity and coherence with regard to norms applied in Europe and there are aspects of departure from general norms of international law. Why these evolutions in Europe, which tend to differentiate it from the general institutions and norms of international law? What is this about? Lack of confidence in the rules applied to the world system? Search for being different and original? Specific interests which would require some specific rules? To what extent they could justify different solutions on some issues, including less protection of human rights for Europeans and for people from other https://tsw.createspace.com/title/9179171/setup/book_interiorcount ries coming in contact with Europe? It is up to the member States of the EU and of the Council of Europe to find ways and means to determine more uniformity in the application of the rule of law in Europe and to stay as close as possible to the rules of general international law.

The Author

CHAPTER I - JUS COGENS - as REFLECTED by the EUROPEAN PRACTICE

Abstract

Jus Cogens -imperative norms of the general international law- is a relatively new concept in international law, launched as part of the codification of the law of treaties and finalized substantially by the 1969 Convention on the law of treaties. Received with some coldness by the analysts in the beginning, it was gradually accepted and promoted by decisions of international and internal courts of justice, even if sometimes under other names. It was also given more substance by the examples of imperative norms enounced, particularly from the field of human rights-the interdiction of genocide, of torture, of racial discrimination, of slavery, but also from the principles of international law-the non-use of force and of threat to force, the right of peoples to self-determination.

The European judiciary-the two regional courts and the internal courts of many States- also reflected increasingly the existence and the effects of imperative norms in relations between European States and to the benefit of individuals affected by alleged violation of their rights..

The concept was also extended to cover unilateral acts meant to create international obligations, reservations to treaties intended to lead to derogations from imperative norms, as well as local and regional customary norms that could try to establish legal derogatory regimes.

Key words: jus cogens, imperative norms, derogatory treaties, obligations *erga omnes*, peremptory norms, reservations to treaties, unilateral acts, customary norms, immunity of jurisdiction of States

Introduction

During the last years, international bodies, representatives of States and international and internal courts refer to the existence of imperative norms of international law[1], give examples of such norms and found their decisions on norms considered imperative.

As we know, the first regulation on this subject was enounced in the 1969 Convention on the law of treaties, the legal instrument elaborated by the International Law Commission (ILC) in the exercise of its mission of codification and progressive development of international law, adopted by the Diplomatic Conference convened in Vienna in 1967 and 1969. Nevertheless, international practice referred also before the Conference to norms

---

[1] A first book on this issue was written as a doctorate thesis, on the basis of the documentation available in the 1960-ies, by a Romanian student at the Institute of High University Studies of Geneva, under the coordination of professors Paul Guggenheim, Michel Virally, Khristina Marek and Denise Bindschedler, defended in 1971. Other works on the subject were published mainly after 1990, taking into account the evolution of the international practice.

from which States should not derogate in their mutual relations, although using different concepts[2].

It is at present generally accepted that there are imperative norms in international law, although there is no agreement on the norms which have this character, neither on criteria to determine them, nor on their effects in different fields and different institutions of international law. International and internal courts recognize the existence of norms of jus cogens and give examples of such norms, most often the interdiction of genocide, of torture and seldom of slavery, of racial discrimination, of the prohibition of the use of force and threat to force and the right of peoples to self-determination or of norms of humanitarian law-without justifying their choice, sometimes incidentally, without advancing the consequences of such norms or retaining different consequences. The International Law Commission noted in 2001 that „the concept of peremptory norms of general international law is recognized in international practice, in the jurisprudence of international and national courts and tribunals and in legal doctrine"[3].

Almost without exception, the specialized doctrine accepts the existence of imperative norms (jus cogens) in international

---

[2] Both the international treaties and the jurisdictional practice reflected undetakings and opinion according to which States could not derogate from some norms in their relation. An extended presentation of such undertakings and opinions by Ion Diaconu, Imperative norms in international law (jus cogens), Editing House of the Academy of Romania, 1977, pp. 162-178.

[3] ILC Commentaries to Draft Articles on Responsibility of States for International Wrongful Acts, Yearbook of ILC, 2001, vol. II, part. 2, p. 282.

law[4]. Even such authors who expressed doubts with regard to the concept of jus cogens itself, accepted that the prohibition of the use of force and of threat to force is an imperative norm from which States cannot derogate in their mutual relations and that jus cogens applies not only with regard to derogatory treaties, but also to unilateral acts in violation of such norms[5].

SECTION I - Evolution of opinions and practice before the 1969 Convention on the law of treaties

With regard to slavery and the slave trade, that the international community of the time wanted to eliminate, the Assembly of the League of Nations adopted on 25 September 1926 the Convention on slavery which expressed the objective of completely suppressing the slavery under all its forms, progressively and as soon as possible. In its art. 3 the Convention stipulated that contracting parties may conclude between them such special arrangements which, in view of their particular situation, seem adequate to lead as soon as possible to the complete the

---

[4] Among the numerous studies on this issue, we note Grigore Geamanu, Jus Cogens in contemporary international law, in Romanian Revue of international studies, 1967, pp. 87 and foll; Ion Diaconu, Imperative norms in international law, 1977, Ed. House of the Romanian Academy; Antonio Gomez Robledo, Le Jus Cogens international, sa genese, sa nature, ses fonctions, in RCADI, 1981, tome 172; Lauri Hannikainen, Peremptory Norms(Jus Cogens) in International Law, Ed. L. Kustannus, Helsinki, 1988; Maurizio Ragazzi, The concept of international obligations Erga Omnes, Ed. Clarendon Oxford Press, 1997; a divergent opinion, quite isolated, Michael J. Glennon, De l'absurdité du droit impératif (jus cogens), în RGDIP, 2006, nr. 3.

[5] Olivier Deleau, La position française à la Conférence de Vienne sur le droit des traités, in AFDI, 1969, pp. 7-23.

elimination of slavery, „but without derogating from the principles established therein".

The Suplementary Convention adoptedd by the United Nations on 7 September 1956 maintained the text of article 3 of 1926 and declared abolished slavery under all its forms asking States parties to take all measures for that purpose. This reflects the constant preoccupation of States to forbid agreements contrary to the prohibition of slavery under all its forms[6]. The Convention of 1982 on the law of the sea provides for the obligation of States to take effective measures to prevent and suppress the transport of slaves by ships under their flag; according to the 1966 Covenant on civil and political rights slavery, slave-trade and servitude are forbidden and this constitutes a norm from which no derogation is admitted.

With regard to the non-use of force and of threat to force, one has to mention the General Treaty on the renonciation to war, adopted within the League of Nations on 27 August 1928 (called also Paris Pact or Briand Kellogg Pact), according to which Contracting parties solemnly declared that they condemn, on behalf of their peoples, the resorting to war in order to solve international conflicts and that they renounce to war in their mutual relations as an instrument of national policy. The United Nations Charter of San Francisco, signed on 26 June 1945, reflecting the evolution of the international practice and preoccupations during the inter-war period and mainly during the Second World War, stipulates in art. 2 paragr. 4, in the Chapter „Purposes and Principles", that „All Members shall refrain in their international relations form the threat or use of force against the territorial

---

[6] Text in RTSN, vol LX, pp. 254 and foll.

integrity and political independance of any state, or in any other manner inconsistent with the Purposes of the United Nations". Already the Convention signed on 9 August 1945 on the judgment of war criminals and the Statute of the Military Tribunal of Nurnberg (confirmed by the resolution nr. 95(I) of 11 December 1946 of the UN General Assembly) qualified the war of aggression as the most serious of international crimes[7].

This principle was reaffirmed in most of the political documents, regional or bilateral, signed after the adoption of the Charter and in numerous documents adopted within the United Nations. One has to mention also art. 52 of the Charter, concerning regional arrangements dealing with such matters relating to the maintenance of international peace and security as appropriate for regional action, according to which such arrangements and their activity are consistent with the Purposes and Principles of the United Nations. The purpose followed was clear: to exclude at the regional level derogatory regimes from the Charter principles, mainly from the non-use of force or the threat to force[8].

As for the jurisprudence before the adoption of the Convention on the law of treaties, the first decision mentioned usually is the Advisory Opinion of the International Court of Justice of 1951 on reservations to the Convention on the Prevention and Punishment of the Crime of Genocide of 1948. This Advisory Opinion gives expression to the concept of imperative norms even if it is in different words. First of all, the

---

[7] Texts in Procès des grands criminels de guerre devant le Tribunal Militaire International, Nurnberg, 14 novembre 1945-1 octobre 1946, Nurnberg, 1947, pp. 11-19, 94.

[8] On this issue J. M. Yepes, Les accords régionaux et le droit international, in RCADI, 1947, vol. 71, pp. 252-253.

Court reminds the origins of the Convention and the intention of the United Nations to condemn and punish the crime of genocide which is"contrary at the same time to the moral law and to the spirit and purposes of the United Nations". Then it affirms that this conception leads to two consequences: the first, according to which „the principles at the basis of the Convention are recognized by the civilised nations as binding upon States even outside of any conventional relationship" and the second, consisting in „the universal character of the condemnation of genocide and of the cooperation necessary to free the world of this odios scourge". The Court concludes that both the General Assembly and Contracting Parties wanted this Convention „as one of effectively universal applicaion" and that States have „all and each of them a common interest, that of safeguarding the higher purposes which are the raison d'ètre of the Convention"[9].

In the Memorandum submitted to the International Law Commission on international crimes, the proposal was made to include, under the title „Threat to the illegal use of force and preparation of such use", as an international crime, „the conclusion of treaties with an aggressive purpose or any arrangement to ensure assistance to another State, in a situation when it would commit an aggression"[10].

In some decisions, the International Court does not mention expressly the imperative character of the norms of international law it has in vue, but uses other concepts where it underlines the importance of such norms as compared to others and gives them more weight in its consideration. For instance, in its

---

[9] ICJ, Advisory Opinion, Recueil 1951, p. 23.
[10] Memorandum presented by Vespassian Pella, doc. Yearbook of ILC, 1950, vol. II, p. 335.

decision in the Corfu Channel case, the Court referred to „elementary considerations of humanity which are even more absolute in time of peace than in time of war"[11]. In the decision Barcelona Traction, the Court refers to the existence of particularly important norms in international law and refers to „obligations which, in the contemporary law, derive for example from the prohibition of acts of aggression and of genocide, as well as from principles and morms concerning fundamental rights of the human person, including protection against slavery and racial discrimination"[12].

In a decision on a different matter, the Court declares that it does not want to approach the issue of jus cogens; neverthelles, it admits that States can derogate from norms of international law through an agreement in special cases or between some parties. At the same time, the Court affirms that in the field of the delimitation of continental shelf international law does not contain any imperative norm and authorises resorting to different principles or methods, as appropriate[13]. Thus, the Court recognizes that in other fields there may be imperative norms of international law from which States should not derogate.

In one of its decisions, the Military Tribunal of Nurnberg declared null and void „as contrary to good moeurs" an agreement between Nazi Germany and the authorities of Vichy concerning the obligation of French war prisoners to work in the German weapons

---

[11] Corfu Channel case, UK. V. Albania, ICJ Reports, 1949, p. 22.
[12] Case Barcelona Traction, Light and Power Company, Limited, Belgium v. Spain, Second Phase, ICJ Reports, 1970, p. 32.
[13] ICJ, Reports, Dispute on the Continental shelf of the North Sea, 1969, p. 42.

factories[14]. The Tribunal refers to the rules and customs of war which were applicable as France and Germany were in a state of war. Without examining the significance of the concept of good moeurs in international law at the end of the Second World War, one has to note that humanitarial law contained a rule according to which prisoners of war could not be obliged to act against their country, including to work for the war industry of the ennemy.

In their individual or dissident opinions, judges of international courts referred in many cases to „provisions which formed an essential part of the reglementation of peace and were adopted …in the interest of the European political order"[15], to a field of jus cogens which would be created by the League of Nations and would have as effect that when States convene on some legal rules and agree that they cannot be modified by some of them, any act in contradiction with this agreement is null and void[16], to the exsitence of principles of „public international order" which have an imperative character and universal value[17], to standards of the international community to which provisions of

---

[14] Trials of War Criminals before the Nurnberg Military Tribunals (under Control Council Law no. 10), vol IX, Washington, 1950, p 1395.

[15] Judge Anzilotti, individual opinion to the Advisory Opinion of the Permanent Court of International Justice on the Customs regime between Germany and Austria, Publications, Series A/B, nr. 41, p. 37

[16] Judge Schucking, dissident opinion to the decision of the Permanent Court in the case Oscar Chinn, Publications, Serie A/B, nr. 63, pp. 149-150

[17] Judge Moreno Quintana, individual opinion to the decision of the International Court of Justice of 1958 on the dispute concerning - The application of the 1902 Convention on the trusteeship of minors, ICJ Report, 1958, p. 106.

previous treaties cannot be opposed[18], to the possibility to derogate from a general norm which does not belong to jus cogens and to have the respective conventional derogatory relationships accepted as valid (*per a contrario* recognizing the different effect of imperative norms)[19].

Although it is a decison of an internal court, it seems useful to refer to a decision of the Supreme Constitutional Court of the Federal Republic of Germany of 7 Aprilie 1965, in a case where a Swiss company contested the legality of taxes imposed by law to nationals and foreigners without distinction in order to create a fund for paying compensations to victims of war and to Germans expelled from other countries. The application of the law imposing that tax to Swiss national citizens was accepted through a Convention between Germany and Switzerland of 1952. The Swiss company invoked, among others, that this Convention was contrary to a general norm of international law according to which foreigners cannot be obliged to contribute to creating income for executing obligations resulting from a war. The Court retained that international customary law is essentially *jus dispositivum* and that only some legal elementary principles can be considered norms which cannot be replaced by treaty: the quality of such peremptory norms can be attributed only to such legal norms that are firmly entranched in the legal conviction of the community of nations and are indispensable for the existence of international law as an

---

[18] Dissident opinions of judges Jessup and Padillia Nervo to the decision of the International Court of Justice of 1966 in the dispute on the South-West African, ICJ, Report, 1966, pp. 440-441, 467-468, 470.

[19] Dissident opinions of judges Lachs and Sorensen in connection with decisions on the Continental shelf of the Northern Sea, ICJ Report, 1969, pp. 229 and 248.

international legal order, and whose respect can be requested by all members of the international community[20]. And the Court concluded that the rule according to which foreigners cannot be obliged to contribute to the execution of obligations of war does not have such a character.

SECTION II - Evolution of practice and concepts after the Vienna Convention

After the UN Conference of codification of the law of treaties and the adoption of the Vienna Convention in 1969, the international practice became gradually more extensive and more clear with regard to the concept and the exsitence of imperatrive norms in international law.

In its Advisory Opinion in the case Legality of the threat and use of nuclear weapons, the Court described many of the norms of humanitarian law as „intransgressible principles of international customary law"[21]. In the Advisory Opinion on Legal Consequences of the Construction of a Wall in the Occupied Palestinian Territory[22], the Court affirms that „This construction, which is added to measures taken previuosly, raises ...a serious

---

[20] Text of the decision and extensive presentation by Stefan Riesenfeld, Jus dispositivum and jus cogens in international law; in the light of a recent decision of the German Supreme Constitutional Court, Editorial Comment, in AJIL, 1966, vol. 60, p. 511, 515.

[21] ICJ Reports, 1996, p. 257, para. 79. The same qualification is given in the case Bosnia and Herzegovina v. Serbia and Montenegro, Application of the Convention on genocide, judgment of 26 February 2007, ICJ Reports, 2007, p. 161.

[22] Legal Consequences of the Construction ...., ICJ Reports 2004, p. 136.

obstacle to the exercise by the Palestinian people of its right to self-determination" and by this violates the obligation of Israel to respect this right[23]. Noting that the construction of the wall violates also human rights provided for in the 1966 Covenant, the Court underlines that „ the State of Israel has to respect the obligation incumbent to it to respect the right to self-determination of the Palestinian people and obligations to which it is compelled through international humanitarian law and international law concerning human rights"[24].

Taking into account this evolution, in the case „Armed activities on the territory of Congo" (R.D. of Congo v. Rwanda), where Congo tried to convince the judges that the Court has legal competence to examine disputes on the application of the Convention of 1948 on genocide (in order to reject the reservation of Rwanda to the article of the Convention concerning the jurisdiction of the Court on disputes with regard to its application), the International Court of Justice made the distinction between imperative norms of general international law (jus cogens) and those concerning its competence. The Court affirmed that the prohibition of genocide has undoubtedly an imperative character, which both States in dispute accepted, while its competence is based on the consent of parties, which is absent due to the reservation of Rwanda[25]. Analysts appreciate that thereby the Court accepted finally and explicitely the existence of imperative norms

---

[23] ICJ, Reports; 2004, para. 122; extensively on this case, Phillippe Weckel, Chronique de jurisprudence internationale, in RGDIP, nr. 4/2004, pp. 1017-1036.
[24] Ibidem, para. 149.
[25] ICJ Reports, 2006, para. 64.

in international law[26]. In several cases, the International Court affirmed the *erga omnes* opposability of the right of peoples to self-determination, recalling that this principle is proclaimed by the UN Charter and developed in the Covenant on civil and political rights of 1966[27].

In the case called *aut dedere aut judicare*, the Court affirmed expressly that the prohibition of torture is part of international customary law and it has become a peremptory norm (jus cogens). It had to consider the request of Belgium to Senegal, to prosecute or to extradite Hissene Habré, the former head of State of Tchad, refugiated in Senegal, for acts of torture and other crimes committed during his violent reign in the 1980-ies in violation of the Convention against torture of 1984. The Court admitted the request of Belgium[28] and Senegal created Extraordinary African Chambers of its courts in order to prosecute crimes committed in Tchad between 1982-1990, where a procedure against Hissène Habré began in 2015[29].

In the more recent case on States immunity of jurisdiction, where the immunity of jurisdiction of State before the courts of another State was invoked, the International Court retained that, by submitting Germany to the jurisdiction of its courts, Italy violated

---

[26] Phillippe Weckel, Guillaume Aréou, Chronique de jurisprudence internationale, Cour Internationale de Justice, in RGDIP nr. 3/2006, pp. 487-494.

[27] Advisory Opinions on Namibia (ICJ Reports 1971) and Western Sahara (ICJ Reports 1975); decision on Western Timor (Portugal v. Australia), Recueil CIJ, 1995, para. 88.

[28] Obligation to Prosecute or extradite, Belgium v. Senegal, ICJ Reports 2012, decision of 20 July 2012, p. 422.

[29] Presentation by Ion Diaconu, Human Rights' Impact in International Law, 2017, Amazon, Create Space, pp. 238-239.

the customary law on sovereign immunity of States and rejected Italy's arguments to the contrary. The Court did not accept arguments according to which immunity of jurisdiction was not applicable if the State was responsible of crimes of war and crimes against humanity[30]. The Court recognized the existence of norms of jus cogens, but did not accept that they set aside the immunity of jurisdiction of States. In a different case concerning the immunity of the foreign minister of D. R. of Congo in Belgium, who was under prosecution for crimes against humanity and crimes of war under the Conventions of 1949 of Geneva, Belgium held that such crimes are offending jus cogens. Without contesting the accusation by Belgium, the Court accepted the immunity of jurisdiction of the Congolese minister as an expression of the State's immunity[31].

In its Advisory Opinion on the Unilateral Declaration of Independence in Respect of Kosovo, the International Court referred to „egregious violations of norms of general international law, in particular those of peremptory character (jus cogens)"[32].

Similarly, in the case „Diplomatic and consular personnel of USA in Tehran", the Court referred to the „fundamental character of the principle of inviolability" of the person of the diplomatic agent and of the premisses of diplomatic missions and referred to the obligation incumbent upon the Iranian government as one having an „imperative character"[33].

---

[30] Germany v. Italy, ICJ Reports, decision of 3 Februsry 2012.
[31] The case Arrest Warrant of 11 April 2000, decision of 14 February 2012, ICJ Reports, 2002.
[32] Advisory Opinion on Accordance with International Law of the Unilateral Declaration of Independence in Respect of Kosovo, Advisori Opinion, ICJ Reports, 2010, p. 403.
[33] ICJ, Reports, 1980, paras.86 and 91.

In many other more recent cases, judges took a clear stand in their individual or dissident opinions in favour of imperative norms in international law, giving examples of such norms and underlining what should be their consequences in international law[34].

The 1969 Convention looks at the imperative norms only from the point of view of treaties and focuses on the effect of these norms on such treaties, which become void from the beginning or when they would derogate from imperative norms accepted after their conclusion. Other international instruments, adopted subsequently also as a result of the activity of codification of ILC, refer to effects of imperative norms on unilateral acts of States, on reservations to multilateral treaties as well as in the field of international responsibility of States and of international organizations for harmful acts; this extends the scope of imperative norms and their impact in international law. In some cases considered by national courts of different States, with regard to civilian responsibility of States for damages produced to citizens of other States in the context of armed conflicts, the relationship between imperative norms of international law protecting human rights and the State immunity is also approached.

The voidness of conventional instruments in conflict with imperative norms is, consequently, not the only effect of the application of these norms. With regard to treaties in conflict with imperative norms, the concept of jus cogens is rather a preventive weapon, because cases of treaties derogating from such norms are not known in practice after the adoption of the Vienna

---

[34] As presented in by Dire Tladi in his second Report on imperative norms in international law, doc A/CN.4/706 of 16 March 2017, pp. 9-14, 21-22, 35, 39, 41-42.

Convention. States would rather resort to unilateral acts of violation of such norms than to conclude derogatory agreements which would raise a strong opposition from the majority of States. The international practice shows that violations of imperative norms take place mainly through unilateral acts of some States, which are harmful acts subject to State responsibility[35]. The International Law Commission adopted in 2006 Guiding Principles concerning unilateral statements of States susceptible to create international obligations, which were submitted to the UN General Assembly. The document adopted affirms from the beginning that statements made public through which a State manifests its will to assume an obligation have the effect to create legal obligations[36]. After enunciating the conditions of form to be fulfilled by such acts, the Guiding Principles affirm that a unilateral declaration which is in conflict with an imperative norm of international law is void. In its decision on the case „Armed activities on the territory of Congo", the International Court of Justice did not exclude the possibility to invalidate a unilateral declaration of the State of Rwanda as being in conflict with an imperative norm, but appreciated that it was not the case[37].

---

[35] Report of the International Law Commission on international responsibility of States for harmful acts, doc. Supppl. No. 10(A/56/10), of which the UN General Assembly took note by its resolution No. 56/83, adopted on 12 December 2001.

[36] On this subject, Guiding Principles concerning unilateral statements of States, susceptible to create international obligations, 2006, adopted by the International Law Commission, doc. A/66/10; also, Ion Diaconu, Human Rights' Impact in International Law, Selected Issues, 2017, Amazon, Create Space, pp. 53-54 and 58-59.

[37] R.D. Congo v. Rwanda, Jurisdiction and Admissibility, ICJ Report 2002, para. 69.

There is also an important practice according to which reservations to norms of international treaties which have an imperative character are not permitted, because they create also derogatory regimes from imperative norms. Consequently, a reservation to a provision of a multilateral treaty giving expression to such a norm would be in conflict with the object and the purpose of the treaty. On this issue, the Human Rights Committee affirms in its General Comment nr. 24 of 1994 that „The provisions of the Covenant which represent customary international law (and *a fortiori* those who have the character of imperative norms) cannot make the object of reservations"[38]. In its General Comment, the Human Rights Committee affirms that a State cannot reserve its right to practice slavery or torture, to subject persons to cruel, inhuman or degrading treatment, to deprive them arbitrarily of life, to arrest and detain them arbitrarily, to deny their right to the freedom of thought, conscience and religion and others. Nevertheless, the Committee recognizes that there is no automatic corelation between reservations which are contrary to the object and purpose of a treaty and those concerning norms from which States cannot derogate, that is imperative norms, and affirms expressly that the prohibition of torture and depriving arbitrarily of life a person are imperative norms[39].

In 2011, in its final report, the Commission adopted Guideliness with regard to the Practice of Reservations to Treaties,

---

[38] Human Rights Committee, General Comment no. 24/1994, doc. HRI/GEN/1/Rev. 9(vol. I), pp. 249-250.

[39] Similarly, by Su Wei, Reservations to treaties and some practical issues, în Asian Yearbook of International Law, vol. 7, 1999, p. 133.

submitted to the UN General Assembly[40], where it maintains its opinion expressed in the preliminary report. The Commission enunciates the basic rule, according to which reservations in conflict with the object and the purpose of a treaty are not permitted, and explains that this means affecting an important element of the treaty which is essential in its general economy and the raison d'être of the treaty.

The Guideliness affirm that a reservation to a provision of a treaty which gives expression to an impetrative norm of the general international law (jus cogens) does not affect the binding character of that provision, which will continue to apply between the reserving State and other States or international organizations. It is also stated that a reservation cannot exclude or modify the legal effect of a treaty in a manner contrary to an imperative norm. Although it is said that reservations are allowed to customary norms provided for in the treaties, it is outlined that reservations are not allowed to provisions of a treaty concerning human rights from which derogations are not admitted in any circumstances, except the case when the reservation is compatible with the essential rights and obligations resulting from the treaty. Without underlining in particular the place of imperative norms in the context of reservations to treaties, the Guideliness affirm with clarity the inadmissibility of reservations to those provisions of treaties which enunciate imperative norms.

Some court decisions and some analysts launched a discussion on the validity of reservations to those provisions of

---

[40] A first report, Preliminary Conclusions with regard to reservations to multilateral normative treaties, including those on human rights, Gen. Ass., Doc. Fifty-second session, Suppl. No. 10(A/52/10); the last report, doc. A/CN.4/647 of 26 May 2011.

treaties concerning compulsory jurisdiction of the International Court of Justice or the competence of other bodies to receive and consider individual claims on violations of human rights, mainly in cases where a violation of an imperative norm is invoked[41]. At the European level, ECHR affirmed in the case Belilos, in the name of European public order, the lack of validity of the declaration by Switzerland having the effect of a reservation, considered contrary to the 1950 Convention; in 1995, in the case Loisidou, ECHR affirmed the lack of validity of restrictions *ratione loci* and *ratione materiae* adopted by Turkey with regard to the application of the Convention to Northern Cyprus[42].

The Human Rights Committee examined the individual complaint of Kennedy v. Trinidad and Tobago, following the formulation by that State of a reservation to Protocol nr. 1 to the Covenant on civil and political rights, which stated that it does not accept the examination of complaints by detainees condemned to capital punishment. The Committee declared the reservation incompatible with the object and the purpose of the Protocol and treated it separately from the act of ratification, examining the substance of the complaint[43]. Similarly, the Interamerican Court of human rights, in the case Ivcher Bronstein, did not accept the withdrawal of the acceptance of the optional clause on the

---

[41] Extensively on this subject Gerard Cohen-Jonathan, Les réserves dans les traités institutionnels relatifs aux droits de l'homme. Nouveaux aspects européens et internationaux, in RGDIP, 1996, no. 4, pp. 915-948.

[42] Case Belilos, decision of 29 Aprilie 1988, prezented by Vincent Berger, Jurisprudence of the ECHR, fourth edition, 2002, IRDO (in Romanian), pp. 182-185; case Loisidou, decision of 23 March 1995, Serie A, no 310.

[43] Communication no. 845/1999, CCPR/C67/D/845/1999-31-12-1999.

jurisdiction of the Court, having in view the authority of treaties on human rights based on the acceptance by States of higher common values, which entail also a special regime of provisions on the compulsory jurisdiction that cannot be submitted to subsequent unilateral acts of States[44].

As a result of the acceptance and the recognition of imperative norms as norms from which States cannote derogate in their relationships, these norms have also different effects in the context of State responsibility for wrongful acts. The wrongful act is defined similarly in case of violation of international obligations, irrespective of whether they have as a source an imperative norm or a norm having a dispositive character; it is defined as a conduct attributed to the State or to the international organization, which is not in conformity with their international obligation. Nevertheless, the codification undertaken by the International Law Commission[45] reached the conclusion according to which the consequences of the wrongful act are different in case of the violation of imperative norms, having in view the importance given to these norms by the international community when accepting and recognizing them as norms from which no derogation is permitted.

If a wrongful act is not in conformity with an imperative norm of the general international law, its wrongfulness cannot be precluded by the consent of the injured State, by invoking the self-defence, by invoking a counter-measure to the wrongful act, by

---

[44] Decision of 24 September 1999 on the competence; Serie C, no. 54.
[45] Report of the International Law Commission on international responsibility of States, doc. Suppl. No. 10(A/56/10), of which the UN General Assembly took note by the resolution no. 56/83, adopted on 12 Dcember 2001.

invoking the force majeure, a situation of distress, or a situation of necessity. It is obvious that by precluding the wrongfulness of an act and by invoking such situations, a State could try to justify a regime which is derogatory from an imperative norm; articles adopted as codification in this field are explicit on this issue, excluding such situations.

Moreover, the document elaborated by the Commission[46] in the process of codification and progressive development of international law in this field contains a chapter on the serious breaches of obligations under peremptory norms of general international law, outlining the different consequences of such wrongful acts. Serious breaches of imperative norms are defined as involving a gross or systematic failure by the responsible State to fulfil its obligation. As particular consequences of a serious breach of such a norm, the document enunciates:

- the obligation of all States to cooperate to bring an end through lawful means to any such serious violation;
- the obligation of all States not to recognize as lawful a situation created by a serious breach as defined, and not to render aid or assistance in maintaining that situation.

More than that, the responsibility of a State can be invoked by any other State for the breach of an obligation which is owed to the international community as a whole, and this is the case for imperative norms.

---

[46] Extensive presentation in Ion Diaconu, International Responsibility in International Law, 2013, Prouniversitaria (in Romanian).

As for counter-measures, as actions of response to unlawful acts, the norms adopted within this process of codification underline that such counter-measures cannot affect: the obligation of States to refrain from resorting to force or to the threat with force, the obligations on the protection of fundamental human rights, the obligations of a humanitarian character which forbid reprisals, or other obligations resulting from imperative norms of international law. Without specifying which are the obligations concerning the protection of human rights or those under humanitarian law which forbid reprisals, the document of codification excludes the counter-measures wich violate them as well as other imperative norms. Wrongful acts which would violate such norms are not allowed even as counter-measures against other wrongful acts, as this would lead to derogations from imperative norms[47].

SECTION III - International and internal judicial practice concerning maninly Europe

Internal and international courts of justice, as well as regional or specialised courts, have used in their decisions, initially very cautiously and using some general terms (norms of fundamental importance, norms of general interest or which create *erga omnes* obligations), then gradually with more courage the concept of imperative norms and gave examples of such norms.

---

[47] Report of the International Law Commission on international responsibility of States, doc. Suppl. No. 10(A/56/10), of which the UN General Assembly took note by the Resolution no.56/83 adopted on 12 December 2001; Report on international responsibility of international organizations, doc. Suppl. No. 10(A/66/10), of which the UN General Assembly took note by its Resolution no. 66/10 of 9 December 2011.

The issue of the competence of the courts in disputes on the application of some norms considered imperative was also raised; this was the question of extending the non-derogatory effect of imperative norms to the clauses relating to the compulsory jurisdiction in cases concerning the application of such norms submitted to courts.

1. International criminal courts, created during the last decades as an answer to serious violations of human rights and of norms of humanitarial law, referred in many decisons to imperative norms of international law. In several decisions, the International Criminal Tribunal for former Yugoslavia, created by the resolution of the Security Council nr. 827 of 5 May 1993, retained as crimes of genocide, according to the Convention of 1948 and according to its Statute, acts committed against some ethnic groups in Bosnia and in Kossovo[48]. The Tribunal declared explicitely genocide as an imperative norm of international law[49] and stated that „there can be absolutely no doubt that the prohibition against genocide in the Geneva Convention falls under customary international law and is now at the level of jus cogens", although it condemned Jelisic for crimes of war and crimes against humanity[50].

In the Furundzija case, the Tribunal had to decide whether acts committed against Bosnian women (threats, attacks with violence, rapes) by a paramilitary group, with the involvement of at least one public official as a *de facto* organ of the State (as it is

---

[48] On the jurisprudence of that Tribunal, Sean D. Murphy, Progress and Jurisprudence of the International Criminal Court for the Former Yugoslavia, in AJIL, 1999, vol. 93, pp. 57-97.

[49] Case Krstic(Srebrenica), sentence of 19 Aprilie 2004; case Prosecutor v. Popovic, judgment case no. IT-05-88-T, T. Ch. II of 10 June 2010, para 807. .

[50] Case Jelisic, IT-95-10-T, T, ch., 14 December 1999, para.60. .

provided for in the Statute of the Tribunal), constituted acts of torture. Noting the existence of the elements of the crime of torture, as in the cases Tadic and Celebic, the Tribunal condemned the accused for acts of torture and attempt to dignity, including rape, as violations of laws and customs of war. In the reasoning of the sentence, the Tribunal affirms that the prohibition of torture imposes to States *erga omnes* obligations and acquired the status of an imperative norm of international law (jus cogens), that is a norm that enjoys a higher rank in the international hierarchy than treaty law and even ordinary customary rules, that the status of the prohibition of torture as a jus cogens norm is linked „to the importance of the values it protects" and that „clearly, the jus cogens nature of the prohibition of torture articulates the notion that…(it) has now become one of the most fundamental standards of the international community" . The Tribunal also considers that the prohibition of torture as a norm of jus cogens is based, *inter alia*, on the extensiveness of prohibition, including the fact that States are prohibited from expelling, returning or extraditing a person to a place where they may be subject to torture, and refers to decisions on this subject by ECHR-Soering v. UK, Cruz and Valas v. Sweden, Chahal v. UK[51].

In the case Delalic, also, the ITCY affirms that the prohibition of torture is a norm of customary international law and constitutes a norm of jus cogens[52].

---

[51] Case Furundzija, decision of 10 December 1998, paras. 151, 153-154.
[52] ITPY, case No. IT-96-21-T, T ch, 16 November 1998, paras.152-153, 454. The same in the Tolimir case, no. IT-05-88/2-T, T ch. II, of 12 December 2012, para. 733.

The International Criminal Tribunal for Rwanda[53] also judged crimes of violence, including sexual acts committeed against Tutsi women (perceived as part of a different ethnic group), qualified as genocide. The Tribunal condemned Akayeshu for genocide, including also sexual violence, as part of the process to destroy the respective ethnic group. The Tribunal also held that rape and other forms of sexual violence constitute themselves crimes against humanity[54] and that many of these acts are in fact acts of torture using intimidation, degrading, humiliation, punishment, control and destruction of the person[55].

2. The European courts also referred to imperative norms of international law, when examining mainly civil law cases concerning damages for violations of human rights alleged by individuals.

The European Court of Human Rights (ECHR) examined a civil law application of a Kuweiti citizen Al-Adsani against UK, because his action for damages produced by acts of torture committed by agents of Kuweit was rejected by the British courts on the ground of immunity of jurisdiction enjoyed by the State of Kuweit in UK. The applicant claimed that the State immunity, recognized by the courts in this case, was contrary to the prohibition of torture which is an imperative norm of international law. The European Court recognized without ambiguity the imperative character of the prohibition of torture, as a norm of

---

[53] Created by the Resolution of the Security Council No. 955 of 8 November 1994.
[54] Akayeshu, ICTR No. 96/4, decision of 13 february 1996, paras. 733-736.
[55] Ibidem, para. 689. More extensively, Diane Marie Amman, International Decisions, in AJIL vol. 93, 1999, pp. 195-199.

primary importance, having a jus cogens value[56], citing decisions of the Criminal Tribunal for former Yugoslavia and the decision of the Chamber of Lords in the case Pinochet[57]. The Court held that in this case the issue was not the criminal liability of an individual for acts of torture, but the immunity of a State in a civil suit for damages in respect of acts of torture committed within the territory of that State, and admitted the exception of State immunity.

In a case Jorgic v. Germany of 2007, the European Court had to solve a contestation of the competence of the German courts to prosecute a foreigner for the crime of genocide. A citizen of Bosnia refugiated in Germany in 1992 and was accused and condemned in 2007 for the crime of genocide committed in Bosnia in 1992. He contested the competence of the German courts to prosecute him. ECHR rejected the contestation, considering that German courts properly investigated and prosecuted him. ECHR retained that „according to art. 1 of the Convention of genocide, the Contracting Parties are obliged *erga omnes* to prevent and to punish genocide whose prohibition is part of jus cogens" and that „ for the national courts, having in mind that the purpose of the Convention....expressed mainly in this article does not exclude jurisdiction for the punishment of genocide by the State whose laws provide for extraterritoriality...(this) should be considered reasonable and convincing enough"[58].

---

[56] Decision of 21 November 2001, ECHR 2001-XI, pp. 79. 101-102

[57] In this case, the House of Lords of UK held that the jus cogens nature of the international crime of torture justifies States in taking universal jurisdiction over torture wherever committed. Case Regina v. Street Metropolitan Stipendiary Magistrate, ex parte Pinochet Ugarte, no. 3, 24 March 1999, 119 ILR, p. 136.

[58] ECHR, application No. 74613/01, decision of 12 july 2007, para 66.

Following a similar approach, the Inter-American Court of Human Rights, in its Advisory Opinion of 17 September 2003 on the situation of irregular migrant workers, appreciated that the principle of equality enshrined in the Covenat on civil and political rights enunciates *erga omnes* rights and obligations of States towards migrants and has the character of a norm of jus cogens. The IACHR affirms that jus cogens is not limited to the law of treaties, but refers to all legal acts, to the foundations of international law[59]. According to the opinion of this Court, the principle of equality and non-discrimination can be considered as an imperative norm of international law „because it is applicable to all States, regardless of being or not parties to a treaty, and produces effects towards third parties, including persons". Consequently, „States... cannot act in contradiction to the principle of equality and non-discrimination so as to cause prejudice to a determined group of persons"[60].

Also in the case Las Dos Erres Massacre v. Guatemala, the IACHR considers that the norm of the common art. 3 of the Geneva Conventions (of 1949 on protection of war victims) belongs to jus cogens on the basis of its customary status[61]. In the case Michael Dominguez v. USA, the IACHR stated that jus cogens norms are derived from superior legal order norms[62].

---

[59] Advisory Opinion no. 18 of 17 September 2003, para. 99.
[60] Ibidem, para. 100.This Advisory Opinion on the existence of imperative norms is cited by the author without sharing the opinion expressed concerning one or the other of the norms considered imperative.
[61] Judgment of 24 November 2009, cited in the Second Report on jus cogens, doc. A.CN.4/706 of 2017, p. 30.
[62] Case no.12285(2002), IACHR, Report no. 62/02, para. 49.

The courts of the European Union also referred to the existence and effects of imperative norms. In a decision of 21 December 2005, the Tribunal of First Instance of the European Union (now the Tribunal) had to consider the legality of a Regulation adopted by the Council of the Union in order to implement a resolution of the Security Council which requested States to take measures of freezing and blocking the fonds of organizations and persons related to Al-Qaeda and to Talibans. The claimants, Kadi and Al Barakaat International, held that some of their fundamental human rights were violated, mainly procedural rights, the right to have accesss to a remedy and the right to property. Although the Tribunal did not consider itself to be competent to control the legality of the Regulation from the point of view of the general principles of the community law concerning fundamental rights, it admitted to be entitled „to control incidentally the legality of the respective resolutions of the Security Council from the point of view of jus cogens, understood as an international public order which is imperative for all subjects of international law, including UN instances, and from which a derogation is not possible"[63]. The Tribunal exercised its control with regard to the respect for the prohibition of inhuman and degrading treatment and for the right to property and reached the conclusion that no fundamental rights relating to jus cogens were violated. The Tribunal recognizes that the prohibition of inhuman and degrading treatment is a norm of jus cogens, but finds that the sanctions applied do not have the object or effect to produce such a treatment. With regard to the right to property, the Tribunal

---

[63] Decisions T 306/1, para. 277, 320, 339 et 344 and T 315/01, para. 226, 274, 284 and 289, reaffirmed in Ayadi and Hassan of 12 April 2006, no. T 253/02 and T 49/04.

considers that only an arbitrary deprival of this right whould violate an imperative norm[64].

The Tribunal affirms nevertheless, with reference to the provisions of the UN Charter, that „International law allows thus to consider that there is a limit to the principle of compulsory effect of the resolutions of the Security Council; they have to respect the peremptory fundamental norms of jus cogens. Otherwise, as improbable as it could be, they would not bind member States and thus neither the European Community"[65]. In its reasoning, the Tribunal outlines, similar to the Interamerican Court on human rights (case Caesar v. Trinidad and Tobago), the conception according to which the prohibition of inhuman and degrading treatment represents an imperative norm.

Although the decision of the Tribunal was appealed and cancelled by the European Court of Justice, which decided to cancel the Regulation for not being in conformity with fundamental human rights recognized by the European Union (without exercising a direct control on the resolutions of the Security Council and without reference to imperative norms), this decision represents an explicit affirmation of the existence of imperative norms; together with decisions of other regional courts, it opened the way of control of internal norms which could be in conflict with norms of jus cogens or other norms protecting human rights, even if such internal norms are implementing resolutions of the Security Council.

Some national courts aso affirmed the existence of imperative norms of international law and adopted decisions in

---

[64] Decision T-306, paras. 290-292.
[65] Ibidem, T-306, para. 281.

cases submitted to them requesting financial compensation for damages suffered by individuals during armed conflicts. Several internal and international jurisdictions had to solve cases where the violation of imperative norms was invoked in order to obtain civilian reparation for damages suffered by individuals during armed conflicts. The States accused invoked the State immunity of jurisdiction. Some judicial courts rejected this exception, as being contrary to the imperative norm affected; others accepted it, finding the case admissible, but without judging on substance.

The Greek courts were the first to invoke an imperative norm in order to adopt a restrictive conception on the State immunity of jurisdiction, denying the immunity of Germany for facts committed by the German army during the Second World War. In the case Prefecture of Voiotia v. Federal Republic of Germany of 2000[66], the Supreme Court of Justice of Grece examined a petition against the decision taken by the court district of Livadia, which granted material compensation for the attrocities committed by the German troops of occupation in the village of Distomo, in June 1944. The Supreme Court invoked the European Convention on the immunity of States of 1972, according to which a State cannot pretend immunity in case of acts producing harm to physical integrity of persons or to private property, as well as decisions given by American courts on the basis of an amendment of 1996 to the Law on foreign State Immunity of 1976, which

---

[66] Prefecture of Voiotia v. Federal Republic of Germany, Case no. 11/2000, decision of May 4, 2000, presented in International Decisions, AJIL, vol. 93, 2001, pp. 198-204; a critical approach by Carlo Focarelli, Immunité des Etats et Jus Cogens, in RGDIP, 2008, nr. 4, pp. 766-780 and Christian Tomuschat, L'immunité des Etats en cas de violation grave des droits de l'homme, in RGDIP, 2005, 1, pp. 51-73.

refused to foreign States immunity in cases of claims concerning financial compensation for damages produced by acts of torture (case Letelier v. Chile and Liu v. People's Republic of China)[67]. The Greek court considered that the facts committed constituted crimes against humanity and violations of imperative norms of international law and therefore cannot be opposed by the immunity of jurisdiction of States.

Similarly, the Italian Court of Cassation reaffirmed in 2008 the conclusion reached by a preliminary decision of 2004 in the case Ferrini (complaint of an Italian citizen deported in Germany, obliged to work for the weapons industry and submitted to inhuman treatment), according to which a State that committed international crimes does not have the right to State immunity and affirmed the primacy of imperative norms on other norms of international law[68].

To the opposite, in the case Al-Adsany, although it did not accept the request of a Kuweiti citizen to receive damages for acts of torture committed against him in Kuweit, on ground of State immunity of jurisdiction, the European Court of Human Rights recognized the imperative character of the prohibition of torture, but did not agree to remove the immunity of jurisdiction of the State in case of a civilian action before other courts than those where facts imputed took place. The Court appreciated that there is no norm of international law requesting to give up the State immunity in the case of civilian actions[69]. In the case Jones also, the Chamber of Lords did not agree to remove the immunity of the defending State as an effect of, while recognizing, the imperative

---

[67] Cited in AJIL, vol. 93, 2001, p. 199.

[68] Presented by Carlo Focarelli, art. cit., pp. 765-773.

[69] Analysis undertaken by Carlo Focarelli, art. cit., pp. 761-793.

character of the prohibition of torture[70]. In the case Yeroda („Mandat d'arrestation" of 11 Aprilie 2000, D. R. Congo v. Belgium), where Belgium invoked the implication of the Congolese minister of foreign affairs in the commission of crimes of war and crimes against humanity, in violation of imperative norms, the International Court of Justice accepted that there is full immunity of jurisdiction of the minister of foreign affairs, resulting from its mission of representation of the State. In individual opinions, some juges did not accept this solution, helding that the immunity of jurisdiction of the minister of foreign affairs is not an imperative norm[71].

In the case Mario-Luiz Lozano v. the General Prosecutor for the Italian Republic, the Italian Courts affirmed that jus cogens norms hold a higher rank than other norms[72].

In the case Youssef Nada V. Switzerland, the Swiss Supreme Federal Court stated that „norms of jus cogens were binding on all subjects of international law"[73].

In the Pinochet case, mentioned above, the House of Lords recognized the jus cogens nature of the prohibition of torture, as

---

[70] Jones v. Ministry of Interior of the Kingdom of Saudi Arabia, presented in AJIL, vol 100, 2006, pp. 910-918.
[71] Decision of 21 November 2001; extensive and critical presentation of this decision in Chronique de jurisprudence internationale, RGDIP, 2002, pp. 178-182. Judges from the minority held that imperative norms exclude the application of the norm concerning the immunity of jurisdiction of States, depriving it of any legal effect.
[72] Appeal Judgment of 24 July 2008, Supreme Court of Cassation, First Criminal Chamber, Case No. 31171/2008, p.6.
[73] Appeal Judgment of 14 November 2007, Case no. 1 A45/2007, ILDC, 461(CH 2007), para.7.

justifying universal jurisdiction over cases of torture wherever committed[74]. It was noted that for the first time a domestic court denied immunity of a former head of State against prosecution for crimes of torture[75].

The German courts also prosecuted a case of genocide referred above, committed in Bosnia at the beginning of the war in former Jugoslavia. A Bosnisn citizen, who was residing in Germany, was arrested in 2005, prosecuted and condemned in 2007 for genocide. The German courts held that they have unversal jurisdiction in that case and rejected the motion of incompetence. The German courts affirmed that genocide represents a crime directed againt the interests of the international community as a whole[76].

In many of the decisions given by European courts they cite decisions given by US courts on similar issues. The most often cited is the case Siderman de Blake v. Argentina, where the US Court of Appeals of the 9-th Circuit stated that jus cogens norms "are derived from values taken to be fundamental by the international community"[77], formulation which reminds the text of art. 53 of the Vienna Convention. This decision was cited with

---

[74] Case mentioned above, pp. 34-35.
[75] According to the ILC Report entitled „Fragmentation of International Law: difficulties arising from the diversification and expansion of International Law", Report of the Study Group of ILC, doc. A/CN.4/L.682 of 13 Aprilie 2006; UN General Assembly took note of its conclusions by the resolution 61/34 of 4 December 2006.
[76] Federal Constitutional Court of Germany, case BvR 1290/99, decison of 12 December 2000.
[77] Doc.965 F.2d 699, 1992, US, App. P. 715.

approval by a number of decisions of other US courts[78]. Decisions where the existence of jus cogens norms was recognized, mainly the prohibition of torture, were also adopted by Canadian courts[79].

One has to retain that in all these cases the courts affirmed the imperative character of the norms invoked-prohibition of torture, crimes of war, crimes against humanity, but accepted the exception of State immunity of jurisdiction before courts of another State (an exception *ratione persone*, not *ratione materiae*). This is not an opposition on substance between two norms, which would diminish, replace or remove the application of an imperative norm by another customary norm of international law. The norm of State immunity of jurisdiction comes into place at the stage of the examination of the competence of jurisdiction, while recognizing the validity of the imperative norm invoked in connection with the substance of the claim.

Taking into account the international practice as presented, in most cases norms advanced as imperative are: the prohibition of torture, of genocide and of slavery, the crimes of war and the crimes against humanity, non-use of force and of threat to force (sometimes naming aggression or self-defence) and the right of peoples to self-determination. Most of the time courts refer to these imperative norms as cutomary rules of general international law, sometimes to multilateral treaties as important elements of those

---

[78] In cases like Siderman de Blake v. Republic of Argentina, Estate of Hernandez-Rojas v. USA, Doe I v. Reddy, cited in the Second Report on jus cogens by Dire Tlady, Special Rapporteur of the International Law Commission, doc. A/CN.4/706 of 16 March 2017, p. 11, mainly footnote 48. See also Robert Kolb, Peremptory International Law: Jus Cogens-A General Inventory, Oxford and Portland, Hart Publishing, 2015.

[79] Doc. A/CN.4/706, 2017, pp.10-11.

customary rules, without examining international practice which led to their imperative character. Interestingly enough, imperative norms invoked by the applicants are recognized as such, even if their application is not always accepted for other legal reasons.

* * *

The evolution of international practice, mainly during the last decade, led to definitively recognizing the existence of imperative norms and to the clarification of many consequences of the application of this concept in different fields of international law, beyond the law of treaties. Of course, not all consequences reveiled in different documents and decisions met with the consensus or are not contested; still, this is the way to crystallize the international practice and to accept norms of international law.

It is gerenally recognized that treaties in conflict with imperative norms are void; a series of norms are recognized as imperative; as for other norms, some of them mentioned above, opinions vary and the international practice is not uniform. International practice is generally uniform with regard to the consequences of imperative norms in relation to derogatory treaties, but is far for being uniform with regard to other norms which in their application could come in competition with imperative norms, like those on the competence of the courts of compulsory jurisdiction or of treaty monitoring bodies, or like those concerning the immunity of jurisdiction of States which commit violations of imperative norms.

There is more clarity with regard to the consequences of imperative norms on unilateral acts of States, as statements of their will to take upon themselves international obligations, which are void if they are in conflict with imperative norms, as well as those in the field of State responsibility, under which some circumstances cannot be invoked to preclude the wrongfulness of acts violating such norms and counter-measures cannot be applied if they are themselves breaches of imperative norms; with regard to ways and meas to promote State responsibility, all States have the right to invoke international responsibility for violations of imperative norms, as well as the obligations to cooperate for eliminating the consequences of such violations and not to recognize as lawful such consequences. Equally clear is the relationship between imperative norms and regional or local customary norms, meaning that they also cannot create legal regimes which would derogate from imperative norms. Although it is less clear, it seems difficult to accept that universal customary norms in conflict with imperative norms of general international law could be formed. International practice does not offer examples of such an evolution.

CHAPTER II - AGAIN ABOUT the NON-USE OF FORCE and OF THE THREAT TO USE FORCE

Abstract

The United Nations Charter and the documents adopted subsequently within the UN established the legal framework of the use of force and of the threat to use force, an objective followed by mankind for some time in order to eliminate the scourge of war and the serious violations of human rights which accompanied it. This legal framework defines precise cases when the use of force is accepted as legitimate in interstate relations.

As it is known, after the adoption of the Charter acts of use of force by some States took place when legitimate reasons provided for the Charter were invoked, but also cases when the States concerned invoked other reasons or gave more extensive interpretations to the provisions of the Charter, without challenging the principles and provisions of the Charter. Several such acts took place since the beginning of the XXI-st century and some European States were involved.

The purpose of this study is to consider these cases from the point of view of the provisions of the Charter and of the positions of different States, having in view to see to what extent they could have determined the development of a generalized practice, recognized by the international community, which could lead to new norms of international law.

Key Words: non-use of force and of threat to force, non-intervention in internnal affairs, territorial integrity of States, inviolability of borders, aggression, the people's right to self-determination, the right to self-defence, territorial disputes, irregular forces, military occupation, responsibility to protect, humanitarian intervention, non-lethal assistance

SECTION I – Legal Framework in Force

As it is known, the UN Charter, adopted in San Francisco in 1945 at the end of the most destructive war in the world's history, postulated as a principle of the relations among States the non-use of force or threat to use force against territorial integrity or political independance of any State, or in any other manner inconsistent with the purposes of the United Nations. The Charter provides only two cases of legitimate use of force, which are individual or collective self-defence against an armed attack (article 51) and the decision of the Security Council concerning actions for maintaining or restoring international peace and security (article 42), in cases of threat to peace, breaches of peace and acts of aggression. On the basis of the principle of the right to self-determination of peoples, the international practice developed a third case of legitimate use of force, by a people which is fighting for self-determination, including also the right to assistance from abroad.

These are presently the elements composing the principle of non-use of force, including also a number of explicite obligations provided for in other documents which solemnly proclaimed and developed this principle, mainly the Declaration

2625 of 24 October 2070 concerning the principles of international law relating to friendly relations and cooperation among States according to the Charter and other subsequent resolutions[80].

According to the Declaration of 1970, a war of aggression constitutes a crime against peace, for which there is responsibility according to international law; every State has the duty to refrain from the threat or use of force to violate the existing international borders of another State or as a means for solving international disputes, including territorial disputes and problems concerning frontiers of State; every State has the duty to refrain from any forcible action which deprives peoples (colonial and those submitted to foreign domination) of their right to self-determination and freedom and independance; States have the duty to refrain from acts of reprisal involving the use of force; every State has the duty to refrain from organizing or encouraging irregular forces for incursion into the territory of another State, as well as from organizing, instigating, assisting or participating in acts of civil strife or terrorist acts in another State, when such acts involve a threat or use of force; the territory of a State shall not be the object of military occupation or of acquisition by another State resulting from the threat or use of force and no such acquisition shall be recognized as legal.

---

[80] Adopted by consensus by the resolution of the UN General Assembly nr. 2625 of 24 October 1970. On the contents of this principle in the Romanian doctrine of international law, I. Diaconu, P. Iliescu, D. Negrea and V. Pacuretu, Renunciation to the use of force and of threat to force-a fundamental principle of international law, in Revue roumaine d'études internationales, nr. 2-3(20-21), 1973 as well as Ion Diaconu, Treaties of Public International Law, vol. I, 2002, Ed. Lumina Lex, pp. 285-297(in Romanian).

According to the principle of non-intervention in internal affairs of other States, developed in the same Declaration, armed intervention and all other forms of interference or threats against the personality of the State or against its political, economic and cultural elements are in violation of international law; no State shall organize, assist, foment, finance, incite or tolerate subversive, terrorist or armed activities directed towards the violent overthrow of the regime of another State or interfere in civil strife in another State; the use of force to deprive peoples of their national identity constitutes a violation of their inalienable rights and of the principle of non-intervention.

The Definition of aggression, after proclaiming that the first use of armed force by a State in contravention of the Charter shall constutute *prima facie* an act of aggression, reaffirms some of the elements of the Declaration 2625 of 1970 and enumerates acts which are qualified as as acts of aggression, such as: the invasion or attack by the armed forces of a State of the territory of another State, any military occupation or annexation of the territory of another State or parts of it as a result of such invasion or attack; bombardment of the territory of another State; blockade of the ports or coasts of another State; sending of armed bands, groups or irregular forces which carry out acts of use of armed force against another State. The Definition emphasizes that a war of aggresssion is a crime against international peace and gives rise to international responsibility, that territorial acquisition or special advantage resulting from aggression shall not be recognized as lawful and that no consideration of whatever nature, political, economic, military or otherwise, may serve as a justification for aggression[81].

---

[81] Resolution nr. 3314 of 14 Dcember 1974. Presentation of the definition and of the proceedings leading to its adoption, Aurel

Many of the obligations of States according to these principles were reaffirmed by other resolutions of the General Assembly, in particular by the resolution nr. 42/22 of 18 November 1987 and the Declaration concerning the inadmissibility of intervention and interference in internal affairs of States, adopted by the resolution nr. 36/103 of 9 December 1981, as well as by the Declaration adopted by the high level meeting of States in connection with the issue of the responsibility to protect (adopted by the resolution 60/1 of 24 October 2005).

As for Europe, many of the norms of international law provided for in the UN documents are reaffirmed in the Declaration on principles of relations between participating States, included in the Final Act of the Conference on Security and Cooperation in Europe, which contains some formulations more precise and extended. The Declaration develops the principles mentioned, but also two others, territorial integrity of States and the inviolability of borders, as well as measures for the practical implementation of the principle of non-use of force and of threat to use force[82].

It is also important to emphsise the jurisprudence of the International Court of Justice in cases submitted to it and in the advisory opinions requested (Military and paramilitary activities in and around Nicaragua-1986, Legality of the use of nuclear weapons and their threat-1994, as well as the more recent Consequences of the Construction of the Wall in the Occupied

---

Preda-Matasaru, Treaties of Public International Law, second edition, 2006, Ed. Lumina Lex, pp. 73-84(in Romanian).

[82] Published in the volume Security and Cooperation in Europe; Documents, 1972-1989, Ed. of the Romanian Academy, 1991, pp. 35-43(in Romanian).

Palestinian Territory-2004 and Armed activities on the territory of D. R. of Congo-2005), which will be mentioned below.

Since the adoption of the Charter, the world was confronted with several cases which raised the question whether this legal framework gives an answer to all concerns and situations when some States resorted to the use of force without being authorised by a decision of the Security Council or when action of the Council was considered necessary, but no decision was adopted due to a veto of one of the five permanent members of the Security Council. Moreover, in 1950 a resolution of the General Assembly was adopted, named Uniting for Peace (nr. 377/V of 3 November 1950), which provided for the competence of the General Assembly to adopt decisions concerning the use of armed force according to the Charter, whenever the Council could not act. This resolution was applied only in the case ot the war in Korea; although it was referred to in several cases for convening special session of the General Assembly (the conflict concerning the Suez Channel 1956, the situation in Hungary 1956, the conflict of Congo 1960, the situation in Palestina 1980, 1982 and others) and more recently in connection with the debates on the responsibility to protect, the General Assembly did not adopt decisions to authorise the use of force except in the case of the war in Korea (1951).

As generally adopted by States members of UN, according to the resolution 60/1 of 2005 following the summit of the heads of State and government, the concept of the Responsibility to protect contains the commitment of the States to carry when necessary a collective determined action, through the Security Council, according to the Charter, including its Chapter VII, if the State concerned does not take itself the necessary measures for protecting its population against serious acts of violation of human rights (such as genocide or ethnic cleansing) and if the diplomatic means used are without result[83]. If for some analysts this formulation would open the way to unilateral action against States which cannot or are not willing to protect their population, for many others this text excludes unilateral acts of use of force, opinion that we share. The majority of States declared that the responsibility of the international community must be exercised collectively, under the authority of the Security Council, and that in no way this could be assimilated with a right to humanitarian intervention[84].

The conflicts in the Golf area, in former Jugoslavia and in Rwanda during the decade 1990-2000 led to actions of use of force, some of them authorised by the Security Council, others not authorised by the Council according to the Charter, as well as to situations where the international community failed to react or did it too late, which raised questions about the efficiency of the mechanism to maintain peace and security as provided by the Charter.

Since the beginning of the XXI-st century this issue is taken up again, both at the level of States and of lawyers; some of them affirm that the regime of prohibition of the use of force instituted by the Charter would be out of date and should be revised in order to better respond to all concerns[85]. With regard to

---

[83] The Responsibility to Protect, Report of the International Commission on Intervention and State Sovereignty, Ottawa, 2001, pp. XII-XIII.

[84] Position expressed, among others, by the non-aligned States in the Final Statement of the Ministerial Conference of Cartagena (Columbia), of Aprilie 2000.

[85] Among others, Michael C. Wood, Towards New Circumstances in which the Use of Force may be Authorized? The Cases of

situations in Ukraine and Syria, some authors[86] and some States[87] referred to the serious threats they create for the system of security based on the Charter, as well as to its limits. Other conflicts, in Irak, Yemen, Lybia, Mali, Central African Republic, Kenia, D. R. of Congo, which provoked also numerous human victims and where other States intervened, invite of course to be analysed from case to case, as well as to review the evaluation of the functioning of the system of security provided for by the Charter.

This reveals two important trends: one extensive, which gives priority to the practice against the provisions adopted, that is tends to admit the use of force by the States which have the possibility to do it and considers that the existing norms have to be adapted to the changing needs of international life (with direct reference to combating terrorism and to humanitarian cases); one called orthodoxe, which considers that respect for the existing norms and for the interpretation given to them by the international community as a whole represents an absolute requirement in order to maintain international legal order outside of the relations of force.

Humanitarian Intervention, Counter terrorism and WMD, in Niels Blokker & Nico Schrijver(eds), The Security Council and the Use of Force, Theory and Reality-A Need for Change? Leiden, Martinus Nijhoff, 2005, pp. 75-90.

[86] Dapo Akande, The Legality of Military Action in Syria: Humanitarian Intervention and Responsibility to Protect, in European Journal of International law, cited by O. Corten and A. Verdebout, Les interventions militaires récentes en territoire étranger: vers une remise en cause du jus contra bellum? in Annuaire Français de Droit International, 2014, p. 136.

[87] Positions expressed by States such as France, USA and others in the Security Council (doc. S/PV.7144 of 19 March 2014, S/PV.7287 of 24 October 2014).

Another issue widely considered refers to the use of force on the territory of another State against organizations which are non-governmental or are acting without the control of any State (the most recent being the military action against djihadiste groups in Mali in 2013, actions of Israel against the Palestinian organization Hamas in 2014 and the military actions against the so-called „Islamic State" in Irak and Syria, some of which still continue at present). The provisions of the Charter are based on the conception of relations between States, that is they forbid the use of force and threat of force by a State against another State and provide the action of the UN mechanism against the State which resorts to the use of force in violation of the Charter provisions.

Moreover, according to the norms based on the Charter, the use of force on the territory of another State without its agreement should be analysed as a violation of the sovereignity of that State, that is as an illegal use of force, unless the State concerned does not itself commit or support from its territory aggressive acts against another State. Each of these cases presents its specificity.

SECTION II – Connsideration of Recent Cases of Armed Intervention on the Territory of other States

In Mali, France inrervened with armed forces to support the government against irregular forces which occupied the northern part of the country, heading to the capital of the State and endangering the territorial integrity of Mali. Initially, France invoked collective self-defence, referring to the request of assistance of the government of Mali, but referred also to the threat against the French community of 6 thousand people living in the country. Subsequently, in the letter adressed to the Security Council, France did not refer any more to the right to collective self-defence, but only to the request of the Malian government as a justification of its action. Besides, according to the Charter (art. 51), a State member which uses force in the exercise of its right to self-defence has to inform immediately the Security Council, which France did not. Rightly so, it is considered that resorting to motivate a military action in the territory of another State on grounds of collective self-defence is useless, if the intervention takes place at the request of the State and on its territory[88]. Moreover, a justification by referring to art. 51 concerning self-defence would not correspond to the jurisprudence of the International Court of Justice, which in the case Legal Consequences of the Construction of a Wall in the Palestinian Occupied Territory affirms that …"article 51 of the Charter recognizes …the existence of a natural right to self-defence in case of an armed aggression of a State against another State, and consequently article 51 is not relevant in this case"[89].

With regard to the military action against non-governmental groups on the territory of Mali, that was publicly supported by the African Union and by other bodies, including by the UN Security Council through the resolution 2100 (2013) of 25 Aprilie 2013. Thus it appears that numerous States supported the use of force against non-governmental forces, on the territory of another State, provided that it takes place at the request or with the agreement of that State.

---

[88] Opinion by Olivier Corten and Agatha Verdebout, art. cit., p. 142.
[89] ICJ, Legal Consequences of building a wall in the Palestinian occupied territory, Advisory Opinion of 9 July 2004, Report 2004, p. 194.

The military action of Israel in the Gaza Streep, in July 2014, was motivated by this State as a self-defence operation in order to respond to attacks and to protect its citizens against a constant threat, without referring to article 51 of the Charter. As Israel does not recognize the Palestinian State, it invokes self-defence against a non-governmental group, not the responsibility of another State. As seen above, the International Court of Justice does not accept the concept of self-defence in such cases. Moreover, although some States recognized in principle the legitimate right of Israel to defend itself, (USA, States members of EU and other Western States), while others denounced the excessive or disproportionate character of the action of Israeli forces (South Africa, Argentina, Nigeria, Russian Federation), which could be interpreted as accepting in principle this type of action of defence, many other States categorically rejected the thesis of Israel, qualifying its action as an aggression in violation of the provisions of the Charter (numerous non-aligned States individually, the Movement of Non Aligned by the Statement of 11 June 2014, the Committee of coordination of the Movement of Non Aligned with the Group of 77 and China by the Statement of 28 July 2014[90], the Organization of Islamic States by its Statement of June 2014, the Executive Committee of the Arab League of 22 July 2014).

Taking into account the specific situation of Palestine, which is recognized as State only by some States, and the fact that Israel did not refer to art. 51 of the Charter, it seems difficult to retain from this case an evolution with regard to the position of

---

[90] Communications conveyed to the Security Council in July 2014.

States on the application and the scope of the provisions of the Charter concerning the non-use of force[91].

The military intervention against the „islamic state in Irak and in Levant"(further called ISIL) raises also specific questions. The so-called State is a group of insurgents which occupied large portions of the territories of Iraq and Syria and claimed authority over the whole of Islamic world. Due to its territorial instability and lack of effectivity as a State power on a territory, as well as due to the illegal way it took place on the territory of some States, this grouping of people does not reunite elements to be considered as a State.

Although ISIL is not a State recognized according to the norms of international law, USA invoked the right of collective self-defence of other States according to art. 51 of the Charter against actions of that grouping, because States where it operates are not willing or not able to prevent attacks which take place or start from their territory. USA justified their military actions against this grouping in Iraq by the fact that this State cannot impede ISIL to act; as for Syria, USA justifies their action against one group (Khorassan), formed of AL-Qaeda elements, in order to respond to the terrorist threat it represents for USA and for its allies[92].

It is obvious that the position of USA means to extend self-defence to non-governmental groupings and to act against them

---

[91] Opinion presented by Olivier Corten, L'applicabilité problèmatique du droit à la légitime défense au sens de l'article 51 de la Charte des Nations Unies aux relations entre la Palestine et Israel, in Revue Belge de droit international, 2012-1, pp. 67-89.
[92] Doc. S/2014/695 of 23 September 2014.

wherever they would find themselves. Moreover, this extends the possibility to use armed force against a threat, which leads to the conception of preventive defense; this conception is not in conformity with art. 51 of the Charter, is not accepted by the majority of world States and was not retained in the context of the responsibility to protect, neither in the document adopted by the heads of State and government in 2005, reflected in the resolution 60/1 of the General Assembly. As for Syria, USA seems to consider itself responsible for activities taking place on Syrian territory by the so-called islamic state; as it is known, Syria was itself in war with ISIL for many years on its territory. It is also retained that neither USA, nor other western powers did request the agreement of Syria for their military actions against ISIL on the Syrian territory[93].

The position of USA is departing from the provisions of the Charter concerning self-defence, both with regard to those against whom actions of self-defence are directed, and with regard to actions to which States can respond in self-defence. If in the case of Iraq there was a request of assistance of that State and other States are also participating in actions against ISIL, only a few States are involved in such actions in Syria and Russia is obviously acting on the basis of an agreement with the Syrian government. Moreover, taking into account the position of other States, it is difficult to maintain that the position of USA with regard to extending the concept of self-defence *ratione materiae* and *ratione personae* would be accepted by a majority of States. Numerous

---

[93] Olivier Corten, Le droit contre la guerre, deuxième éd., Paris, Pedone, 2014, p. 262.

States requested that actions to combat the so-called islamic state be conducted with respect for the principles of the UN Charter[94].

On the other side, an ambiguous position of the Syrian authorities was noted with regard to actions taking place on its territory against ISIL; officially, Syria communicated to the Security Council that it will consider any military action on its territory without its agreement as a violation of its territorial sovereignity[95], but also that it was open to armed actions on its territory led by an international coalition to which it would participate, on the basis of a previous full and complete cooperation[96].

The Security Council did not adopt a resolution concerning a military action *in Syria or against it*. During 2012 USA and France refused to launch military operations in Syria in the absence of an authorisation of the Council. In 2012, when accusations appeared that the Syrian government would use chemical weapons against internal opponents, they announced military operations against Syria without the authorisation of the Council, while the British authorities invoked humanitarian considerations related to the use of chemical weapons. As it is known, the Syrian gouvernment accepted the destruction of its chemical weapons under international control. Numerous States opposed to the use of force against Syria, without the authorisation of the Council (among them China, Russia, Brazil, Argentina, but also Germany

---

[94] During the discussions in the Security Council, September 2014.
[95] Letters addressed by the Permanent Representative of Syria on 17 September 2015 to the U N Secretary general and to the flPresident of the Security Council, doc. S/2015/719.
[96] Letters addressed by the permanent Representative of Syria on 21 September 2015 to the U N Secretary general and to the President pf the Security Council, doc. A/70/385, S/2015/727.

and Belgium), including in the debates within the Security Council. A resolution of the Council was adopted, which reaffirms the authority of the Council to adopt such measures according to Chapter VII of the Charter (with regard to the use of chemical weapons-resolution 2118 of 27 September 2013), which does not authorize any action against Syria.

Military actions against ISIL continued to take place on the territory of Syria against ISIL, although in spite of the cruelty of its actions the right of a humanitarian intervention against it was never invoked. A civil war also continues in Syria, where rebel forces against the government are supported from abroad. According to international law, intervention in internal affairs of another State is forbidden, in particular when it is directed towards changing its regime. According to decisions of the International Court of Justice, States are in principle forbidden to support irregular forces in another State[97]. States which support rebel forces tried to justify the assistance granted to them maintaining that these forces conduct a legitimate struggle to protect a population whose right to self-determination was violated by the government of the country, that is invoked the right of peoples to self-determination. These arguments lack clarity and consistence, taking into account the structure of the State and of the population of Syria, unless the whole population of Syria is taken into account, which is placing the discussion on a political ground of the struggle for power[98].

In connection with the war in Syria, some Arab States held that Syrian rebels have the right to full military assistance; at the

---

[97] Case Military and paramilitary activities in and against Nicaragua, CIJ Recueil, ICJ Reports 1986, p.108; case Military Activities on the territory of Congo, ICJ Reports 2005, pp. 226-227.
[98] Olivier Corten and Agatha Verdebout, art. cit., pp. 153-154.

high level meeting of Doha in 2013, the League of Arab States adopted a statement proclaiming the right of every member State to offer all means of self-defence, including military, to the Syrian people. There is no reference to art. 51 of the UN Charter; it seems that it was considered that the entire Syrian people has this right and should be supported to exercise it against the existing government. Western European States did not accept this conception, having in view their hesitation to support in principle irregular forces, and granted only a limited unlethal support, which is not expressly forbidden in international law. Numerous States criticize both ways of action, including some Western States and many among the non-aligned, as well as China, while the Russian Federation is directly involved in assisting the Syrian government against the rebels. The majority of States continue to support the principles of non-use of force and of non-intervention in internal affairs of other States, including for changing its regime.

With regard to its military action in Syria, France never invoked the consent of Syria, which was not requested, due to its position towards the government of this country. France justifies its military actions against ISIL on the territory of Syria since September 2014 till September 2015 by the request of assistance addressed to the U N by the Iraqi government, that is as an action of collective self-defence against an armed attack according to art. 51 of the UN Charter. After the terrorist attacks against France of 13 November 2015, assumed by ISIL, the French government invoked the right to individual self-defence according to art. 51 of the Charter[99]. Authors of international law examined the position

---

[99] François Alabrune, Fondements juridiques de l'intervention militaire française contre Daech en Irak et en Syrie, in RGDIP, 2016-I, pp. 41-49.

of the French government in relation to the provisions of the Charter and of norms of international law in general and expressed serious doubts concerning the justification of the French bombardments on the territory of Syria on the ground of self-defence: *ratione personae*, because it is not a case of use of force by a State against France or by armed forces sent by another State; *ratione materiae*, after 13 September 2015, because it is considered difficult to accept that terrorist attacks of Paris would represent an armed attack of the type of those referred to in international documents in order to justify self-defence according to art. 51 (meaning acts of a massive character and of an exceptional seriousness); *ratione conditionis*, because the respective armed actions would not respond to the criteria of necessity and of proportionality affirmed by the International Court of Justice[100].

The text of the resolution 2249 of 20 November 2015, adopted by the Security Council on proposal by France, shows that it does not include in clear terms an authorisation to use force on the territory of Syria and makes no reference to the Chapter VII of the Charter, but asks all States to take all necessary measures in accordance with international law. In spite of this, being adopted by the Council by consensus, it is obvious that it places the action of France against ISIL within the framework of application of the UN Charter[101]. On the basis of this resolution, France requested the support of member States of the European Union, invoking art.

---

[100] Cases Military Activities in and against Nicaragua, decision of 27 June 1986, ICJ Reports 1986, p. 103; Oil Platforms, decision of 6 November 2003, ICJ Reports, 2003, p. 187 and Military Activities on the territory of Congo, decision of 19 December 2005, ICJ Reports, 2005, p.223.

[101] As analysed by Franck Latty, Le brouillage des repères du jus contra bellum, in RGDIP, 2016, I, pp. 21-24.

42.7 of the Treaty of European Union (the clause of European collective self-defence in case of aggression); UK and Germany declared themselves ready to engage in a military action against ISIL in Syria.

An evaluation of the reference to this provision of the Treaty of European Union shows that France could invoke art. 222 of the Treaty on the functioning of the EU, which provides explicitly a prrocedure of allert and of solidarity in case of a terrorist major attack (which means with the involvment of the institutions of the Union). It is affirmesd that by choosing the solution to invoke the armed aggression, that is self-defence, France pursued the objective to preserve the control over its operations, while at the same time obliging the Union to support its actions against terrorism, mainly in Syria[102].

It is our opinion that both the military actions of the USA and that of France on the territory of Syria cannot be justified under international law on the request by Irak or its agreement for armed assistance against ISIL, because the agreement given by Iraq cannot generate rights or obligations concerning a third State, unless the latter would support directly or indirectly the terrorist group in question in its acts against Iraq.

With regard to *Lybia,* the resolution of the Security Council nr. 1973 (2011) recalls, by the terms used, the resolution adopted by the General Assembly on the Responsibility to protect. The Security Council authorised the adoption of all necessary measures in order „to establish an area of aerial exclusion" and to

---

[102] Fabien Gouttefarde, L'invocation de l'article 42.7 TUE ou la solidarité militaire européenne a l'épreuve de la guerre contre le terrorisme, in RGDIP, 2016, I, pp. 51-67.

„protect the population and the civilian areas threatened by attacks". States participating in military actions in Lybia justified their participation by this resolution. The resolution adopted concerning Lybia cannot be interpreted as opening the way to a unilateral intervention for humanitarian or other purposes; on the contrary, it confirmed the normative framework existing according to the UN Charter and did not endorse the conceptions aiming at extending the cases of legitimate use of force.

A resolution partially similar to that concerning Lybia was adopted with regard to *Cote d'Ivoire*. The resolution 1975 (2011) of 30 March 2011 authorized France to take all necessary measures „to protect all civilians threaten by acts of imminent violation to the limit of its capacities and in its areas of displacement, including to prevent the use of heavy weapons against the civilian population". In both cases, of Lybia and Cote d'Ivoire, it was noted that the mandate given by the resolutions of the Council was exceeded. In the case of Lybia, the powers which intervened interpreted that the protection of the population of the areas threatened by attacks included also the bombing of the infrastructure, then actions aiming at changing the regime and finally supporting the rebel forces opposed to the regime. In the case of Cote d'Ivoire, the action to protect civilians threatened by imminent physical violence led the French forces to aim one of the forces involved in the struggle for power and to arrest its head, a former prim-minister. It is ascertained that there was an extended interpretation of the resolutions of the Security Council, which did not mention in any way the changing of the regime as a purpose of the actions authorised, but implied neutrality in the internal conflict[103]. As a matter of fact, many States reacted against this

---

[103] Olivier Corten and Agatha Verdebout, art. cit., p. 160.

evolution, more in the case of Lybia, less in the case of Cote d'Ivoire. This led to more caution in the adoption of other resolutions of the Council to authorize such actions, which was immediately obvious in the attitude of Russia and China with regard to the adoption of resolutions of the Council to authorize similar actions against Syria.

The case of *Ukraine* represents also a challenge for the mechanism of protection of territorial integrity of member States against the use of force and of guarantee of international peace and security according to the Charter. The conflict concerning Crimeea, a territory which *de jure* is part of Ukraine, started with the attitude of the authorities of this peninsula of insubordination towards the new authorities of Kiev, considered unconstitutional after the eviction of the former president Yanukovici by the popular movement in the capital town of Ukraine. The intervention of the Russian Federation and the presence of Russian forces made possible the proclamation of the independance of the „Republic of Crimeea" on 11 March 2014, then approved by a referendum on 16 March, recognized by Russia and annexed through an agreement of 18 March, confirmed by a law of 21 March of the Parliament of Russia concerning the „admission of Crimeea and Sevastopol in the Russian Federation". The Russian representative in the Security Council affirmed on 13 March 2014, in order to justify the situation created, that „it is about to protect our citizens and compatriots, as well as the most important human right, the right to life". He referred to the new Ukrainian government as one „which came to power following a violent and unconstitutional coup d'état undertaken by radical nationalists who violated the rights of the Ukrainian people".

One has to retain that the Russian government does not invoke a right to intervene in favour of rebels, or a right to self-determination of the population of Crimeea, but the agreement of the local authorities, which has no relevance with regard to norms of international law concerning the non-use of force and respect for territorial integrity of States. The Russian representative also referred to an appeal of the president evicted Yanukovici, who obviously did not represent Ukraine at that time, to the unconstitutional coup d'Etat which took place in Kiev and to the violation of the rights of Ukrainian people[104], which represent of course the position of the Russian Federation on events in Ukraine. The question is whether the situation created could justify, according to norms of international law, the intervention of the Russian Federation and in the end the annexation of part of the territory of another State. The position of the Russian Federation was not accepted by the majority of States members of the UN, expressed in the resolution of the General Assembly nr. 68/202 of 27 March 2014. The resolution affirmed the attachment of the General Assembly to the sovereignty, political independance, unity and territorial integrity of Ukraine within its borders recognised at the international level and asked all States to stop and to renouce to any action aiming to disrupt partially or totally the national unity and the territorial integrity of Ukraine, as well as to refrain from threats, use of force or other illegal means to change the borders of this country.

Analysts appreciate that both the western powers and Rusia do not adopt coherent positions on the issue of supporting rebel forces in other States: in Syria some of the western powers

---

[104] Doc. S/PV. 7125 of 3 March 2014, pp. 3-4, 8-9 and 17; doc. S/PV.7134 of 13 March 2014, p. 17.

support openly rebel forces and try to justify this position refering to the norms of democracy and respect for human rights, while with regard to Ukraine they consider illegal the support of rebel forces by the Russian Federation, while the latter supported rebel forces in Ukraine as far as the proclamation of the independance of Crimeea, and in Syria acts along with the government against the rebel forces. These different positions derive from political considerations, related to a different evaluation of the legitimacy of the cause of rebel forces, but in substance by different opposed political interests[105].

Taking into account the position officially presented by the Russian Federation, which does not contest the principles of non-use of force and of non-intervention in internal affairs of other States, but seeks to justify its actions by arguments which are placed outside of the obligations deriving from these principles, as well as the fact that these arguments were rejected by the majority of States, it is our opinion that this case does not call in question the contents or the validity of the obligations adopted according to the UN Charter and other international documents. On the contrary, it confirms the necessity to strengthen respect for the non-use of force and non-intervention in internal conflicts and for the norms of international law which forbid supporting rebel forces in another State, even if it is considered that they pursue a legitimate objective[106].

---

[105] Opinions defended mainly by O. Corten and A. Verdebout, art. cit., p. 167.
[106] With the same meaning, cases Military and Paramilitary Activities in and against Nicaragua and Armed Activities on the territory of Congo, which refer to the Declaration 2625 concerning principles of international law, mentioned above; in the specialised writtings of international law Olivier Corten, La rébellion et le droit

In connection with some of the cases mentioned, mainly after the terrorist attacks against USA of 11 September 2001, a question appeared concerning the relationship between self-defence and combating terrorist attacks. USA invoked the right to self-defence after the attacks of 2001, which was recognized by the resolutions of the Security Council 1368 and 1373 of the same year and it was not contested by other States. It was considered that the extension of attacks, implying the projection of airplanes transporting passengers against civilian and military targets in several places in the USA, poducing thousands of human loss, represented an armed attack, and the respective attacks were claimed by the group Al-Qaeda, which had its base of action in Afganistan and maintained close relations whith the Talibans. France also invoked the right to individual self-defence in connection with terrorist attacks of 13 November 2015. Some authors held that a customary norm would develop according to which an armed attack within the meaning of art. 51 of the Charter could be performed by terrorist groups, like Al-Qaeda or ISIL, if the respective attacks have a massive character and are particularly serious[107].

This conception is not in conformity with generally recognized norms concerning the definition of aggression, as it was given in the resolution 3314 of 1974(such terrorist acts were not referred to in ithe resolution), as well with the more recently elaborated definition as part of the Statute of the International Criminal Court, although the object of this last definition is the

---

international: le principe de neutralité en tension, in Recueil des Cours de l'Académie de Droit International, tome 374, p. 164.

[107] A Cassesse, Article 51, in J.P. Cot, A. Pellet, M. Forteaux, La Charte des Nations Unies. Commentaire article par article, Paris, Economica, 2005, p. 1352.

aggression as committed by individuals submitted to the jurisdiction of the Court, which does not include neither in terms nor implicitly terrorist attacks[108]. According to the definitions mentioned, the armed attack incriminated as aggression has to come from another State or to be attributed to it, as the right to self-defence is exercised against it, which is usually not the case of acts committed by terrorist groups. As a well known international specialist affirms, „a transnational extension of self-defence inevitably leads to attacking one or the other (of the States) for acts which, hypothetically, are not attributed to them"[109]. USA held that acts of self-defence would be justified against a State which is unwilling or unable to take measures against terrorist groups from its territory, which commit terrorist attacks against other States. This conception tends to justify acts of self-defence against a State on the basis of the fact that terrorist groups are situated on the latter's territory. Analysts affirmed and rightly so, that this is only an evolutive interpretation of the right to self-defence[110], which is not sustained by the generally recognized norms on the non-use of force , nor by a consistent international practice.

*   *   *

When considering these situations and their consequences on the corresponding principles and norms set forth in the UN Charter and developed in documents adopted thereafter by

---

[108] Definition adopted by the Conference of Kampala of States parties to the Statute of the Court, May-June 2010, doc. ICC-ASP, 10/32 of 11 June 2010.

[109] J. Verhoeven, Les étirements de la légitime défense, in AFDI, 2002, p. 62.

[110] Franck Latty, art. cit., pp. 29, 39.

consensus, which can be considered as authentic interpretations of the provisions of the Charter, we start from the methodology developed by the International Court of Justice, namely to evaluate to what extent a new right or a new interpretation advanced by some States are accepted by the international community of States, with a special care for those norms recognized as imperative norms of the general international law[111]. It is not our purpose to examine the legitimate character of the actions which took place, but the arguments invoked with regard to the principles and norms of international law, in order to see whether thereby the respective States understand to contest these principles and norms or to depart from them and whether the position of other States opens the prospect to see developed new norms or to modify those which exist by a generalized practice accepted by the majority of States.

According to this methodology of evaluation, we note that in none of the situations mentioned there were doubts expressed with regard to the validity of the obligations resulting from the UN Charter or clear cut positions that the respective provisions of the Charter were modified or obsolete. In most of the situations, the majority of the States do not accept the justification offered by the State concerned. In several cases, the agreement of the State on whose territory the respective action takes place is invoked and it cannot be equated with collective self-defence, as it is sometimes stated, for which other conditions are required. In the case of the

---

[111] Contained in the reasoning of the decision in the case Military Activities in and against Nicaragua, ICJ Reports, 1986; about imperative norms in the Romanian doctrine, Ion Diaconu, Normele imperaative în dreptul international (jus cogens), Editing House of the Romanian Academy,1986 (in Romanian) and recently in Human Rights' Impact in International Law, Selected Issues, 2017, Create Space, Amazon, pp.28-39.

action of Israel in the area of Gaza against Hamas, a non-state group, neither art. 51 of the Charter, nor an attack from another State is invoked, while the specific situation of Palestine, recognized only by some States, makes it difficult to draw conclusions with regard to a valid precedent for extending the concept of self-defence to non-state actors.

With regard to actions against the so-called islamic state on the territory of Iraq, there is a request of assistance from this State; as for the terrritory of Syria, there was an agreement for action by Russian Federation, while western States did not make such a request for political reasons. They acted on the territory of Syria invoking terrorist threats of ISIL and of elements of Al-Qaeda against other States, thus extending self-defence provided for in art. 51 of the Charter to terrorist attacks, some of which could hardly be equated with an armed aggression, and to non-state elements acting from the territory of a State without its support or control. Or, the request by Iraq or its agreement cannot justify acts of use of force on the territory of another State. Whatever it may be, in the case of Iraq the mandate given by the Security Council cannot justify military actions in Syria and therefore it is difficult to retain arguments in favour of an extension of the notion of self-defence. Moreover, the Security Council did not authorize military actions against Syria as requested by some States; the non-lethal support given by some States to rebel forces in this country, in fact also military material, invoking humanitarian considerations, comes closer to supporting or encouraging acts of civil war, forbidden by norms of international law.

In the case of the military action on the territory of Cote d'Ivoire, there was also a departure from the mandate given by the Security Council by the intervention in the civil war in favour of one of the opposed forces. With regard to the situation created in Ukraine, the protection of citizens and of their right to life, as well as the violation of the rights of the Ukrainian people were invoked, namely an argumentation which refers to elements which cannot justify a military action on Ukrainian territory according to norms of international law generally recognized.

In most of these cases the majority of States opposed those military actions on the territory of other States, that is did not accept an extension of the mandate given by the Security Council. Moreover, there is no generalized practice accepted by the majority of States, with regard to the use of armed force on the territory of other States without their agreement, nor with regard to extending the concept of self-defence to other acts than those of armed attack committed by a State against another State or in support of an aggression of the latter. Consequently, there is no significant evolution of the regime established in international law concerning non-use of force and of threat to force; some States invoke the same norms, but give them their own interpretation of these norms in order to justify their actions; such interpretations are not accepted by other States. In fact, this is confiming the respective norms, instead of contesting or modifying them[112]. New international documents accepted by consensus reaffirm the norms as previously set force; with regard to responsibility to protect, these documents underline the duty of each State to protect its population against serious violations of human rights, the obligation of the international community to apply diplomatic, humanitarian and other peaceful adequate measures, in accordance with Chapters VI and VIII of the Charter, in order to support the protection of the populations against such serious violations

---

[112] O. Corten, A Verdebout, art. cit., pp. 136, 167-168.

(crimes of genocide, crimes of war, ethnic cleansing and crimes against humanity), and when such means prove to be inadequate, take a collective action through the Security Council, in conformity with Chapter VII of the Charter[113].

On the other side, according to the UN Charter, the action of self-defence ia exercised until the moment when the Security Council takes himself measures to maintain international peace and security. Analysts note that, when the Council authorizes the use of force by some States or implicitly accepts such actions without explicitly authorizing them, the Council is not exercising this mission according to the Charter, living to the discretion of individual States the adoption of such measures, including their duration and the control over respect for norms of international law related to armed actions on the territory of other States (norms concerning respect for human rights, norms of humanitarian law, on the protection of the environment and others)[114].

CHAPTER III - EUROPEAN UNION and INTERNATIONAL LAW

---

[113] A More Secure World.Our Shared Responsibility, The Report of the High-Level Panel on Threats, Challenges and Change, UN Doc. A/59/565, 2004; Final Document of the World Summit of 2005, adopted on 16 December 2005, General Assembly, doc. A/760/L.1. Extended presentation by Ion Diaconu, Human Rights'Impact on International Law, part II, Chapter VII, pp. 174-177.

[114] Similarly, Franck Latty, art. cit., pp. 38-39.

Abstract

The relationship between general international law and norms of law developed in one or the other of the regions of the planet was allways a fascinating subject. This problem became topical mainly after the adoption of the Charter of the United Nations in 1945, considered as a real codex of peaceful relations in the world which proclaimed in its art. 103 that in the event of a confict between obligations of member States under the Charter and their obligations under any other international treaty, their obligations under the Charter shall prevail.

It was allways generally accepted that in the regulation of their relations at the regional level the respective States can go beyond the norms of general intenational law, meaning that they can take up more extended obligations; this derives from the homogeneity of the region, from the specificity of their relationships, sometimes from historic evolutions, which make possible, sometimes necessary, more extended obligations between the regional members than towards those from other regions. The questions appeared, though, to what extend can they depart from the norms of general international law, what are the consequences for other States and for the international system as a whole, and how these evolutions can be managed to avoid adverse effects and more human sufferings in the world.

The European Union is the first experience of an organization of integration, in which member States renounced to some of aspects of their sovereignty, which are exercised according to the treaties of the Union by its institutions, with the participation of member States. The Union has exclusive competences in some fields, in other fields competences are exercised in common with member States, and in others it has competences of coordination and support of the activity of member States.

This complex system of competences often exercised with mixt participation leads sometimes to consequences both at the internal level of member States and on international norms and relations which have to be well understood and carefully managed. In the final analysis it bestows to member States to ensure the harmonization of regional regulations with the general norms of international law, who were adopted with the participation of European States. It is not contested that Europe was allways in the forefront of initiatives for building relations and structures of cooperation based on norms of general international law.

Key Words: imperative norms, derogation, internal order, standards, equitable and comparable protection, autonomy of EU law, legal certainty, incompatibility of obligations, political conditionality, denial of justice, illegal migration, threat to security, access to justice, protection of the environment, fundamental human rights, the dualist conception.

Introduction

As it is well known, the European Union developed as an independent legal order, which prevails over the national legal systems of member States and is of a direct application on their territories.

That means that the European Union's law can also derogate from norms of international law, creating a different legal regime within its area of application and among its member States. Does it mean that the European Union's law can derogate from all norms of international law, for instance from imperative norms of the general international law? . The Vienna Convention on the law of treaties of 1969 contains clear provisions on imperative norms as recognized and accepted by the international community of States as norms from with States cannot derogate in their relations (art. 53 and 64). The Vienna Convention on the law of treaties between States and international organisations and between such organisations, adopted in 1986, as a result of codification of international law in this field (although it is not in force because of imposing to host States obligations which they did not accept), contains identical norms concerning imperative norms of international law as compulsory for international organizations.

A correct interpretation of the norms concerning imperative norms of international law leads to the conclusion that international organisations, similarly to States, cannot derogate from imperative norms of general international law (like the non-use of force and of threat to force, interdiction of genocide, of slavery, of torture and others), by the means of treaties they conclude with States or with other international organisations, or by unilateral acts or statements.

On the other side, does it mean that the European Union can decide not to execute international obligations it assumes as a party to a treaty, invoking its legal internal order? This would be in contradiction with article 26 and 27 of the Vienna Convention on the law of treaties and the corresponding article of the Convention on the law of treaties between states and international organisations and organisations among themselves, according to which „Every treaty in force is binding upon the parties to it and must be performed by them in good faith"; „A party (to a treaty) may not invoke the provisions of its internal law as justification for its failure to perform a treaty".

Questions may be raised also with regard to human rights (those which are not protected by imperative norms of international law); one may consider this issue solved by the adoption at the level of the primary law of the Union of the Charter of fundamental rights and by other provisions in the EU Treaties, according to which the Union respects human rights and fundamental freedoms and the level of protection of human rights offered by the Charter shall never be inferior to that offered according to the European Convention of 1950 on human rights and fundamental freedoms, adopted within the Council of Europe, to which all EU State members are parties. And still, as we will see, some differences were noted between the system of protection of the EU and that functioning under the Council of Europe.

No opinion or argument was expressed in the international arena, meaning that imperative norms would not be compulsory for international organisations and that they could derogate from such norms. Of course, in each case one has to start from the existence of an imperative norm according to the criteria established by the general rules of the law of treaties, and then consider whether there is an act of the international organisation aiming to derogate from the imperative norm. With regard to human rights in general, the Lisbon Treaty contains the decision of EU to adhere to the European Convention of 1950, which would ensure a more harmonious functioning of the two systems of protection. We try to understand why this is not yet fulfilled. Let us also consider from that perspective some practices of the European Union, especially in the context of the recent flow of migration.

A second issue to consider refers to the EU participation in some treaties on the protection of environment, along with member States, and to the obligations of the Union as a party to such treaties. To what extent the Union has to be treated differently from other parties to such treaties? Can it invoke internal regulations and structures in order not to implement some provisions of these treaties? One has to have in mind the provisions of the Vienna Conventions on the law of treaties and the overall position of the Union in favour of the protection of the environment all over the world.

A third issue is the conception of EU bodies with regard to international law as a whole and its relationship with the EU law.

SECTION I -European Union and norms on human rights and freedoms

According to the Lisbon Treaty, the European Union adheres to the European Convention of 1950 on human rights and fundamental freedoms. Almost 9 years elapsed since the Treaty is in force and the Union is still not a party to the Convention of 1950, to which member States of the Union are parties. Since then, the Charter of fundamental rights of the Union is also in force. This means that the 28 (still) member States are parties to two systems of protection of human rights-the Convention of 1950, functioning within the Council of Europe, under the control of the European Court of Human Rights, and the EU system, based mainly on the Charter of fundamental rights, under the control of the Court of

Justice of the European Union. The two systems evoluated and still may develop differently, in spite of the provision of the Charter according to which the protection ensured by the Charter shall never be inferior to that guaranteed by the European Convention.

Obviously, there are differences of interpretation between the European Court of Human Rights (ECHR) and the European Court of Justice (CJEU) with regard to the exercise of some human rights; one of them is the direct access of individuals to challenge any act which would violate their rights according to the Convention of 1950 (having in vue also acts of the EU as such), which is not ensured by the EU law[115]; the apllication of different standards by the two courts in the field of human rights (for instance with regard to the right to an equitable process)[116]; the equivalent or the comparable protection offered by the two systems, which opens the possibility of different interpretations[117]; the possibility to consider both the Union and a member State or one of them as responsible for a violation of human rights[118]; the possibility to submit to ECHR disputes between State members of the EU with regard to violations of human rights provided both in

---

[115] Ion Gâlea, Accession of the European Union to the European Convention of human rights, Critical Analysis, 2012, Ed. C. H. Beck, pp. 49-58; also Jean Claude Piris, The Lisbon Treaty, A Legal and Political Analysis, Cambridge University Press, 2010; Lock Tobias, Walking on a tightrope: the draft accession agreement and the autonomy of the EU legal order, Law and governance in Europe Working Paper Series, 12/2011, Center for Law and Governance in Europe, London; Lemmens P., The Relationship between the Charter of Fundamental Rights and the ECHR, Maastricht Journal of European and Comparative Law, no. 8/2001.
[116] Ion Galea, pp. 58-62.
[117] Ibidem, pp. 40-49.
[118] Idem, pp. 108-116, 119-125.

the Charter of fundamental rights and in the European Convention of human rights[119].

According to the Opinion of the European Court of Justice on the draft agreement negotiated between the EU Commission (on the basis of a mandate given by the EU Council) and the Council of Europe[120], the draft agreement is not comptible with the EU treaties for many reasons, among which: it would not take into account the interpretation by CJEU of the 1950 Convention and of the Charter and would extend the external control of ECHR on acts adopted within the Common Defence and Security Policy; ECHR would be able to ascertain the responsibility for violations of human rights by the EU, by member States or by both of them; the 1950 Convention allows that States parties grant a higher level of protection of human rights, while the EU treaties do not allow this; according to the 1950 Convention a State party can present a petition against another State party for not respecting the Convention, while according to the EU treaties disputes between member States have to be considered within the EU; a Protocol to the 1950 Convention allows that courts of a State party ask for an advisory opinion of ECHR on the interpretation of its provisions; if States members of the EU would use this opportunity, this would affect the autonomy of the EU law(which contains the institution of preliminary questions) in cases where the rights guaranteed by the European Convention correspond to those guaranteed by the EU Charter.

---

[119] Idem, pp. 106-108.
[120] Opinion nr. 2/13 of December 2014, Accession of the European Union to to the European Convention on the protection of fundamental human rights and fundamental freedoms(2014), ECLI, EU, C/2014, 2454.

One has to note that the Opinion of the Court is not based on an analytical comparison between the provisions of the Convention and those of the Charter or of the jurisprudence of the two courts on human rights issues. It is not based on an analysis of the situation of human rights in Europe, but on concerns related to the competences of EU institutions, to the interpretation and the use by State membres of the EU of the possibilities open to them by the adhesion of the EU to the 1950 Convention and to the external control on acts of the EU, mainly on decisions of the CJEU.

As a result of this Opinion, the Union cannot for the time being become a party to the 1950 Convention on the protection of human rights; it cannot implement this provision of the Lisbon Treaty. The 28 EU member States are parties at the same time to the two systems of protection of human rights; they form also the majority of members of the Council of Europe, parties to the 1950 Convention. These States and mainly their citizens are interested to be protected by a clear and coherent system of human rights and of institutions monitoring the application of the legal instruments enunciating human rights. Everybody-institutions and States- have to accept that human rights are universal and there is no valid reason to be interpreted and applied differently by different institutions, *a fortiori* on the same continent. Beyond politics and good governance, it is a question of legal certainty. Besides that, EU was always in the forefront of promoting human rights in the world; could this position be maintained if on the continent it remains behind the level of protection granted under the conventions of the Council of Europe?

The solution is to come back to the table of negotiations, to continue to discuss and to eliminate some concerns which may be not justified or exagerated. Ideas were also advanced to consider modifications to the Lisbon Treaty or of its annexes concerning the adhesion to the 1950 Convention. This would of course depend on political evaluations and of evolutions within Europe.

SECTION II - Concerns for human rights in a situation of economic and financial crisis

A situation in which the European Union involved itself and which shows lack of preoccupation for respecting human rights is that concerning measures that the Greek government had to take to face economic and financial crisis of 2009-2010, following decisions taken with the participation of the European Union[121]. In 2010 and 2012 member States of the Euro zone and the International Monetary Fond granted financial assistance under the conditionality of eliminating the bugetary excessive deficit and resuming financial discipline. In this respect Greece adopted measures of economic recovery which led to a strong recession and to a massive unemployment[122].

The European Committee on Economic and Social Rights (CEDS) received a number of collective petitions from the trade unions and other organizations of workers and of public officials from Greece and found that these measures had a negative effect on social rights. The Committee established from the beginning

---

[121] Presentation in Chronique du droit de l'Union Européenne, AFDI, LXI, 2015, pp. 476-479.

[122] Between 2010 and 2015 the Greek PIB diminished by 25% and unemployment increased with more than 20%. As envisaged by Francesco Martucci, L'hybridation juridique et institutionnelle de la zone Euro sous les effets de la crise, in Chronique de droit de l'Union Européenne, 2015, p. 496.

that the responsibility for the measures adopted, that is for the violation of the provisions of the Charter on social rights, adopted within the Council of Europe in 1965, rests upon the Greek government. The respective measures were adopted by Greece in order to have access to funds from creditors, among them the European Union, and to be able to cover for the obligations relating to the payment of the foreign debt.

In front of CEDS, the Greek government declared that „the rights guaranteed by the Charter were restricted in conformity with other international obligations it has, that is those it assumed in the context of credit subscribed to the EU institutions and to the International Monetary Fond"[123]. The Committee affirmed that the fact that the national measures tend to satisfy another international obligation than those provided for by the Charter does not exonerate the State from the application of the Charter, and that the commitments to the European Union are not a cause of exoneration of responsibility[124].

The Greek government accepted the Protocol to the agreement which established the conditions related to the facility of financial assistance granted. The Protocol was signed by the European Commission on behalf of the European Mechanism of Stability created by the EU treaties to maintain the financial discipline by Euro member States (MES), by the International Monetary Fond and by Greece. This troika has no legal personality

---

[123] Presented by Valérie Michel, La crise des devoirs de l'Etat membre, in Chronique de droit de l'Union Européenne, Annuaire Français de Droit International(AFDI), vol. LXI, 2015, p. 477.

[124] CEDS referred to the decision of the European Court on Human Rights in the case Cantoni v. France, petition nr. 17862/91, decison of 15 November 1996.

in order to be liable as such. No doubt, the Greek government had a week margin of negotiation. Some of the subsequent complementary decisions were adopted as acts of the seconday law of the Union. The Council of the Union adopted in 2010 a decision which asked Greece to increase the budgetary surveillance and to reduce the excessive deficit, but also requested to adopt a reform of the legislation concerning the protection of employment with regard to the prolongation with one year of the period of stages for the new recruitments, and another one in 2011, resuming the request to increase the budgetary surveillance and reduce the deficit, but requesting also a reform in order to facilitate an increasing use of temporary contracts and resorting to partial time employment[125]. Representatives of the European Commission referred openly to the reduction of pensions and of benefits, but left to the appreciation of the government to establish the scope of the respective rights[126].

It appears that the mesures adopted by Greece coincide with those requested by the Council in its decisions, which are acts attributed to the European Union. The Union signed and promoted acts which created for a member State obligations contrary to human rights, for which the Greek State commited through

---

[125] Beyond the need for such measures, which are applied in many Western European States, their requirement by the Council of the Union in the context of the crisis and the obligations imposed upon Greece in order to receive the financial assistance leave no doubt about the involvement of the European Union as such in the adoption of the respective measures.

[126] Decisions of the Council of the Union of 2010 and 2011 cited above and the answer of M. Moscovici as representative of the Commission of 11 August 2015 to the question E-005025 concerning the violation of the European Social Charter in Greece by the Commission as a member of troika.

uncontested international instruments. Beyond the direct responsibility of Greece for these violations, the European Union did not show any concern for the observance of human rights in this case, in spite of an obligation resulting from its basic treaties to respect human rights and to see that member States respect them.

In the collective petition of the General Confederation of Labour of Greece against its State[127], the petitioner refers to the violation by Greece of the Charter, in particular to the licensing of workers without prior notification during the first 12 months of activity, as a consequence of decisions of the European Union. In its response to the petition, the Greek government referred to the restriction of the social rights provided for by the Charter as a result of obligations resting upon Greece from the credit subscribed to the EU and the IMF, that is to a conflict of obligations. If for CEDS the situation is clear (position publicly affirmed also by the European Commission, meaning that the Greek side is responsible for these violations and that its commitments to the EU cannot exonerate it of responsibility), the overall situation seems to be more complex with regard to other participants. Fisrt of all, the troika signatory of the documents which provided for the conditionality of the credit has no legal personality and thus cannot be considered responsible.

The Protocol of agreement which defined the conditionalities was signed by the Commission on behalf of MES and by Greece. Because Greece approved this Protocol (considered as an international treaty), it adopted according to the law of treaties an agreement through which it assumed an

---

[127] Collective petition nr. 111/2014, declared admissible on 19 May 2015; presented extensively by Francesco Martucci, art. cit., pp. 476 et ss.

obligation which is contrary to an obligation resulting from a previous treaty. At the same time, one cannot ignore the decisions of the Council of the Union, as acts of the Union mentioned above, which asked that Greece adopts these measures[128].

Thus, member States can find themselves in a situation where, in order to respect obligations imposed to them any time within the European Union, either resulting from acts of secundary law of the Union or from commitments they have to accept in situations of crisis (economic and financial or resulting from the influx of migrants, as we will see later-on), they have to adopt measures which are not respecting human rights provided for in international treaties accepted previously. The institutions of the Union do not seem to be concerned with requirements to respect human rights in cases of incompatibility of obligations which may result for member States and of the international responsibility encoured by them according to international treaties and to decisions of EU bodies.

Taking into account the universal character of human rights, to which the European Union and member States adhered through the Union's treaties and through numerous other international treaties, it seems difficult to accept that member States could be placed in the dilemma to choose between respecting obligations assumed within the Union (whose violation would lead to harsh sanctions) and respect for other international obligations (for the violation of which they bear international responsibility, under its different forms). It is our opinion that it belongs to the 28 member States of the Union to find a solution of principle, of a general application, so that their international

---

[128] As analysed also by Valérie Michel, art. cit., p. 478.

obligations in the field of human rights are not contradicted by acts or obligations accepted within the European Union.

Questions were raised, and rightly so, with regard to the legality and the legitimacy of the political conditionality included in the agreements for granting financial assistance to Greece. The elements of the political conditionality were negotiated with the Greek side by IMF, the European Commission and the European Central Bank. As said above, in order to achieve the objective of financial discipline, budgetary balance and reduction of excessive deficits, some of the main means established by the respective agreements aimed at reducing pensions and benefits, licencing persons and other measures concerning human rights. The political conditionality represented in fact restraining some human rights so that the Greek State can pay off his debts to foreign banks and States. The European Commission received from the Council of Governers of MES „the mission to negotiate the protocol which defines with precision the political conditionality and to survey that it is respected"[129]. CJEU examined the legality of the involvment of the Commission in this activity and retained that this is compatible with the law of the Union, which allows member States to involve institutions of the Union in executing missions beyond the framework of the Union[130]. It is thus recognizing that this mission was beyond the framework of the Union. The Court retained that by doing this the Commission promotes the general interest of the Union[131] and can see that the conditionality is

---

[129] According to the presentation of Francesco Martucci, art. cit., p. 506.

[130] Several Opinions of the Court, the last of them nr. 1/09 of 8 March 2011.

[131] Conception retained by CJEU in its décision in the case Pringle, C-370/12, of 27 November 2012.

compatible with the law of the Union. One could then question to what extent did the Commission see that this conditionality is in conformity with the fundamental human rights, which form part of the Union's law? Is the protection of human rights not within the general interest of the Union? Can the Commission receive missions beyond the framework of the Union which imply departing from the Union's law?

Of course, the conditionality was established by international agreements, by acts of the Council of the Union as sanctions for excessive deficit and by provisions of the internal law of the State. The national judge can consider the legality of measures adopted by the government on the basis of such agreements and decisions. The Constitutional Court of Portugal retained the violation of fundamental human rights by the law adopted on the basis of the conditionality (similar to that established for Greece)[132]. In Greece, the State Council declared the political conditionality justified by „exceptional circumstances of the national economy"[133] and refused to transmit to CJEU a prejudicial question with regard to the second plan of assistance[134].

The Tribunal of CJEU examined actions against institutions of the Union related to the clauses of political conditionality. The Tribunal rejected as inadmissible actions for annulment and for damages against the Commission and the ECB which challanged the validity of their statements and of acts asking

---

[132] Tribunal Constitucional du Portugal, case no. 187/13, décision du 5 avril 2013.
[133] Conseil d'Etat de Grèce, no. 1285-1286/2012, décision du 2 avril 2012; no. 1116-1117/2014, décision du 21 mars 2014.
[134] Conseil d'Etat de Grèce, no. 1507/2014, décision du 28 avril 2014.

for the restructuring of the banking sector and of the financial system of Cyprus, on the ground that the Commission and the ECB are not parties to the agreement concluded by Cyprus with the MES[135]. With regard to Greece, the Tribunal examined actions of redress for failure and for damages introduced against the European Parliament, the European Council, the Council of the Union, the Commission and the ECB, challenging the consequences of the political conditionality imposed to Greece[136]. These remedies were also rejected on the same procedural grounds.

As the analysts affirm, this shows that justiceable individuals and persons affected by the measures of application of the political conditionality are exposed to the denial of justice, because the political meetings of the Eurogroup have an informal character and are not competent to adopt legal decisions, while the Commission would have only the roll to assist the financial institutions and the State in negotiations[137]. That means that Eurogroup has no legal personality, no responsibility, but the EU institutions execute its decisions. The only documents which could be contested before the Court are the decisions of the Council of the Union, but this way is considered very difficult to follow due to the conception of CJEU on admissibility, which is submitted to the condition of the direct and individual interest of the petitioner in the act contested; moreover, actions with regard to the responsibility of the Union can be introduced only in a case of a characterised violation (see article 263, al. 4 of TFUE).

---

[135] Décisions du Tribunal no. T-327-331/2014, ordonnance du 16 octobre 2014, ainsi que no. T-290-294, ordonnance du 10 novembre 2014.

[136] Décisions du Tribunal no. T-350/14, T-35/14 et T-413/14, ordonnance du 5 juin 2015.

[137] Opinion presented by Fr. Martucci, art. cit., p. 509.

SECTION III - European Union and the crisis of illegal migration

After a first quarter of 2015, when measures of limited intensity were taken, the increase of the influx of refugees and the tragic events in the Mediterranean led to the adoption during the following months of a series of measures of emergency to establish a mechanism of intervention to support Italy and Greece by a programme of urgent relocalisation and a plan of action against the trafficking of migrants, then a new plan of relocalisation, a manual on return and a package of measures for the protection of external borders of EU. Then the majority of the EU countries introduced again the control to the interior borders, while Slovenia and Hungary raised walls to prevent the entry of migrants. EU concluded new agreements of readmission, tryed to obtain from the South-Mediterranean countries the limitation of the flow of migrants to Europe and concluded with Turkey the well known agreement of 20 March 2016 (in exchange of a contribution by EU of 3 billion Euro and of the elimination of visas for Turkish citizens). According to this agreement migrants will be retained in centres in Turkey and Greece would receive from Turkey only Syrian refugees who did not enter previously illegaly on the territory of EU member States, while Turkey would receive back, at the rate of 1 to 1, other migrants who entered illegaly form Turkey to Greece[138].

---

[138] Presentation made by Ségolène Barbou des Places, L'Union Européenne et la crise de l'asyle. A la recherche de la légalité

During this period of time, the European Commission and some member States associated more and more the migratory movements with threats to security. This allowed a disproportional emphasis on measures of preventing the access to the territory of member States, ignoring at least in the beginning a minimum of human rights and guarantees of security, integrity and health of migrants and then reducing their rights in the process of examination of their requests within fair procedures with respect for norms of European law. Public interest was strongly emphasized, without taking into account the interests and the rights of those willing to reach Europe. Such measures had a collective character, aiming at migrants in groups, and not on the basis of evaluating their individual situation. At the same time, by the accelerated procedures and by rejecting the migrants at the borders or in transit areas to States of origin considered safe, the burden of proof to dismiss this presumption, that is a proof to the contrary, was shifted to the indivudual, making it practically impossible to justify the need for international protection in each case.

Some of the decisions of the Union were adopted without the agreement of the Parliament and without consulting all interested parties; the Commission justified this departure from some provisions of the treaties by the extreme emergency nature of the crisis of migrants and refugees.

The agreement concluded with Turkey in March 2016 also raises many questions. From the legal point of view, it was concluded by EU and Turkey through a joint Declaration and Conclusions of the European Council, both of which refer to a Plan of action EU-Turkey and to an agreement of readmission

---

communautaire, in Chronique de droit de l'Union Européenne, AFDI, vol LXI, 1915, p. 483.

between Turkey and Greece, which means it did not follow the usual procedures of ratification or approval. EU is a party to this agreement with Turkey, although it did not follow the norms of EU on the conclusion of agreements (the agreement was negotiated by the European Council with Turkey, without the participation of the Commission and without involving the European Parliament). With regard to its substance, this agreement is departing from norms adopted by the EU concerning the treatment of migrants (directives Procedures, Return and Qualification). Despite imperfections concerning its conclusion,these agreements represent nevertheless international treaties, presented as such by the parties and are currently applied[139].

From the point of view of human rights, this agreement was met with a lot of criticism for not offering sufficient protection to asylum seekers in Greece and in Turkey and for leading to their return to less safe countries[140]. The obligation to protect asylum seekers bestows again to Greece, although ECHR decided in many cases that both the system of examination of asylum requests and the conditions of detention in this country present systemic failures. With regard to Turkey, which would retain on its territory most of migrants, it is underlined that conditions of granting international protection are very unequal in different parts of its territory.The agreement is not referring in any way to the guarantees provided for in the Directive Return, nor to respect of human rights provided for in other international instruments. By its very nature and contents, the Agreement of readmission between Turkey and Greece, to which the agreement between EU and

---

[139] Ségolène Barbou des Places, art. cit., pp. 488-489.
[140] Ibidem, pp. 485-487. Similar opinion by M. Heikkila and M. Mustaniemi-Laakso, art.. cit., p. 192.

Turkey refers, does not respond to these concerns. The agreement provides for the retaining of migrants in and returning them to Turkey, without a commitment of this State to respect their human rights and without guarantees with regard to the consideration of their requests for asylum.

On one side, Turkey ratified the Protocol of 1967 to the Convention of 1951 Convention on the status of refugees mantaining a reservation of a geographic scope, meaning that it is not obligated by the provisions of the Convention towards non-European asylum seekers. On the other side, according to its law of 2014 on the reform of the right to asylum, Turkey grants to Syrian citizens (who form the bulk of asylum seekers targeted by this agreement), in case of a massive influx, a temporary status which offers limited rights as compared with the 1951 Convention. A doubt was expressed whether in these conditions Turkey was a safe country in the understanding of the EU law. Even if it would be accepted that Turkey was a safe country, one could ask why the EU institutions cautioned by the agreement of 2016 a protection limited as compared to that provided by the Directive Return. According to this Directive, a State is considered safe if it allows a person to request a status of refugee and, in case this status is granted, it offers the protection provided for by the Geneva Convention of 1951. Or, by the conclusion of this agreement, member States of the Union organized the transfer of asylum seekers outside the EU, in conditions which do not respect the regime provided for by the regulations of EU and by those of international law concerning the status of asylum seekers. Analysts also appreciate that measures of collective control do not take into account the vulnerability of some persons who may be part of the respective groups, such as pregnant women, children, aged or sik persons, because it does not ensure the individual evaluation of each person[141].

It is considered that, in circumstances of crisis and in the absence of solidarity and of an agreement among the State mambers with regard to the relocalisation of asylum seekers, the European Union adopted simplifying procedures and moved away from the Union's legality[142]. The most serious failure is, in our opinion, the fact that by the agreement with Turkey the Union renounced to the protection of a category of persons who are extremely vulnerable, in accordance with its own regulations, and accepted the risk that these individuals are exposed to an inhuman and degrading treatment either in the transit countries or in those where they would be retourned.

Migration remains an eternal phenomenon, with changing directions and dimensions. These are human realities to which international instruments and internal laws cannot offer rigid solutions, applicable everywhere and everytime. The only criterion which should be constantly applied is to ensure respect for fundamental human rights and freedoms and even in circumstances of massive influxes of migrants, to ensure the observance of a minimum of rights of persons crossing the borders of another State, in accordance with international treaties in force with regard to different categories of migrants (asylum seekers, those legally admitted on the territory of other States and those considered illegal).

Analysing the situation from this point of view, international organisms in charge with different subjects in this

---

[141] Ségolène Barbou Des Places, art. cit., pp.488-495.
[142] Ibidem, pp. 487-490.

field expressed opinions which give a clear evaluation of the measures to be taken. The UN High Commissioner for Refugees declared that even in the most difficult circumstances States are obliged by the art. 33.1 of the Convention of 1951 on the status of refugees to respect the principle of non-refoulement (that is not to expel or return in any way a refugee to the borders of territories where he would be subject to inhuman treatment on grounds of race, religion, nationality, belonging to a specific social group or on ground of political opinion), from which no dergation is admitted[143].

Other international bodies also underlined the need for a high level of a situation of emergency in order to justify derogations from some of the fundamental human rights and freedoms. According to the Covenant on civil and political rights of 1966 and to the European Convention on human rights of 1950, a public emergency, such as a war or a natural catastrophy, would have to represent a situation which endangers the life of a nation. The Human Rights Committee, as a body created to monitor the application of the Covenant, affirmed that „not any trouble or catastrophe is qualified as a public emergency which threatens the life of a nation"[144]. Similarly, ECHR considered as public emergency which could justify derogations from some human rights only an „exceptional situation of crises or emergency which

---

[143] UNHCR, Advisory Opinion on the Extrateritorial Application of Non-Refoulement Obligation under the 1951 Convention relating to the Status of Refugees and the 1967 Protocol(2007).
[144] CCPR. General Comment no. 29: Art. 4; Derogations during a State of Emergency(31 August 2001), CCPR/C/21/Rev. 1/Add. 11, para.3.

threatens the whole population and constitutes a threat to the organized life of the community"[145].

It seems necessary to underline that according to the provisions of the two documents on human rights mentioned, even in case of danger for the life of nation (of war, according to the European Convention), States cannot derogate from some human rights, in particular from the right to life, the interdiction of torture and of inhuman and degrading treatment, the interdiction of slavery and servitude and the interdiction of punishment for action or omission which were not incriminated by law at the time they took place. Thus, the problem of a possible derogation comes into place for other human rights, and even for them, under condition that a derogation is not contrary to other obligations according to international law and does not involve a discrimination on grounds of race, colour, sex, language, religion or social origin. With regard precisely to the policies of imigration, ECHR affirmed in the case Hirsi Jamaa that „problems concerning control of migratory flows cannot justify resorting to practices which are incompatible with obligations of the State according to the European Convention"[146]. In another case, the Court recognized that countries forming the external borders of the Union are confronted with considerable difficulties to face the increasing flow of migrants and asylum seekers, but it does not consider this situation as a justification for failing to respect obligations resulting for them from art. 3 of the Convention[147].

---

[145] ECHR, Lawless v. Ireland(Nr. 3), decision of 1 July 1961.
[146] Hirsi Jamaa and others v. Italy, petition nr. 27765/09, decision of 23 February 2012.
[147] MSS v. Belgium and Greece, petition nr. 30696/09, decision of 21 July 2011.

SECTION IV – European Union and European agreements in the field of environment

The European Union became a party to several agreements concluded among European States for the protection of environment. Its participation was considered a mark of interest for a healthy environment on the continent and around it, for support of the functioning of the respective agreements and of the monitoring bodies created by them. It is a party to the Agreement of 1994 of Sofia on the protection of the environment on Danube, to the Espoo Convention of 1991 on environmental impact assessment in a transboundary context and to the Aarhus Convention of 1998 on access to information, public participation in decision-making and access to justice in environmental matters.

Committees of independent experts were created to monitor the application by the parties of the Espoo and Aarhus Conventions. According to their mandates, they considered also the application of the two conventions by the EU, as a party to them.

The Aarhus Committee held, in its findings under the complaint ACC/32 of 2008 concerning the European Union, finalized in 2016 and taken up in the recommendations to the Committee of Parties, that „The Party concerned fails to comply with art. 9, paragr. 3 and 4 of the Convention, with regard to access to justice by members of the public, because neither the Aarhus Regulation, nor the jurisprudence of the CJEU implements or complies with the obligations arising under those paragraphs". The

Committee recommended either to change the Aarhus Regulation (adopted by EU institutions) or to see that a new direction is given to the jurisprudence of the CJEU, in order to fulfil these obligations.

The European Commission did not agree with the findings of the Aarhus Committee that EU does not comply with article 9, parag. 3 and 4 of the Convention concerning access of the public to justice. The Commission proposed to the EU Council to adopt a decision to reject the findings of the Committee[148]. In particular, the Commission affirms that the principles of separation of powers and of institutional ballance in the Union makes it impossible to implement the recommendations of the Committee through the CJEU jurisprudence, as the EU courts are independent and that the findings would challenge constitutional principles of EU law that are fundamental. It finds it impossible to open the judicial review to numerous potential litigants in areas going beyond the scope of environment. It also submits that the Aarhus Regulation is not meant to implement article 9.3 and 4 of the Convention and that its provisions correspond to the Treaties of the Union (mainly the Treaty on the functioning of the Union, art. 263.4).

The Committee of experts answered to the opinion of the Commission in an open statement that: it did not propose a modification of art. 263.4 or of other provisions of EU treaties; it did not challenge the constitutional principles of EU, it referred to provisions of the secondary legislation and to the jurisprudence concerning the right of access to the judiciary; EU can choose to apply the recommendations of the Committee through the Court's jurisprudence or by changing the Aarhus Regulation; the

---

[148] Doc. COM (2017) 366 final of 29 July 2017.

Committee treats all parties equally and cannot offer a special status to constitutional principles of regional organizations of economic integration; according to international law, the constitution of a party is not accepted as a justification for not fulfilling its obligations under a treaty (citing art. 27 of the Vienna Convention on the law of treaties of 1969); the extent of obligations of such organizations according to the Convention is a matter of international law and falls within the mandate of the Committee. The Committe reminds that the system of preliminary referals (by the national courts to the EU Court) does not respond to the requirements of art. 9 concerning access of the public to justice with regard to decisions, acts and omissions of institutions and bodies of EU.

The EU Council adopted a decision[149] which responds partially to the request of the Commission. The Council reminds the Declaration of the EU when it ratified the Convention, according to which „Within the institutional and legal context of the Community (the ratification took place in 2005, when the Community was the subject of international law; according to the Lisbon Treaty, the EU ensures the continuity for all agreements concluded before by the Community)..., the Community institutions will apply the Convention within the framework of their existing and future rules on access to documents and other relevant rules of the Community law in the field covered by the Convention". The Council takes up the argument on the separation of powers in the Union and says that it cannot give instructions or make recommendations to CJEU concerning its judicial activities and decides that recommendations related to the Court and its jurisprudence cannot be accepted.

---

[149] Doc. 2017 (015/NLE) of 13 July 2017.

The Council affirms that EU continues to fully support the important objectives of the Aarhus Convention and that „the Union should explore ways and means to comply with the Aarhus Convention in a way that is compatible with the fundamental principles of the Union legal order and with its system of judicial review". This is an important statement and it shows the way the issues raised could be solved.

However, the Council decided that the Union can accept the recommendations proposed by the Committee of experts, subject to changes among which: to eliminate all references to the Court of Justice of the EU; instead of „Endorses the recommendations that the party concerned take measures…" say „Takes note of the recommendation that…". Other minor changes could be agreed during the meeting of coordination wich will take place during the meeting of the State parties. That meant that the Commission or some members of the EU should propose officially these amendments to the Meeting of parties and normally they could be accepted, due to the majority detained by EU members. But the rule usually applied within the meetings of parties is the consensus (resorting to vote is also possible) and many States parties opposed resorting to vote, for reasons concerning their own interests.

No decision could be taken during the meeting in Budva (Montenegro) in September 2017, the amendments of the EU were not accepted due to a strong opposition by Norway and Switzerland and the conclusion adopted was that the respective findings on the EU should be considered during another meeting of the parties. Obviously, this is weakening the findings of the Committee of experts to such an extent that the monitoring of this Committee with regard to the application of the Convention by the

EU becomes useless. This opens also the door for other parties to challenge the recommendations of the Committee and use the argument that their judicial system is independent and they cannot give recommendations to their constitutional or supreme courts.

Within the EU it is accepted by everybody that agreements concluded by the Council are binding on the EU institutions and member States; such agreements form an integral part of the Union's legal order and the EU Court ensures compliance with them. Such agreements take precedence over legal acts adopted as secondary law. What the Committee of experts requested through its recommendations is in conformity with this principle. At the same time, these agreements are treaties under international law and their interpretation and the monitoring of application follow the rules and practices of international law. This includes also the competences of the committees of experts created for this purpose with the agreement of all parties to the respective treaties. Their recommendations are not compulsory decisions, like the decisons of the ECHR, but they are meant to promote the application of the respective treaties and to determine efforts of all parties to a treaty to comply with its provisions. That means they have to be considered in good faith so that ways and means are found by the parties to understand their substance and to ensure the conformity of their practices with the Convention.

One has to remind that in May 2017, at the meeting of States parties to the Espoo Convention, EU opposed to the adoption of the report of this Committee on the application of that Convention by EU and determined the postponement of the meeting for 2018, without a decision. The situation was different with the findings of the Aarhus Committee, but the result may be equally damaging with regard to the functioning in the future of the two committees of experts as monitoring bodies concerning all parties to these conventions. How can one explain the attitude of the EU Commission with regard to the two committees of experts?

EU is also in the forefront of efforts and actions to protect the environment all over the world; its position with regard to the two European conventions should be coherent with this mission.

SECTION V - Position with regard to international law in general

This position was expressed mainly with regard to the cases Kadi, submitted first to the Tribunal and then to the Court itself. Yassin A. Kadi and Al Barakaat International Foundation requested to the Tribunal the annulation of the Regulations of the Commission (nr. 467 and 2062/2001) and of the Council (nr.881/2002) which transposed in the EU law sanctions imposed by resolutions of the UN Security Council against Al-Qaeda and the Talibans; the petitioners invoked the violation of fundamental rights such as the right to a fair trial and the right to property. The Tribunal recognized the priority of the norms of the UN Charter, but affirmed the competence of the EU courts to control the compatibility of the Resolutions of the Security Council with the norms of jus cogens[150]. The Tribunal demonstrates that the priority of UN norms derives from the customary rules of international law, codified by the 1969 Convention of the law of treaties. It concludes that the European Union should be considered linked by the

---

[150] Case T-315/01, Y. A. Kadi v. the Commission and the Council (2005), Repertory of CJEU, II-3649, paragr. 177.

obligations under the UN Charter similarly to member States, by the virtue of the treaties which created it. The Tribunal proceeded nevertheless to a control of the resolutions of the Security Council in relation to jus cogens norms concerning human rights (which are no doubt part of international law) and concluded that such norms were not violated by the resolutions.

In appeal, the CJEU did no accept the way followed by the Tribunal[151]. The Court starts from the juridical specific nature of the Community(the Union), based on the state of law, affirming that an international agreement cannot change the attribution of competences based on EU Treaties and consequently the autonomy of the legal system of the Community (Union). The Court declared that obligations imposed by an international agreement cannot have the effect of departing from the constitutional principles of the European treaties, including among them the principle according to which all community acts have to respect the fundamental rights as a condition of their legality. The Court exercised its competence with regard to measures of execution taken by the institutions, not with regard to the resolutions of the Security Council. It is the same conception as that mentioned with regard to human rights agreements.

While the Tribunal considered the relationship between the EU law and international law in a „monist" perspective, the Court takes a clear „dualist" perspective, considering that the validity of acts of the Union's institutions should be evaluated on the basis of their conformity with norms established by the treaties of the Union, not with norms established at the international level, that is

---

[151] Cases C-402/05 P and C-415/05 P, Kadi, Yusuf and Al Baracaat v.Commission and Coucil (2005), Repertory of the Court, I-6351, paragr. 311-313.

that the EU law is autonomous with regard to international law, including the UN Charter.

In its decision in the case Kadi II[152], the Tribunal noted that „doubts were expressed in the juridical media with regard to the full conformity of the decision Kadi of the Court with international law, mainly with article 25 and 103 of the Charter" and affirmed that such criticism is not without justification; the Tribunal adopts itself a critical position to the decision of the Court, mainly for the fact that „it deprived of effect the priority of the norms of international law of the UN Charter", and refers to the serious inconvenients invoked by the intervenient institutions and States.

We retain also that, following the decision Kadi of CJEU, ECHR also revised its jurisprudence adopted in cases Behrami v. France and Sramati v. France, Germany and Norway[153], in which it did not retain the responsibility of these States, accepting that obligations resulting from the UN Charter, according to art. 103 of the Charter, prevail over other obligations of member States.

In the case Jedda v. UK, concerning the treatment suffered by the petitioner under the conditions of occupation of Iraq, ECHR considered that there is no contradiction between the resolution of the Security Council nr. 1546/2004 concerning the control by the British forces of the respective zone in Iraq and the obligation for UK to respect art. 5.1 of the European Convention. For that purpose, the Court refers to the objective of UN to promote respect for human rights and to the obligation of the Security Council, in fulfilling its responsibility of maintaining international peace and

---

[152] Case T-85/09, A. Kadi v. Commission (2010), paragr. 2015(cited by I . Gâlea, op. cit., pp. 74-75).
[153] Petitions nr. 72412/01 and 78166/01, decision of 2 May 2007.

security, to act in accordance with the purposes and the principles of the Charter. On this basis, the Court considers that in the interpretation of the resolutions of the Council, States should start from the presumption according to which the Council does not understand to impose to member States an obligation which would contravene to fundamental principles concerning the protection of human rights. In case of ambiguity, the Court should retain the interpretation which corresponds better to the provisions of the Convention and which allows to avoid the conflict of obligations.

With regard to the petition examined, the Court retains that the resolution mentioned does not impose explicitly or implicitly to UK to incarcerate without a limit of duration and without prosecuting a person who would represent a danger for security. In other words, the Court considers that obligations established for the States concerned by the resolution of the Security Council cannot prevail over the provisions of the Convention, because they are not accompanied by guarantees at the level of European standards. The Court retained a violation of art. 5.1 of the Convention (the right of freedom of the person except in cases of lawful detention or arrest according to a procedure prescribed by law). It is appreciated that by this decision the European Court confirmed that the obligations resulting from the European Convention are compulsory for the States parties in each situation when their agents, representatives or authorities exercise control or authority in a territory which does not belong to them, irrespective of the situation prevailing on that territory[154].

---

[154] Petition nr. 27021/08, decision of 7 July 2011.

Similarly, in the case Nada v. Switzerland[155], ECHR reaffirmed the obligation of States to respect human rights in the context of the struggle against terrorism and approached once again the question of the relationship between obligations resulting from the resolutions of the Security Council and the obligations concerning respect for human rights imposed by the European Convention. In this case, an Italo-Egyptian citizen, living in the locality Campione, enclaved in Switzerland, was inscribed on the lists of those who would have cooperated with Al-Qaeda and the Talibans and was sanctioned by the Swiss authorities by freezing her assets and forbidding the entry and transit in and from their territory. Although the respective person was taken out of the lists at the request of Italian government, the European Court considered necessary to examine whether her rights were violated . Switzerland invoked its obligation to observe the decision of the Security Council, affirming that the application of the respective sanctions could not be attributed to her, and was supported in this respect by the intervenient States France and UK. The Court retained nevertheless that States act on their behalf when they execute a resolution of the Security Council and that they can assume responsibility on the basis of the national acts of application. The Court did not retain the presumption of compatibility between the resolution of the Council with obligation to respect human rights under the Convention, because the resolution provided explicitly the freezing of assets and the interdiction of entry and transit. In this situation, the Court applied the reasoning according to which the UN Charter does not impose to States a model of application of the resolutions of the Security

---

[155] Evaluation made by David Szymczak and Sebastien Touzé, Cour Européenne des droits de l'homme et droit international général (2011), in AFDI, LVII, 2011, pp.636-637.

Council, that it imposes only obligations of result and leaves them the free choice of means of application. This way, the Court could conclude that Switzerland did not take all the measures to adapt the regime of sanctions to the situation of the petitioner, did not respect the principle of proportionality, and retained a violation of art. 8 in conjunction with article 13 of the European Convention.

* * *

With regard to the situations considered before, one has to remind that international organizations are subjects of international law. Norms of general international law are applicable to international organizations, whatever may be their level of integration, as they are fully applicable to federal States. International organizations have their internal law, which is applied within their framework, between them and their members and among the members, but international law complements the internal rules; internal rules of international organizations cannot derogate from norms of jus cogens. If international organizations become parties to international treaties, they have to fulfil the provisions of such treaties as any other parties. One can maintain that member States of international organizations can ask that some norms of international law are applied within the international organization, on the basis of fundamental principles of international law. Of course, international law is fully applicable between the organization and other organizations and to their relations with non-member States.

An international organization can try to derogate from norms of international law in its relations with non-member States (except from norms of jus cogens), but this depends on the agreement of these other States. Thus, an international organization cannot be considered as having a status completely departing from norms of international law (such as the law of treaties, the peaceful settlement of disputes, responsibility for unlawful acts and other customary norms). To proceed differently, the organization would be exposed itself to disputes on many aspects of its foreign relations and therewith its international personality in the world's arena would seriously suffer.

EU member States are known to be fully committed to respect principles and norms of international law. Two of them are permanent members of the UN Security Council. Will they accept that the organization they created as a form of European integration is and remains outside international law, while at the UN they are promoting respect for international law, first of all for universal human rights and freedoms? Will other States accept as a partner an organization which is placing itself above principles and norms of international law, that is which pretends to be free to create its own rules of behaviour and ignore international law? These are prospects which have to be taken into account by all those who define the political line of EU for a medium and long term period of time.

CHAPTER IV - FREEDOM of EXPRESSION and OPINION-EVOLUTIONS and CONCERNS at the EUROPEAN LEVEL

Abstract

Freedom of expression and of opinion is a fundamental human right, which is essential for a democratic society, for the functioning of a state of law, based on the respect of law and of human rights. Although its main elements are defined in the basic documents on human rights, the exercise of this right may come into conflict with other human rights: presumption of innocence, the right to reputation, the right to private life, equal rights and non-discrimination, the freedom of thought, of conscience and of religion.

This leads to responsibilities and preoccupations to keep the freedom of expression into reasonable limits, so as to ensure the coherent respect of all human rights. International documents recognize the right to refuse the protection of the freedom of expression in some cases and to establish by law restrictions to the exercise of this freedom, in as much as they are necessary to protect other human rights.

These preoccupations found their expression in decisions of national and international courts, mainly of the European Court of Human Rights; nevertheless, many aspects of the exercise of this right remain still uncertain or controversial, while the decisions adopted are not following one course, being very often determined by the context of the facts brought before the judge.

Key Words: freedom of expression, duties, responsibilities, freedom of opinion, restrictions, racist speech, abuse of right, denial of holocaust, anti-Semitism, Islam-phobia, discrimination, racial hate, facts, judgments of value, right to reputation, defamation, internet

SECTION I - International and regional regulations

1. At the international level, the Covenant on civil and political rights, adopted within the UN in 1966, to which more than 150 States are parties, stipulates in this field in articles 19 and 20. According to article 19.1, everyone shall have the right to hold opinions without interference. Everyone shall have the right to freedom of expression; this right shall include freedom to seek, receive and impart information and ideas of all kinds, regardless of frontiers, either orally, in writing or in print, in the form of art or through any other media of his choice (art. 19.2). It is also provided for that the exercise of the right to freedom of expression carries with it special duties and responsibilities; it may be subject to certain restrictions, such as those provided by law and necessary either to respect of the rights or reputations of others or for the protection of national security, of public order or of public health or public morals (19.3).

Article 20 adds the obligation of States to prohibit by law any propaganda for war and any advocacy of national, racial or religious hatred that constitutes incitement to discrimination, hostility or violence.

The Human Rights Committee, created by this Covenant to monitor the application of its provisions, adopted the General Comment nr. 34 of 21 July 2011 concerning article 19, entitled Freedom of opinion and expression[156]. The Committee emphasizes from the beginning the importance of the freedom of opinion and information as a basis for the full enjoyment and exercise of a wide range of other human rights and refers to other general comments adopted previously, concerning other human rights, for whose protection of the freedom of expression is necessary.

The Committee holds that the freedom of opinion (art. 19.1) cannot be subject to any derogation during a public emergency, as a right to which the Covenant permits no exception or restriction; all forms of opinion, in all fields, are protected; detaining an opinion cannot be subject to stigmatization, intimidation or any sanction or other form of coercion. The Committee also expresses its position according to which a reservation concerning the right to hold opinions (art. 9.1) or to the entirety of forms of exercise of the freedom of expression (art. 19.2) would be contrary to the purpose and the object of the Covenant. The Comment enumerates the forms of expression of ideas and opinions (political discourse, commentary, discussion on human rights, journalism, cultural and artistic expression, teaching and religious discourse) and refers to any means of expression, including those electronic and the internet. This includes even expressions regarded as deeply offensive, but the Comment

---

[156] Comment nr. 34, Article 19: Freedom of opinion and expression, doc. CCPR/C/GC/34, 21 July 2011.

mentions that they can be subject to restrictions according to articles 19.2 and 20 mentioned above

The Comment underlines the importance of the press and other media, free, uncensored and unhindered, mainly with regard to political and public issues, as well as of ensuring the independence of the new means of information and access to them, and of services of public information. At the same time, it gives importance to the access to information detained by public bodies, notably to the protection of personal data, of those of a medical nature and those concerning criminal accusations; the Committee underlines the duty to provide reasons for a refusal to offer public information and to provide a remedy in such cases. The Comment also gives particular significance to the freedom of information for exercising political rights, mainly regarding participation in public life and in elections.

With regard to restrictions which may be applied to the exercise of the freedom of expression, the Committee stresses that they cannot affect the substance of this human right and can be justified only in the cases provided for in article 19.3 and if they fulfill the condition of proportionality. States are asked to adopt measures in order to protect against any attacks which curtail or annihilate the freedom of expression, as well as to investigate such cases and prosecute the perpetrators. It is also underlined that restrictions of the freedom of expression enshrined in traditional, religious or other such customs are not compatible with the Covenant.

With respect to national laws which establish some restrictions to the freedom of information, the Comment stresses that they have to observe all the provisions of the Covenant, they have to be motivated in conformity with article 19.3 and they have to respect human rights universally recognized, mainly the principle of non-discrimination, as well as that they must be proportional with the threat to the object protected. In particular, with regard to restrictions which may be applied in some fields, the Committee expresses concern about restrictions to the distribution of material during electoral campaigns and to the access of opposition parties and of politicians to media outlets, as well as about measures to limit the freedom of expression in political debate, including critics to authorities and personalities, irrespective of the level they occupy in the State's hierarchy. In the same order of ideas, States are reminded that regulations with regard to media have to provide for objective and reasonable criteria, to be clear and non-discriminatory, to promote the pluralism of the media and to avoid control which would lead to restricting the freedom of expression. It is also pointed out that measures to restrict the freedom of journalists and other persons who exercise the freedom of expression are not permitted. Even with regard to measures to combat terrorism, the Committee underlines that they have to be compatible with the provisions of art. 19.3 and that such measures should not lead to restrictions of the freedom of information which are not necessary or are disproportionate.

Even with regard to laws condemning defamation, the Comment insists that they should not lead in fact to stifle the freedom of information, that they should take into account the interest of the public for the information disseminated, to avoid excessively punitive measures and to apply penal sanctions only in the most serious cases. It is also underlined that the prohibition of dissemination of information for lack of respect towards a religion or another system of belief is not compatible with the Covenant, with the exception of the case provided for in art. 20.2 mentioned above; discriminatory law in favour of a religion or certain religions or belief systems in this field (namely forbidding dissemination of such information only about one religion) would be unacceptable, as well as the prohibition of criticism of religious leaders and of comments about religious doctrines. Similarly, laws which would incriminate the expression of opinions with regard to historic facts would be incompatible with the Covenant, even if they would include opinions considered erroneous or incorrect interpretations of past events.

The Comment analyses also the relationship between articles 19 and 20, affirming that article 20 refers also to acts which are submitted to restrictions according to article 19.3, which means that such restrictions have to respect the conditions provided. The only difference would be that for restrictions referred to in article 20 States have to adopt a law to prohibit them, while for those restrictions referred in article 19.3 the adoption of a legislative act is not necessary. In our opinion, article 20 provides for an interdiction by law of acts of war propaganda and of those promoting national, racial or religious hatred that constitutes incitement to discrimination, hostility or violence, which leaves no margin of discretion to States, while under art. 19.3 certain restrictions with regard to other types of information shall be provided by law when they are necessary and, as the Committee affirms, have to be proportional to the object protected. That means that in the adoption of the law concerning restrictions under art. 9.3 States can evaluate to what extent such restrictions are necessary and eventually some conditions how to apply them, while the adoption of a law introducing a legal prohibition under article 20 is compulsory.

Another committee monitoring the application of an international document in this field is the Committee for the Elimination of Racial Discrimination, which adopted also a General Recommendation nr. 35[157] with regard to the freedom of expression in relation to the racist hate speech[158]. The Committee starts by affirming the compatibility of the freedom of expression with the prohibition of the racist speech and presents the interdiction of the racist hatred speech and the flourishing of the freedom of expression as being complementary, not as a zero-sum game in which the protection of one would lead to diminishing the other; the conclusion is that both human rights-to equal rights and freedom from discrimination and to freedom of expression have to be fully reflected in laws, policies and practices of States.

Taking as a starting point the text of the Convention on the elimination of all forms of racial discrimination, adopted within the UN in 1965 (mainly its art. 4), the Committee recommends that States parties declare and effectively sanction as offences punishable by law: dissemination of ideas based on racial or ethnic superiority or hatred, by whatever means; incitement to hatred, contempt or discrimination against members of a group on grounds of race, color, descent or national or ethnic origin; threats or incitement to violence against persons or groups on the grounds mentioned; expression of insults, ridicule or slander of persons or groups, or justification of hatred, contempt or discrimination on such grounds, when it amounts to incitement to hatred or to

---

[157] General Recommendation no. 35, Combating racist hate speech, doc. CERD/C/GC/35, 26 September 2013.

[158] On racist speech and the freedom of expression in the context of the 1965 Convention, Ion Diaconu, Chapter XIII-Racist speech and freedom of expression and information, in Human Rights' Impact in International Law, Amazon, 2017, pp. 334-355.

discrimination; participation in organizations and activities which promote and incite racial discrimination. The Committee also recommended that public denials or attempts to justify crimes of genocide and crimes against humanity, as defined by international law, should be declared as offences punishable by law, provided that they clearly constitute incitement to racial violence or hatred.

At the same time, the Committee underlined that, beyond the legal provisions requested by the Convention, the roll of independent and impartial courts is crucial in order to assess the facts and to give the proper legal qualifications in individual cases, in conformity with international standards of human rights (with a direct reference to the Universal Declaration of Human Rights, which enunciates the entirety of human rights, including the freedoms of expression and association). The Committee also indicates a series of contextual factors which should be taken into account when considering such cases, namely: the content and form of the speech allegedly racist; the economic, social and political climate prevalent in society at the time the speech was made; the position and the status in society of the author and the audience to which the speech is directed; the rich of the speech and the means of transmission of the speech; the objectives of the speech.

The General Recommendation underlines the importance of the obligations taken by States to adopt immediate and effective measures in the fields of teaching, education, culture and information with a view to combating prejudices which lead to racial discrimination, to promoting understanding, tolerance and friendship among nations and racial or ethnic groups, as well as to propagating universal human rights principles. The importance of the education system, of educational programmes and materials, of intercultural education and of encouraging the knowledge of history, culture and traditions of racial or ethnic existing groups is also emphasized. The Recommendation also refers to the important role of the informed, ethical and objective media, including of the social media and the internet in promoting responsibility in the dissemination of ideas and opinions, and asks States to encourage the adoption of codes of professional ethics that incorporate respect for the principles of the Convention and other fundamental human rights standards, as well as the plurality of media.

Other human rights committees referred also to the freedom of expression as an important factor for promoting the respective rights of women, children, persons subject to torture and inhuman treatment or punishment, disabled persons and for the elimination of discrimination against these persons, in the comments adopted by them and in the recommendations addressed to States parties to the respective treaties.

2. The European Convention for the protection of human rights and fundamental freedoms, adopted in 1950 by the Council of Europe, resumes in substance the provisions of article 19 of the Covenant as indicated above. Moreover, the European Convention stresses in its article 10.2 that the exercise of the freedoms of expression and of opinion may be subject to such formalities, conditions, restrictions or penalties as are prescribed by law and are necessary in a democratic society, in the interests of national security, territorial integrity or public safety, for prevention of disorder or crime, for the protection of health or morals, for the protection or the rights of others, for preventing the disclosure of information received in confidence, or for maintaining the authority and impartiality of the judiciary.

At the same time, according to article 14 of the European Convention, the enjoyment of the rights and freedoms set forth in the Convention shall be secured without discrimination on any ground such as sex, race, color, language, religion, political or other opinion, national or social origin, association with a national minority, property, birth or other Status; similarly, other provisions have to be borne in mind such as those of art. 16 (nothing in articles 10 and 14 of the present Convention prevents the States parties from imposing restrictions on the political activities of aliens), of art. 17 (nothing in this Convention may be interpreted as implying for any State, group or person any right to engage in any activity or perform any act aimed at the destruction of any rights and freedoms set forth therein or at their limitation to a greater extent than is provided for in the Convention) and those of art 18 (the restrictions permitted under this Convention to the said rights and freedoms shall not be applied for any purpose other than those for which they have been prescribed).

The American Convention on human rights, adopted in San Jose-Costa Rica in 1969, treats the freedom of expression jointly with the freedom of thought. In substance, the American Convention adds interesting aspects concerning: the prohibition of previous censorship on the exercise of the freedom of expression; the interdiction of restrictions of the right to expression by indirect means, such as the governmental or private control on the means of communication and of circulation of ideas and opinions; the possibility of submitting to censorship the public advertisement with the view to regulating access to it for the moral protection of children and adolescents; the right to reply of the person affected by statements or ideas, using the same media, without excluding other legal responsibilities.

The African Charter of human rights and the rights of peoples, adopted in Nairobi in 1981, enunciates in general terms the right of everyone to receive information and to express and disseminate his opinions according to the law. The Arab Charter of human rights adopted in Tunis in 2004 contains also similar provisions of a general nature.

Within the limits of this study, it does not seem necessary to present national legislations in European States about the freedom of opinion and expression; as all States of the region are members of the Council of Europe, they have such laws, which offer some variety, having a different emphasis on aspects considered of particular interest. This is shown by a number of cases examined by the European Court of Human Rights, as presented below.

SECTION II - Exclusion *de plano* by the European Court of Human Rights of the Protection, for Abuse of the Freedom of Expression

After the well-known decision in the case *Handyside v. United Kingdom*[159], where the Court affirmed that „the freedom of expression applies not only with regard to information or ideas received favorably or considered inoffensive or indifferent, but also with regard to those which hurt, shock or trouble the State or

---

[159] Handyside v. UK, decision of 7 December 1976; on this case also Frederic Krenk, La liberté d'expression vaut pour les propos qui heurtent, choquent ou inquiètent. Mais encore ? in Revue trimestrielle des drots de l'homme, no. 106, 2016, pp. 311-350.

one of the fractions of the population", other decisions which followed are marked by questions, hesitations and uncertainty.

Having in mind the provisions of articles 17 and 10 mentioned above, the Court refused to grant protection in cases were the freedom of expression was exercised by a serious and manifest violation of the basic principles of the Convention and of some human rights.

The Court excluded applications related to a category of acts considered as representing an abuse of right, in conformity with art. 17, namely as acts aiming at the destruction of rights and freedoms of other persons or directed against the values protected by the Convention.

This category includes first the racist speech. In its decision adopted in the case *Jersild v. Denmark*, the Court retains that statements like "A black person is not a human being, is an animal" or also that "Take simply a picture, dear friend, of a gorilla and then look at a black person, it is the same physical structure and all, my friend, a plate front and all is this way", do not benefit from the protection of 10 of the Convention[160]. Similarly, the Court excluded from the protection of art. 10 affirmations which aim at the denial of holocaust. In connection with this, in the case

---

[160] Case Jersild v. Denmark, decision of 23 September 1994. This is an *obiter dictum* of the Court, as the object of the petition was to contest the condemnation by the Danish courts of the journalist who took the interview. The Court retained that the action of the journalist was a contribution to the discussion of an issue of general interest, that is an action which should not be sanctioned unless there are particularly serious reasons (para. 35).

Garaudy v. France[161], where the applicant invoked the freedom of expression for his book "Founding myths of the Israeli policies", the Court retained that "contesting crimes against humanity appears as one of the sharpest forms of racial defamation against Jews and of incitement of hatred against them. Denying or reviewing historic facts of this type raises doubts about the values which underlie the combat against racism and antisemitism and are of the nature to seriously disturb the public order. As they injure the rights of other persons, such acts are incompatible with democracy and with human rights, and their authors pursue obviously objectives among those prohibited by art. 17 of the Convention".

More recently, the European Court considered the application of *Dieudonne M'Bala M'Bala* invoking the violation of his freedom of expression by the French courts[162]. The French courts condemned the applicant for transforming a theatre performance into a public meeting with the unique purpose to turn into derision the deportation and the extermination of Jews by the Nazi regime during the Second World War. By its decision, the Court rejected the application as being *ratione materiae* incompatible with the provisions of the Convention and refusing

---

[161] Case Garaudy v. France, decision of 24 June 2003; similarly, in the case Faurisson v. France submitted to the Human Rights Committee, opinion of 8 November 1996, in view of the statement according to which „I have excellent reasons not to believe in this policy of extermination of Jews or in the magic chamber a gas". Doc. CCPR/C/58/D/550/1993.

[162] Case M'Bala M'Bala v. France, decision of the Court of 20 October 2015. An extended analysis of this decision by Mustapha Akroukh, La Cour européenne condamne énergiquement toutes les formes de négationnisme et d'antisémitisme, in Revue Trimestrielle des Droits de l'Homme, nr. 107/2016, pp. 759-774.

the protection provided for by art. 10. The Court underlined the usefulness of art. 17 against the abusive use of freedom of expression, namely as a clause of interdiction even with regard to the freedom of artistic expression, affirming that the expression of a position penetrated by hatred and of antisemitism, apparently disguised as an artistic production, is as dangerous as a direct and abrupt attack. The Court affirms that art. 17, to the extent that it concerns groups or persons, has the objective to make it impossible to derive from the Convention a right which would allow them to perform an act aiming at the destruction of rights and freedoms recognized by the Convention[163].

In a case on the same subject (*case Ivanov*), the Court applied art. 17 with regard to the petition of a Russian citizen, refusing to consider that he exercised his right to the freedom of expression, because he expressed himself for the exclusion of Jews from social life[164]. The Court also declared inadmissible, on the basis of art. 17, the application of a British citizen (*case Norwood*) who invoked his freedom of expression for Islamo-phobic affirmations. He placed on the window of his house a posting of the National British Party which represented the twin towers of New-York in flame accompanied by the appeal „Islam out-Let's protect the British people". The Court retained that „An attack so vehement, of a general nature, against a religious group, which establishes a relationship between the whole group and a serious terrorist attack is contrary to the values proclaimed and guaranteed

---

[163] Decision of the Court, case M'Bala M'Bala, decision of 20 October 2015, para. 32.
[164] Case Ivanov v. Russia, decision of 20 February 2007.

by the Convention, namely tolerance, social peace and non-discrimination"[165].

Still, the Court did not always follow the same way to resort to art. 17 (considered by authors as „a guillotine clause") with regard to positions expressed concerning antisemitism, islamophobia and acts of genocide. In the case *Perincek v. Switzerland*[166], the Court did not accept to apply art. 17 with regard to affirmations concerning a crime of genocide committed by the massacre of Armenians in 1915 by the ottoman empire, affirming that art. 17 should be used only if it is clear that the aim followed was „to use the freedom of expression for purposes obviously contrary to the Convention". The Court retained that the affirmations of the applicant could not be assimilated to calls to hatred, violence or intolerance against Armenians, that they are different from those concerning the denial of holocaust and that in Switzerland „there is not an imperious social value which would justify repression against the words of the applicant".

The Court also applied art. 17 in the case *Vejdenland and others v. Sweden*[167], where the applicant was condemned by the local courts for distributing to young people brochures with offensive contents against homosexuals. The Court underlined that discrimination based on sexual orientation is as serious as that based on race, ethnic origin or colour and that the brochures were disseminated to children of a small age. The Court did not retain a violation of the freedom of expression, but affirmed that the

---

[165] Case Norwood v. UK, decision of 16 November 2004.
[166] Case Perincek, decision of 15 October 2015
[167] Case Vejdenland and others v. Sweden, decision of 14 February 2012; ECHR Annual Report, 2012, p. 95.

sanctions imposed by the Supreme Court of Sweden were excessive.

Consequently, the Court applies art. 17 according to a conception of an absolute prohibition of the racist speech, excluding *de plano* the respective applications from the ambit of the freedom of expression and without examining whether the conditions required by art. 10 are reunited. This differs from the conception retained by the Human Rights Committee with regard to the interpretation of art. 19 and 20 of the Covenant on civil and political rights. According to the conception of the Court, in the case of acts falling under the provision of art. 17 any claims formulated by invoking the freedom of expression are directly inadmissible and there is no need to prove that the respective measure is necessary and to proceed to a test of proportionality with the objective followed.

Besides the cases where it had to apply art. 17 and to exclude *de plano* the examination of application for recognizing the right to freedom of expression according to art. 10, the Court had to make the distinction between statements about facts (for which it can ask the author to prove their existence, in order to grant the protection under art. 10), from statements which represent judgment of value of the author, and for which it cannot request such a demonstration. The Court accepted from the beginning that „the requirement to establish the veracity of judgments of value is not feasible in practice and injures the freedom of opinion, which is a fundamental element of the right guaranteed by art. 10"[168], but underlined that even the judgments of value should have a

---

[168] Cases Norwood v. UK, decision of 16 November 2004, Pedersen and Baadsgaard v. Denmark, decision of 17 December 2004, Oberschlick v. Austria, decision of 23 May 1991.

sufficient factual basis. With regard to statements concerning facts, it says that they can essentially be proved; the author has to prove them and, if this is not done, sanctioning him is considered in conformity with art. 10 of the Convention as indicated above, meaning that he is deprived of the protection of this provision. The Court underlined that the author of the statement has to have an effective possibility to prove the facts invoked, and in the case of the judgments of value, to show that they are justified by a sufficient basis of facts[169].

It is not always easy to make the distinction between a statement about facts and a judgment of value. As a rule, the Court appreciated that this qualification is part of the margin of discretion of national courts. Nevertheless, in some cases the Court intervened and invalidated the decisions of national courts which qualified some statements as concerning facts and requested proof of their existence, considering that they are in fact judgments of value[170].

---

[169] Cases Colombani and others v. France, decision of 25 June 2002; Morice v. France, decision of 13 April 2015.
[170] Cases Scharsach and News Verlagsgesellschaft GmbH v. Austria, decision of 13 November 2003; Brosa v. Germany, decision of 17 April 2014.

SECTION III - Protection of the freedom of expression and of information according to the decisions of the ECHR- general aspects

Much more numerous are the cases where the European Court examined the exercise of the freedom of expression having in view the contents of the expression in the light of the conditions established by art. 10. The Court affirmed that States have the duty, by virtue of their positive obligations according to article 8 of the Convention, „to regulate the exercise of the freedom of expression so as to ensure an adequate protection by the law of the reputation of persons"[171].

In the case *Seurot v. France*, the Court held that the application of that person (who was dismissed from the post of professor) concerning the violation by the State of art. 10 was manifestly unfounded and that "the article in dispute (published by the professor of history and geography in a bulletin for students) has an indisputable racist character and is incompatible with the duties and responsibilities incumbent upon the applicant"[172].

---

[171] Case Cumpana and Mazare v. Romania, decision of 17 December 2004.

[172] Case Seurot v. France, decision of 18 May 2004. In the article incriminated the professor affirmed that „Those illusionists did not foresee that in exchange of the hopeless running away of these damned French from North Africa, the Muslim hordes who are not assimilable will lend and will reach the farthest away of our canton; they are now 5 million, they build everywhere mosques and when they say they will were veils...don't enjoy too much, these will be only on their dirty and arrogant girls".

In the case *Feret v. Belgium*, the chairman of the National Front, author and editor in Belgium, was condemned for materials which "clearly, although sometimes implicitly, incited if not to violence, at least to discrimination, to segregation and hatred towards a group, a community or their members on grounds of their race, colour, descent or national or ethnic origin" and appreciated that „it was inevitable that such a discourse raise up within the public, mainly a less informed public, feelings of rejection, for some even of hatred towards aliens". The Court held that incitement to hatred does not necessarily request an appeal to certain act of violence or other criminal act and that the facts committed „are sufficient for the authorities to privilege the struggle against racist speech versus an irresponsible exercise of the freedom of expression which injures the dignity, even the security of these parts or groups of the population"[173]. Therefore, even without invoking art. 17, the Court considers that incitement to hatred or the intimidation of a vulnerable group justifies in principle to restrain the freedom of expression and retains that there is no violation of art. 10[174].

In a different case concerning a dictionary in the Turkish language (*Aksu v. Turkey*), containing expressions felt by an ethnic vulnerable minority as humiliating and insulting, the Court appreciated, taking into account the general character of a dictionary and the fact that this is not recommended for schools by the Ministry of Education, that the authorities did not go beyond their recognized margin of discretion by not ordering to delete the respective definition from the dictionary. At the same time, the applicant criticized a publication which would represent an attack

---

[173] Case Feret v. Belgium, decision of 16 July 2009.
[174] Cases Feret v. Belgium and Vona v. Hungary, cited above.

to the identity of the Roma community and consequently a violation of his private life. The Court retained that any negative stereotype concerning a group can have an impact on the self-esteem and confidence feeling of members of the group and can be considered as affecting their private life. The Court affirmed that the vulnerable position of Roma imposes that States give a special attention to their needs and to their different way of life both in the legislative framework and in decisions taken in specific cases[175].

The Court applied art.10 also with regard to studies and works which referred indirectly to crimes committed against Jews during the Second World War, besides the cases Garaudy and M'Bala M'Bala v. France mentioned above, where the Court rejected *de plano* the applications of the respective persons as being an abuse of rights. In the case *Giniewski v. France,* the Court found that the condemnation of a journalist for public defamation of the community of Christians, because of the publication of an article entitled „Obscurity of error", with regard to the Vatican's encyclique Veritatis Splendor. On the basis of this encyclique, the author affirmed that numerous Christians recognized that anti-judaism it describes „formed the ground on which the idea and the execution of Auschwitz sprouted". The Court retained that by this article the author wanted „to elaborate a theory with regard to the contents of a dogma and to its possible connections with the origins of the holocaust", namely that the respective text participates in a reflection on the possible causes of the holocaust, that is as part of a debate of a general interest in a democratic society[176]. Similarly, in the case *Lehideux and Isorni v. France*, the

---

[175] Case Aksu v. Turkey, decision of 27 July 2010; presented in ECHR, Annual Report 2012, p. 88.
[176] Case Giniewski v. France, decision of 30 January 2006.

Court retained that art. 10 was violated by the condemnation of the applicants for the apology of crime and collaboration, because they published in the journal Le Monde an article entitled „French, you have a short memory", where they made a eulogy to marshal Petain for his action during the war. The Court noted that marshal Petain was presented in an exclusively favourable light, without mentioning facts for which he was blamed, and which led to his condemnation to death by the French judiciary. At the same time, the Court underlined that the applicants dissociated in an explicit manner from the Nazi atrocities and persecutions and from the barbarian action of the German power and that the purpose followed by them was to promote the pertinence and the legitimate character of reviewing the condemnation of Petain[177].

Other cases considered by the Court refer to freedom of expression with regard to religious beliefs and denominations. This issue was examined for instance in cases such as *Otto Preminger-Institut v. Austria and Wingrove v. UK*, in which the Court considered that the threshold which would characterize a serious or unnecessary offence of religious feelings was not exceeded[178]. It is also *the case Giniewski* presented above, concerning the Vatican's encyclique „Veritatis Splendor" and its presentation as one of the dogma which led to holocaust. More recently, in the case *I. A. v. Turkey*, after affirming that a State „may legitimately adopt measures to repress some forms of behaviour, including the communication of information and ideas considered incompatible with the freedom of thought, conscience and religion of others", the Court retained that the condemnation by the Turkish

---

[177] Case Lehideux and Isorni v. France, decision of 23 September 1998.

[178] Cases Otto-Preminger v. Austria, decision of 20 September 1994; Wingrove v. UK, decision of 25 November 1996.

jurisdiction of an editor for publishing a novel containing some texts considered blasphemy could reasonably respond to a socially imperious need[179]. According to the Court, persons of the Muslim faith could legitimately consider themselves attacked without justification and offensively by the respective texts, which justifies the condemnation of the author aimed to ensure protection against offending attacks on questions considered sacred by Muslims. In a different case, the Court considered a serious offense of religious feelings as representing unjustified sufferings[180]. In connection with this subject, some authors appreciate that the religious feelings, of affection and belonging to a community are, for the jurisprudence of the European Court „an integral part ... of the elements which have to be taken into account in order to determine the limits of the freedom of expression within the public debate"[181].

Although in the case *Refah Partisi v. Turkey*, the court underlined the incompatibility of Sharia with the fundamental principles of democracy[182], in the same year, in a different case (*Gunduz v. Turkey*) the Court held that „the mere fact of defending Sharia in a television programme, without calling to violence to impose it, cannot be considered as a hate speech which would go beyond the limits admissible under art. 10[183].

In the case *Sekmadienis Ltd. v. Lithuania*[184], this closing company was fined by the national courts for displaying a series of advertisements using models and captions referring to "Jesus" and

---

[179] Case I. A. v. Turkey, decision of 13 September 2005.

[180] Case Murphy v. Ireland, decision of 10 July 2003.

[181] Céline Ruet, Sentiments et droits de l'homme, dans Revue trimestrielle des droits de l'homme, nr. 106, 2016, p. 352.

[182] Case Refah Partisi v. Turkey, decision of 13 February 2003.

[183] Case Gunduz v. Turkey, decision of 4 December 2003.

[184] Petition nr. 69314/17, decision of 30 January 2018.

"Mary". The Lithuanian courts considered that these advertisements were an offense to public morals. The European Court found, in spite of a number of complaints received including via the Roman Catholic Church in Lithuania, that these advertisements were not gratuitously offensive and did not incite hatred. As national authorities did not provide sufficient justifications for why such use of religious symbols had been contrary to public morals, and did not strike a balance between the protection of the public morals and the company's right to freedom of expression, ECHR found a violation of art. 10.

A different case referred to the conviction of *Mr. Belkacem*, the leader and spokesperson of the organization "Sharia4Belgium" which was dissolved in 2012, for incitement to discrimination, hatred and violence because of remarks he made in You Tube videos, calling on viewers to overpower non-Muslims and teach them a lesson. The Court considered that these remarks had a markedly hateful content, had sought to stir up hatred, discrimination and hatred against non-Muslims and were incompatible with the values of tolerance, social peace and non-discrimination underlying the European Convention on human rights. The Court rejected the application as incompatible with the provisions of the Convention and as an attempt to deflect article 10 from its real purpose[185].

SECTION IV - Protection related to specific professions or public functions

---

[185] Belkacem v. Belgium, petition nr. 3467/14, decision on admissibility on 20 July 2017.

Numerous cases considered by the Court refer to persons who due to their profession are more directly involved in the exercise of the freedom of information, either in the meaning of an extended freedom, or of a more reserved attitude due to the nature of the profession exercised. Besides the case *Jersild,* referred above, were the Court clearly differentiated the freedom of expression from the racist speech, in many cases the Court refers very often to the freedom of information exercised by *journalists* and underlines their roll[186]. In the case *RTBF v. Belgium*, concerning the temporary interdiction of the diffusion of a television documentary requested by the person named in the programme, the Court affirms that, although the interdiction of diffusion of a material at the TV (preventive control) is not *per se* contrary to art. 10, such restrictions represent significant risks for the freedom of expression. Therefore, the Court considers that they have to be envisaged within a particularly strict legal framework which prescribes the limits of the interdiction and offers an efficient jurisdictional control against potential abuses. The Court retained that both the legal framework and the jurisprudence of the Belgian courts do not respond to the conditions of the restrictions required by the Convention[187].

In the case *Leroy v. France*, the Court considered that the publication of a drawing representing the twin towers of New-York in flames, accompanied by the legend „We all dreamed this...Hamas did it" represents complicity to the apology of

---

[186] Among the more recent cases Couderc and Filipacchi Associates v. France, decision of 10 November 2015 and Haldimann and others v. Switzerland, decision of 24 February 2015.

[187] Case RTBF v. Belgium, decision of 29 March 2011; presented also in ECHR, Annual Report 2011, pp. 99-100.

terrorism, affirming that everyone who invokes the freedom of expression takes also duties and responsibilities[188].

In the case *Haldimann and others v. Switzerland*, the Court examined the case of an audio-video registration of an interview with the agent of an insurance company without his knowledge and consent, which was diffused afterwards at TV. The journalists were penalized by a fine according to the criminal code for registering and diffusing the conversation without the previous agreement of the agent. The Court accepted that there was a basis in internal law for sanctioning the journalists but retained that their purpose was not to present details from the private life of the agent, but to draw attention of the public on the practices of the industry for which he worked, and that they acted in good faith to protect the clients from false information offered by companies[189].

In the case *Rosiianu v. Romania*[190], a journalist who presented for more than 6 years TV programmes on local posts about how public money was used by the local administration, asked for information on this matter from the mayor's office. He made three repeated requests. He initiated an action to the administrative court asking for an order of the court to oblige the mayor to disclose the information requested. The Court of appeal accepted the plea of the journalist and adopted an order to the mayor to disclose the information. The answer given by the office of the mayor was to invite him to come to copy some documents. The Court of appeal considered that it was not a correct execution of its decision.

---

[188] Case Leroy v. France, decision of 2 October 2008.
[189] Case Haldimann v. Switzerland, ECHR Annual Report 2015, pp.169-170.
[190] ECHR, petition nr. 27329/06, decision of 24 June 2014.

The European Court held that, by refusing to implement the judicial decision which ordered to disclose the information requested, the State authorities deprived the journalist of his right to an effective access to justice. This was considered to be a violation of art. 6.1 of the Convention.

In another case concerning Romania (*Sipos.v. Romania*)[191], a TV journalist complained that she was replaced without explanation. As she did not receive any explanation, she addressed to the press alluding to restoration of censorship at the State television. The director of SRTV responded by a press-release, considered insulting and defamatory. She initiated a criminal action against the director and the press officer. The courts did not condemn the two, affirming that they did not act with the intention to insult or defame and expressed only the position of the SRTV regarding accusations of restoration of censorship. The Court of appeal also dismissed her request but retained that the answer given in the press-release contained some defamatory affirmations.

The Court retained first that art. 8 obliges the State not only to refrain from an arbitrary interference with the exercise of the right to respect the private and family life, but also creates the positive obligation to adopt measures to ensure respect of private life in the relations among individuals. It noted that the press-release did not contain only a factual presentation, but also allegations about a political manipulation to which she was subject, about her emotional state, as being marked by family problems and creating difficulties in working relations. The Court noted that the alleged political manipulation was not proved, while the remarks

---

[191] ECHR, petition nr. 26125/04, decision of 3 May 2011.

about her emotional state were based on elements of her private life whose disclosure was not necessary.

The Court accepted the petition of an Icelandic journalist who was found guilty of defamation for publishing an article about individuals who represented a Christian rehabilitation center until allegations of sexual abuse surfaced. The applicant appealed the ruling under art. 10. The Court held that there had been a violation of his right to the freedom of expression as granted by art. 10 of the Convention[192].

The Court also extended the protection granted to *non-governmental organizations* which bring to the attention of the public subjects of public interest, including the *associations acting for the protection of human rights*[193]. The Court recognized the protection provided by art. 10 also to *unofficial militant groups* which distribute information of public interest[194] and accepted the idea of journalism by internet[195], in view of the development of the means of communication. In the case *Animal Defenders v. UK*, where this organization complained against a law which forbids political promotion, and which impedes it to diffuse a TV program as part of a campaign concerning the treatment of primates, the Court accepted that the organization drew the attention on some issues of public interest and exercised its roll of guardian similar to that of the press. The Court affirmed also that the right of n. g. o's to distribute information and ideas of general interest for the public has to be balanced with the willingness of authorities to protect the

---

[192] Erla Hlinsdottir v. Iceland, petition nr. 54125/10, decision of 21 October 2014.
[193] Supra, p. 9.
[194] Case Steel and Morris v. UK, decision of 15 February 2005
[195] Casel Bartnik v. Poland, decision of 11 March 2014.

democratic debate and to avoid its distortion by powerful financial groups which have an advantage in terms of access to media. The Court appreciated nevertheless that the restrictions are limited, there are other means available to distribute the respective information and that reasonable arguments were presented to justify the interdiction of political advertisement paid at the radio and television[196].

The Court applied also the temporal context; the Court took into consideration the long duration of a criminal trial (6.5 years), which did not lead to a condemnation, but were the applicant was prosecuted for publishing an article affirming that an officer of a high rank tried to influence the political life in Turkey. The Court retained a violation of art. 10 because the author approached a problem of public interest and the proceedings against him could dissuade him as well as other journalists to express critical comments about the relation between the military and political life in Turkey[197].

A non-governmental organization *GRA Stiftung gegen Rassismus and Antisemitismus*, in a petition against Switzerland, complained that its right to freedom of expression had been infringed because the domestic courts found a defamation against a politician by classifying as "verbal racism" his remarks at a speech during a campaign during the referendum on minarets, and imposed a penalty to the organization. ECHR found a violation of article 10, because in the context of the debate the use of these words has not been without factual foundation and the authorities

---

[196] Cases Animal Defenders International v. UK, decision of 22 April 2012 and Tarsasag and Szabadsagjogokert v. Hungary, decision of 14 April 2009.

[197] Case Dilipak v. Turkey, ECHR Annual Report 2015, p. 170.

had not given due consideration to the principles and criteria laid down by the Court in its case-law for balancing the right to respect private life and the right to freedom of expression[198].

In a different case, members of a Turkish group called Anti-militarist Platform met in front of the Israeli Consulate in Istanbul, and one of them, Mr. Savda, read out a statement for the press entitled "We are in solidarity with the Israeli conscientious objectors". Criminal proceedings were brought against him and he was sentenced to a five-months prison sentence on the ground that he had incited the population to evade military service by that statement. Mr. Savda complained about his conviction in criminal proceedings as a violation of article 10. The Court found his petition admissible and ruled that a violation of art.10 occurred, ordering also non-pecuniary damages to the applicant[199].

The Court examined also cases concerning the exercise of the freedom of expression by using the *new means of information*. In the case *Delfi v. Estonia*, the Court retained at first that through the internet „words which are unlawful, mainly defamatory, of hatred or which call to violence can be distributed as never before in the entire world in a few seconds and sometimes remain on line indefinitely". The Court examined the case of the owner of a site of news, namely whether he violated the freedom of expression by distributing comments which represented a speech of hatred or of incitement to violence. The Court underlined the obligation of the owner of the site to withdraw from his site such comments immediately after publication, when one could understand at first

---

[198] Petition nr. 18597/13, decision of 9 January 2018.
[199] Case Savda v. Turkey, petition nr. 2458/12, decision of 15 November 2016.

view that they are clearly unlawful[200]. The Court affirmed nevertheless that what it retained in this case does not concern other types of forum on the internet, the sites of electronic dissemination or the platforms of the social media. The Court retained that a State may request that a site of news exercise a monitoring of the comments so as to be able to eliminate immediately such comments which are clearly unlawful, even without a notification from an alleged victim or from a third person.

In the case *Editorial Board of Pravovoye Delo and Shtekel v. Ukraine,* journalists were sanctioned to pay fines because they republished a letter from the internet, considered defamatory by those concerned, accompanied by a comment where they indicated the source and dissociated themselves from the respective text. The national jurisdiction asked them also to publish a retraction and present excuses. The European Court affirmed that art.10 should be interpreted so as to impose to States the positive obligation to create an adequate legal framework which ensures the adequate protection of journalists who use materials from the internet and that the sanctions imposed were not in conformity with the law as requested by art. 10.2. It also underlined that the law should take into account the specific features of this technology in order to protect and promote the respective rights and freedoms[201].

In another case which is more obvious, *Ahmet Yldirim v. Turkey*, the Court had to take a stand on a decision to block a website, having as effect to impede the access to the entire field of

---

[200] Case Delfi A.S. v. Estonia, decision of 16 June 2015, ECHR Annual Report 2015, pp. 164-165.

[201] Case Editorial Board of Pravovoye Delo and Shtekel v. Ukraine, ECHR Annual Report 2011, p. 100.

the Google sites, as a preventive measure in the context of a criminal procedure against a third person. The Court affirmed again that internet became one of the main means through which individuals exercise their right to information and expression and offers essential means to take part in activities and discussions on political or other issues of public interest. Measures which make inaccessible a large quantity of information have a considerable impact on those using the internet and represent a violation of art. 10[202]. Similarly, in the case *Wegrzimowski and Smolenski v. Poland,* concerning the request to delete from the website of a newspaper un article already published, the Court rejected this request referring to the right of the media professionals and to the critical part of electronic archives for preserving and communicating information to the public. The Court affirmed that art. 10 protects also the legitimate interest of the public to have access to press archives through the internet and did not accept the roll to rewrite history by deleting from archives any traces of publications found in the past as defamatory[203].

In the case *Cenghiz and others v. Turkey,* concerning blocking the access to You Tube used by professors in their professional activity, on ground that some video materials were offensive to the address of the memory of Ataturk, the Court noted that this measure affected for longtime the right of professors to receive information and ideas which could not be received by other means and retained that the national courts were not competent to block any access to You Tube[204].

---

[202] Case Yildirim v. Turkey, ECHR Annual Report 2012, pp. 95-96.
[203] ECHR Annual Report 2013, pp. 111-112.
[204] ECHR Annual Report 2015, pp. 172.

Regarding *members of parliaments* and other persons elected, the Court emphasized as a rule their freedom of expression and its importance for fulfilling their mandate[205]. In connection with the freedom of expression of members of parliaments, the Court is inclined to accept its protection more when this includes the discourse made within the framework of the assembly they are part of than for positions expressed in other contexts[206]. Initially, in the case *Lingens,* the Court accepted that in case of *politicians* the limits admitted to criticism are wider and that by the nature of their quality they must show more tolerance[207]. On this ground, many condemnations adopted by national jurisdictions for criticism of elected politicians were considered contrary to art. 10^{208}. Nevertheless, in some cases the Court accepted sanctions applied by national jurisdictions, emphasizing the responsibility of those who pretended to exercise their freedom of expression.

In the case *Lindon, Otchakovski-Laurens and July v. France*, the Court considered as being compatible with the requirements of the freedom of expression the condemnation by the French judiciary for defamation caused by the publication of the novel of J. M. Lindon „The Process of Jean-Marie Le Pen". In this novel, the author presents the French politician as a „head of a band of killers", as a „vampire who feeds himself with the sorrow of his electors, but sometimes also with their blood, as well as with

---

[205] Cases such as Jerusalem v. Austria, decision of 27 February 2001; Brasilier v. France, decision of 11 April 2006; Jean-Jacques Morel v. France, decision of 10 October 2013.

[206] Cases A.v. UK, decision of 17 December 2002; Cordova v. Italy, decision of 30 January 2003.

[207] Case Lingens v. Austria, decision of 8 July 1986.

[208] For instance, the case Lopes Gomes Da Silva v. Portugal, decision of 28 September 2000 (concerning a "reactionary rudeness, of fascist bigotry and of vulgar antisemitism").

the blood of his enemies". The Court considered that the admissible limits of the freedom of expression were exceeded[209]. Similarly, in the case *Feret v. Belgium,* were the chairman of a right-wing party was condemned for disseminating articles full of hatred against minority groups, considered as incitement to racial discrimination, the Court underlined the importance that politicians avoid to disseminate in their political discourse „messages which could produce intolerance" and that the quality of members of parliament cannot be considered as a „circumstance which attenuates their responsibility[210]. The Court held the same position in the case *Willem v. France*, affirming that „in his quality as a mayor, the applicant had duties and responsibilities", including a duty to be cautious in his acts when they engage the territorial collectivity he represents[211], although it decided that the public announcement of his intention to boycott Israeli products on the territory of his commune does not represent a violation of art.10.

As mentioned above, in the case *Lehideux and Isorni v. France*, concerning the presentation by journalists of Petain in a favorable light, the Court held that art. 10 was not violated, as the journalists dissociated themselves from the crimes committed by the Nazi against Jews[212]. Similarly, in the case *Jelsevar and others v. Slovenia*[213], the Court had to evaluate whether it was compatible with art. 8 of the Convention (and consequently with art. 10) that an author uses the life of individuals as a source of inspiration to describe some characters of a book. The applicants, members of a

---

[209] Case Lindon, Otchakovski-Laurens and July, decision of 22 October 2007.
[210] Case Feret v. Belgium, presented above, pp. 126-127.
[211] Case Willem v. France, decision of 16 July 2009.
[212] Presented above, pp. 129-130.
[213] Presented in ECHR Annual Report, 2014, p. 129.

family, recognized the novel and the characters as referring to their family, mainly in the description of their deceased mother in texts considered offensive for her memory. The Constitutional Court of Slovenia rejected the request, affirming that the usual reader does not see the facts presented as referring to real individuals. The European Court considered reasonable the approach of the Constitutional Court of Slovenia as establishing a balance between the competing interests, underlining the importance of the artistic freedom in the context of the literary fiction works in which a person can be used as a prototype for a character, without being named as such, and declared the application as inadmissible.

The Court examined also, in conformity with art. 10 of the Convention, cases concerning the expression of opinions with regard to *heads of State*. In the *case Eon,* the condemnation for an offence addressed to the president of France, on the occasion of a visit to an enterprise, by displaying a sign reminding an insulting appeal of the former president Sarkozy addressed to another individual, was considered contrary to art. 10[214]. Similarly, in the *case Otegi Mondragon,* concerning the condemnation of a representative of a movement of Basques for the offence of serious injury addressed to the king of Spain, the Court noted that the king's position of neutrality, of arbiter and symbol of the unity of State is not making him free of criticism in the exercise of his official functions, that the immunity for criminal responsibility of the king cannot be an obstacle to a free debate concerning his institutional responsibility , even symbolic, as a head of State. The Basque representative affirmed that the king, as a supreme commander of the Spanish army, „is the responsible head of torturers and that who protects torture and imposes to the

---

[214] Case Eon v. France, decision of 14 March 2013.

people…his monarchic regime by torture and violence". The Court noted that „these words did not question the private life of the king, his personal honor and did not contain a useless attack against his person" and that the principles established in the jurisprudence of the Court concerning the republican systems are valid also for monarchic systems[215].

The Court considered also the case *Couderc and Hachette v. France*, concerning the publication in a review of an interview with a woman who pretended that Albert de Monaco was the father of her son. The court of Nanterre penalized with a fine the publication of this interview. The Court considered that a violation of art. 10 took place, because the national court did not take into account the principles of the Convention which require a balance of the private life with freedom of information, respectively the test of the proportionality of the restriction applied to the press with the protection of the private life in the respective case. The Court developed also some criteria which have to be applied in such cases, namely: a) the public interest cannot be confused with the pubic thirst of information about the life of others or with the desire of the reader of sensational news; b) the proactive function of the press to reveal and to submit to the public information able to raise interest and generate a debate in the society; c) the duty and the responsibility of the journalist to verify the impact of the information proposed, to show caution and care when approaching events which require protection of private life[216].

---

[215] Case Otegi Mondragon v. Spain, decision of 15 March 2011, presented in ECHRtbc Annual Report 2011, p. 99.
[216] Cases Couderc and Hachette v. France, ECHR Annual Report 2015, p. 165; Hachette Filipacchi Associates v. France, decision of 23 July 2009.

The Court examined also cases of the exercise of the freedom of expression concerning the *public officials*. Although it admitted that as the politicians they are exposed to more extended criticism than other persons due to their function, the Court considers that they do not have to be treated as politicians regarding their behavior, because they are supposed to act according to the law in fulfilling their mission[217].

The Court also examined the case of an official of the Romanian Service of Information, who disclosed information obtained in the exercise of his function, considering that it presents irregular practices of the Service in violation of the right to private and family life (case *Bucur and Toma v. Romania*)[218]. He disclosed this information in a press conference, after informing the head of the Service who did not take it seriously. He was condemned to 2 years of prison. He asked the European Court to retain a violation of art.10 on the freedom of information, and of art.6.1 on the fair trial because of the lack of impartiality of the court. Mr. Toma, a journalist among those mentioned in the information disclosed, complained about violation of his right and the right of his daughter to private and family life. ECHR recognized that preventing and punishing offenses related to national security was a legitimate aim, but the interference was not necessary in a democratic society when the information was of such a significant public importance. The Court also held that the Romanian court failed to consider whether the interest of maintaining the secrecy of the information outweighed the interest of the public to receive it. The Court retained a violation of art.10 and of art.6 for Mr. Bucur

---

[217] Among others, cases Janowski v. Poland, decision of 21 January 1999; Thoma v. Luxembourg, decision of 29 March 2001; Radio France and others v. France, decision of 30 March 2004.

[218] ECHR, petition nr. 48238/08 decision of 8 January 2013.

and for Mr. Toma and his daughter a violation of art.8 and of art.13 of the Convention, since there was no provision in the legislation that allowed them to challenge the arbitrary retention of their personal data.

The Court also accepted that those involved in judicial procedures, first of all the *judges*, have the right to freedom of expression, but have also the duty of caution, similarly to the public officials[219], and that the State has the legitimate right to impose to them an obligation of reserve. Usually, the Court accepts that judges can be the object of criticism sometimes virulent from the press[220], from those amenable to justice[221], form counsels[222] and from researchers[223]. In the case *Morice v. France*, the applicant, a counsel, complained with regard to the attitude of the judges in a letter published by the press. The judges complained about public defamation and the French court condemned the applicant for complicity to defamation. The European Court affirmed that „Justice needs the confidence of citizens in order to prosper", so that it may be necessary to be protected against serious prejudicial attacks without serious basis, but that, beyond such attacks, „judges as such can be subject to personal criticism, within admissible limits, not only in a theoretical and general measure"[224].

---

[219] Cases De Haes and Gijsels v. Belgium, decision of 24 February 1997; Cornelia Popa v. Romania, decision of 29 March 2011.

[220] Case Bezymyannyy v. Russia, decision of 8 April 2010.

[221] Cases Morice v. France, decision of 23 April 2015; Rodriguez Ravelo v. Spain, decision of 12 January 2016.

[222] Cases Morice v. France, cited supra; Mor v. France, decision of 15 December 2011.

[223] Case Mustafa Erdogan v. Turkey, decision of 27 May 2014.

[224] Case Morice v. France, cited above, presented extensively in ECHR, Annual Report 2015, p. 20.

The Court underlined also the special roll of *counsels* as independent professionals in the administration of justice and the need that a counsel could draw the attention on potential deficiencies in the justice system, and the judiciary could benefit of a constructive criticism. The Court retained the violation of art.10 by condemning the counsel, considering its remarks not as unfounded attacks, but as criticism addressed to the judge as part of a debate about an issue of public interest; even if they could be considered tough, they represented value judgments with a sufficient value factual basis[225]. At the same time, in many cases the Court gave attention to the protection of the reputation of judges and thereby of the authority of the judicial power against the attacks of the press, of those amenable to justice and of their counsels, which are considered excessive[226], including in a case concerning attacks aiming at judges and the clerk's officer of the European Court itself[227].

The Court gave a different appreciation in the case of a criminal sanction imposed to a *counsel* for defamatory statements with regard to an expert in a criminal procedure. The counsel complained that the expert manipulated data to obtain the result wanted by the prosecutor and consequently, he was condemned for defamation. The Court retained that the offensive statements of the counsel did not contain an objective criticism of the activity of the expert, aiming only at depreciating his work and at declaring useless its results, and affirmed that authorized experts have to be

---

[225] Ibidem, p. 20.
[226] Cases Prager and Oberschlick v. Austria, decision of 26 April 1995, Perna v. Italy, decision of 6 May 1993, Lolo v. Poland, decision of 11 March 2014, Kincses v. Hungary, decision of 27 January 2015.
[227] Case Rehak v. Czech Republic, decision of 11 May 2004.

able to perform without interference and their activity can be protected against offensive and abusive attacks. It declared the application of the counsel inadmissible[228].

Extended freedom of expression is recognized to the counsel, as a defendant of those amenable to justice, in order to ensure to his best the defense of his client, namely in connection with the independence of the profession of a counsel, which is considered essential for an equitable administration of justice[229]. This concerns the exercise of his freedom first of all before the court, but also to the extent it is necessary, in the media. The Court accepts that his expression can be „acerb, even sarcastic, but never injurious"[230]; the Court considered contrary to art. 10 sanctions or threats with sanctions addressed to a counsel whose words before the court concerned a prosecutor, the public ministry or a judge[231], considered as having a dissuading effect for fulfilling its mission as defendant. With regard to the exercise of the freedom of expression outside of the court, the Court pointed out that its mission of defendant is exercised with priority before the court and that he can resort to the media only when imperative needs of the defense require it[232]. The counsel is considered as an actor of justice, an independent one who is called to exercise a constant critical control on the functioning of the judiciary, of institutions in general[233]. The

---

[228] Case Fuchs v. Germany, ECHR, Annual Report 2015, p. 162.

[229] Among other cases Wille v. Liechtenstein, decision of 28 October 1999; Rekvenyi v. Hungary, decision of 20 May 1999; Kudeshkina v. Russia, decision of 26 February 2009.

[230] Case Morice v. France, cited supra, pp. 144-145.

[231] Ibidem.

[232] Cases Stuer v. The Netherlands, decision of 28 October 2003; Nikula v. Finland, decision of 21 March 2002; Kyprianou v. Cyprus, decision of 15 December 2005.

[233] Case Morice v. France, cited supra, pp. 144-145..

Court appreciates that a limitation of the freedom of expression of the counsel of defense, even by a light criminal sanction, can be considered necessary in a democratic society[234] only in exceptional cases. In the case *Brodovic and Vujin v. Serbia*, a counsel initiated a judicial procedure for defamation, because he was compared with „a blonde" by the journalists in a local newspaper. The Court retained that the journalists exercised their freedom of expression and that the council should show more tolerance[235].

The Court adopted a clear standing also in favor of the freedom of expression of *the academic world*. The Court affirms on this issue that the freedom of expression is not limited to scientific or university research but includes also for authors to express freely their opinions, even if they are controversial and unpopular, in their fields of research, competence and professional experience[236]. The Court is less clear with regard to the freedom of expression of *trade unions representatives*. In the case *Palomo Sanchez and others v. Spain*, the Court first affirms that these representatives must be able to express their claims to the employer, but it continues saying that some manifestations of their freedom of expression are not admissible in the labor relations; the Court affirms that an injury to the honorability of persons by insulting or injurious expressions in the professional framework has a particularly disturbing and serious character which can justify severe sanctions[237]. During the same year, the Court accepted a more virulent character in the expression of trade union

---

[234] Case Amihălăchioaie v. Republic of Moldova, decision of 20 April 2004.
[235] Case Brodozic and Vujin v. Serbia, decision of 23 June 2009.
[236] Case Mustafa Erdogan v. Turkey, decision of 27 May 2014.
[237] Case Sanchez and others v. Spain, ECHR Annual Report 2011, pp. 98-99.

representatives, when they respond to public accusations concerning the professional and personal behavior of members of their trade union[238].

In several cases, the Court examined also the right of *members of a minority group* to exercise their right to free expression *in their mother tongue*. In the case *Sukran Aydin and others v. Turkey*, some candidates and those who supported them in parliamentary and municipal elections were condemned to imprisonment or fines for violating the Turkish law which forbids the use of a language other than Turkish in electoral campaigns. The Court retained a violation of art. 10 of the Convention for prohibiting the use of another language than the official one in public life; it retained that the case was not about the use of the Kurdish language in the communication with public authorities or before them, but in relations with other private persons. The Court affirms that the right to disseminate political opinions and ideas and the right of other persons to receive them could not have a meaning if the possibility to use the language in which they can be transmitted in the most adequate manner would be restricted as a result of a threat with criminal sanctions[239]. Similarly, in the case *Egitim ve Bilim Emeckcileri Sendicast v. Turkey* the European Court affirmed that art. 10 of the Convention includes the freedom to receive and to distribute information in any language which gives the possibility to participate in public exchanges of cultural, political and social information and ideas: it includes, therefore, not only the substance of the ideas and information expressed, but

---

[238] Case Vellutini and Michel v. France, decision of 6 October 2011.
[239] Case Sukran Aydin and others v. Turkey, ECHR Annual Report 2013, p. 123.

also the form of their transmission and the language of their expression[240].

The Court examined as a violation of art. 10 also *the refusal of the* authorities or *the omission to disclose the information* requested or which is necessary. In the case *Guseva v. Bulgaria*, concerning the refusal of authorities to give information regarding the treatment applied to street animals captured in towns, the Court retained as a violation of art. 10 the refusal of the authorities to disclose official information on an issue of public interest[241]. In the case *Vilnes and others v. Norway*, the applicants divers complained that they did not receive useful information concerning the risks associated with tables of rapid decompression and as a result they developed problems of health which made them disabled. The Court established that the State had the obligation to offer these individuals access to essential information so that they foresee the risks taken. The State also did not take steps to ensure that the private companies which hired them were transparent with regard to the consequences of these tables and allowed that these companies keep them secret[242].

In the case *Haralambie v. Romania*[243], the petitioner complained among others about obstacles to access to his personal file created on him by the former security services. The Court

---

[240] Case Egitim ve Bilim Emeckcirli Sendicast v. Turkey, ECHR Annual Report 2012, p. 95.

[241] Case Guseva v. Bulgaria, ECHR Annual Report 2015, p. 171.

[242] Case Vilnes and others v. Norway, ECHR Annual Report 2013, pp. 112-113; the refusal to offer the relevant information was also considered contrary to the freedom of expression in the cases Kenedi v. Hungary and Youth Initiative for Human Rights v. Serbia, Annual Report, pp. 123-124.

[243] Petition nr. 21737/03, decision of 27 October 2009.

underlined the vital interest of those who were subject to personal files detained by State authorities to have access to them; it also stressed the duty of the authorities to offer an effective procedure to have access to this information. The failure of this duty was retained by the Court, as a violation of art. 10 of the Convention.

Finally, the Court emphasized that *the protection of the honor and reputation* of the usual citizen should be stronger, on the basis of art. 8 of the Convention, as part of the right to private life[244], affirming among others that the right to respect the private life and the freedom of expression „deserve *a priori* equal respect"[245]. The Court also distinguished the protection of reputation of natural persons from that of legal persons. In the case *Uj v. Hungary*, a journalist was recognized guilty of defamation because he wrote about a wine produced by a company that „hundreds of thousands of Hungarians drink with pride this sheet"; the Court considered that the injury brought to the commercial reputation of a society lacks a moral dimension[246], but did not find a violation of art. 10. In the case *Kharlamov v. Russia*, were a professor criticized in a conference of the university the election of the rector and the procedure of selection of the direction of the university, and was sanctioned for defamation, the Court held that the applicant may express himself in a structure of university life with regard to an issue of general interest and did not use an offensive and tough language. The Court appreciated that the protection of the reputation of a university according to the

---

[244] Case Pfeifer v. Austria, decision of 15 November 2007.
[245] Case Couderc and Hachette Filipacchi Associates v. France, decision of 10 November 2015.
[246] Case Uj v. Hungary, decision of 19 July 2011.

Convention cannot be equated with the protection due to an individual, and retained a violation of art. 10[247].

Following the same idea, in the case *Guja v. Moldova*, where an individual working in the private sector initiated a criminal complaint against the employer and made public the alleged criminal behavior of the latter, the Court retained that the dismissal of the applicant represented an interference contrary to the exercise of the right to free expression and retained a violation of art. 10[248]. Similarly, in the case *Heinisch v. Germany* the Court affirmed that the protection of reputation and interests of a company specialized in health care is subject to limitations and that the interests of the company are outweighed by the interest of the public to be informed about deficiencies in offering specialized care to older persons[249].

The Court also examined cases concerning the *reputation of some individuals* and of the right to their image; in the case *Von Hannover v. Germany*, it had to evaluate the sanction applied for publishing photos from the private life of a celebrity person, without her knowledge. The Court examined whether in this case there was a general interest for a question of public debate, which could justify the exercise of the right to expression, and whether other provisions of the Convention were not violated, in particular art. 8 concerning the protection of the right to private life[250].

---

[247] Case Kharlamov v. Russia, decision of 8 October 2015.
[248] Case Guja v. Moldova, ECHR Annual Report 2011, p. 100.
[249] Case Heinisch v. Germany, ECHR Annual Report 2011, p. 100.
[250] Case Von Hannover v. Germany, nr.2, ECHR Annual Report 2012, p. 99.

Similarly, in the case *Axel Springer AG v. Germany*, where a newspaper published information about the detention and the condemnation of a television actor, this applicant asked the interdiction of the newspaper which published this information. This case raised the issue of the freedom of information and of the protection of private life, in relation to the interest of the public to be informed about penal proceedings. In connection with this case, the Grand Chamber of the European Court set forth the criteria which should guide the evaluation of the right to free expression versus the right to private life, namely: if the person concerned was sufficiently known to the public; what is the legitimate expectation that his private life is respected; by what means did the journalist obtain the information, its accuracy; to what extent the anonymous name of the actor was respected; the contents and the form of the respective articles, including the use of expressions meant to attract the attention of the public[251].

In a similar case, *Bohlen v. Germany*[252], a pop singer enjoying celebrity published a book made known by a legal proceeding. A tobacco company used his first name as part of its advertising campaign for a brand of cigarettes. The applicant claimed compensation for the unlawful use of his name in a civil action which was dismissed by the Federal Court of Justice and invoked the failure of the State to protect his private life, according to art. 8. The ECHR retained that the first name is part of the name and consequently the provisions of art. 8 are applicable. The Court had to evaluate whether a fair balance was struck between the competing interests and noted the interest raised by the book

---

[251] Case Axel Springer AG v. Germany, Annual Report 2012, pp. 93-94.
[252] Case Bohlen v. Germany, decision of 19 February 2015.

published, the fact that the applicant was a well-known personality and was looking for publicity, the fact that the advertising did not reveal any details of the private life of the applicant and did not link his personality with the promotion of the cigarettes, as he was a non-smoker. So, the Court retained the freedom of expression of the company and no violation of art. 8.

Similarly, in the case *Kahn v. Germany*[253], the applicants, minors of a famous sport personality, obtained a court order against a publisher, requesting him to refrain from publishing their photos. The publisher continued to do it and paid repeatedly fines to the State. Then the applicants asked for compensation, invoking the failure of the State to protect their right to private life. The Court noted the margin of appreciation available to the State in such circumstances, that fines were paid and that applicants did not ask to increase them so as to stop publishing. ECHR also accepted the finding of the domestic courts that the infringement of the applicant's right was not so serious as to warrant the payment of damages to them. Finally, it affirmed that art. 8 of the Convention could not be construed as requiring in all circumstances the payment of monetary compensation to victims for breach of personality rights.

In a different case, *Stojanovic v. Serbia*, the applicant complained that he was not the author of defamatory information. The defamatory words appeared in an article wrote by a journalist after an interview by telephone with the applicant. The Court affirmed that the extent of the responsibility for defamation should not exceed the mere words of the person. As the applicant argued effectively that the internal court denied him the right to express

---

[253] Case Kahn v. Germany, decision of 17 March 2016.

himself and attributed to him in the interview(whereby he criticized the Ministry of health) statements he did not make, the Court considered that art. 10 was violated with regard to two statements wrongly attributed to him, and the sanction applied could dissuade him to address criticism[254].

Regarding sanctions that States can apply to individuals for infringement of the rights of other persons by exercising the freedom of expression, the Court accepted for some violations criminal penalties (denial of holocaust, racist discourse, defamation)[255]. Nevertheless, as a rule, the Court held that *it was difficult to consider compatible with art. 10 of the Convention a sanction with imprisonment*[256]. In many cases, the Court did not consider necessary to apply a criminal penalty, even denouncing the severity of the sanction applied and indicated that there are „other means of interference and of rejection, notably through the ways of civil law"[257]. As mentioned above, the Committee for the Elimination of Racial Discrimination also indicated, in its General

---

[254] Case Stojanovic. v. Serbia, ECHR Annual Report 2013, p. 125.

[255] Cases Garaudy v. France, Feret v. Belgium, Lindon, cited above. Also the case Coutant v. France, decision of 24 January 2008, where a counsel, member of the bar of Paris was condemned for defamation of a public authority because she denounced in terms particularly virulent the conditions under which the authorities treat, pursue and prosecute persons suspected of terrorist activities.

[256] Case Cumpana and Mazare v. Romania, decision of 17 December 2004, where the Court affirms that „a punishment to imprisonment for an offense committed in the field of the press id not compatible with the freedom of journalist expression guaranteed by art. 10 of the Convention except in exceptional circumstances, mainly when other fundamental rights are seriously affected, as in the case of a hate speech or of incitement to violence".

[257] Decision in the case Lehideux and Isorni, cited above, pp. 129-130.

Recommendation nr. 35 of 2013, that penal sanctions, even in the case of the racist speech, should be applied only for the most serious violations; others could be treated through other means considering the nature and the context they take place, their impact on the individuals and the groups targeted.

* * *

No doubt, there is a sinuous evolution of the practice of the Court and of the motivation of its decisions, in time and with regard to different aspects of the exercise of the freedom of expression. If initially the Court proceeded to a less rigorous control of the interference of authorities (case Handyside v. UK, cited above), subsequently the decisions of the Court show a stricter control (cases Sunday Times v. UK, where the Court retained a violation of art. 10 for prohibiting the publication by the journal of comments with regard to compensations to the victims of Thalidomide, affirming that the guarantee of the authority and the impartiality of the judicial power can be defined at the European level and that these comments could not be forbidden for what was considered as a contempt of the court)[258].

A strict control can be observed in other cases (case Open Door and Dublin Well Woman v. Ireland) concerning the cessation of disseminating the addresses of the British hospitals were voluntary abortion can be practiced[259], a diminished control concerning restrictive measures taken against the questioning about the behavior of a judge towards persons prosecuted in criminal proceedings[260], a more severe control in the case Jersild v.

---

[258] Case Sunday Times v. UK, decision of 26 April 1979.
[259] Petition nr. 14234/88, decision of 29 October 1992.
[260] Case Prager and Oberschlick v. Austria, cited above, p. 145.

Denmark, mentioned above, with regard to the dissemination by a journalist of racist affirmations of some young extremists and one very permissive in the case Otto-Preminger Institute v. Austria, where the Court did not consider violation of art 10 the confiscation of a film allegedly containing a blasphemy that an association of film lovers prepared to present[261].

Sometimes with regard to the same country and in the same year the Court is very liberal in a case (*Obershlick v. Austria*, mentioned above[262], were it considers contrary to art. 10 the condemnation of a journalist for injuries addressed to J. Haider, a right wing politician, and the case *Worm v. Austria*[263] were it did not accept as a violation of art. 10 the condemnation of a journalist who denounced the arrogance to the court of a minister prosecuted for fiscal fraud, in terms which prejudged on the guilt of the latter and were considered an interference in the mission of the courts.

During a first period of time after the entry into force of the Protocol 11 of 1998 to the Convention (according to which the Court remained the only body to receive and examine individual applications), the Court resumed its liberal approach with regard to the freedom of expression. This is obvious in cases *Bladet Tromso and Stensaas v. Norway* of 1999 (where the Court accepted as valid the obligation to allow a debate on the hunting of wales, although this questioned the practices of some hunters)[264], *News Verlag GmbH and KoKg v. Austria* of 2000 (where it considered contrary to art. 10 the interdiction to publish the photo of a neo-Nazi militant suspected of attempts with bomb letters), as an excessive

---

[261] Case Otto Preminger v. Austria, decision of 20 September 1994.
[262] Case Oberschlick, v. Austria, mentioned above. p. 145.
[263] Case Worm v. Austria, decision of 29 August 1997.
[264] Petition nr. 21/980/93, decision of 20 May 1999, Rec. 1999-III.

limitation of the freedom of information on an issue of legitimate concern for the public[265], the case *Bergens Tidende v. Norway* (where it considered a violation of art. 10 the condemnation of a newspaper which published testimonies which seriously questioned the operations of esthetic surgery), taking into account the legitimate public interest[266], or *Colombani v. France* (concerning the incompatibility with art. 10 of a provision of the law on the press which incriminated the offence against a foreign head of State, while forbidding the proof of the facts affirmed, as not fulfilling the requirement of proportionality[267].

After that, the Court was not so favorable to the freedom of expression. In the case *Von Hannover v. Germany* the Court established a criterion on the evaluation of publications, according to which those proposing to satisfy the curiosity of the public concerning details of the private life of some personalities, without a connection to the public debate, did not enjoy the protection of art. 10[268], and in the case *Pedersen and Baadsgaard v. Denmark*, where the Court retained the absence of a violation of art. 10 and affirmed that the exercise of the freedom of expression should be accompanied by caution and based on sufficiently precise and credible data, and considered proportional to the nature and the strength of the allegation in dispute[269]. This orientation will continue in cases such as *Lindon, Otchakovski and July v. France*, although it accepts that the novel in question (entitled the Trial of Jean-Marie Le Pen, in which crimes of homicide and racist attacks

---

[265] Petition nr. 31457/96, decision of 11 January 2000, Rec. 2000-I.
[266] Petition nr. 26132/95, decision of 2 May 2000, Rec. 2000-IV.
[267] Petition nr. 512, decision of 25 June 2002, 2002-V.
[268] Case presented above, p. 151.
[269] Petition nr. 49017/99, decision of 17 December 2004, Rec. 2004-XI.

are attributed to him) is part of a debate of general interest, the Court accepted the decision of the national courts according to which it is necessary to maintain a minimum of moderation and the reputation of a politician even controversial should benefit from the protection of the Convention[270], as well as in the case *Stoll v. Switzerland* where the Court insists on the importance of respecting the journalist deontology and on the need to preserve the secret of exchanges between a diplomat and his department, retaining the absence of a violation of art.10, and the journalist was condemned[271]. Similarly, in the case *Swiss Raelian Movement v. Switzerland*, the Court gives great importance to the national margin of discretion and considers that there was no violation of art. 10 by the prohibition by the authorities of Neuchatel of displaying postings of the Raelian Movement in public places, taking into account the doctrine of this Movement (which promoted human cloning in order to cultivate geniocracy and sexual abuses on minors), as well as the capacity of proselytism of these ideas, in view of protecting morals and rights of other persons and to prevent crime[272].

In spite of these restrictive decisions, it is considered that the liberal approach remains dominant for the time being in the decisions of the Court[273]. In recent cases *(Eon v. France)*, the Court retained that the decision of the internal court represents a violation of art. 10, in case of alleged offense to the president of the republic (resuming expressions used by the president), affirming that „the

---

[270] Case presented above, p. 140.
[271] Petition nr.69698/01, decision of 10 December 2007, Rec. 2007-V.
[272] Petition nr. 16354/06, decision of 15 July 2012, Rec. 2012.
[273] Opinion presented by Patrick Wachsmann, La liberté d'expression..., in INTRODUCTION...., p. 767.

satire is a form of artistic expression and of social comment, which is characterized by the exaggeration and the deformation of the reality and is aiming naturally to provoke and to shake"[274]; similarly, in the case *Roland Dumas v. France*, the Court also retained a violation of art. 10 by the condemnation of the applicant for defamation, because in a volume of memories he recalled what he told to a judge representing the public ministry during a criminal trial against him that „during Vichy he would have been a zealous servant", considering that it was the right of the justiceable to relate the proceedings[275].

The way the decisions of the Court are adopted, with weak majorities, sometimes at the limit, and the dissident opinions expressed, show deep divisions within the Court between the two trends-one in favour of a wider freedom of expression and of the press, and the other one more restrictive, which insists on respecting some requirements, mainly on the need to reconciliate the freedom of expression with those human rights and freedoms which can be affected and with the principle of non-discrimination.

---

[274] Case Eon v. France, cited above, pp. 142-143.
[275] Petition nr. 34875/07, decision of 15 July 2010.

CHAPTER V - ECONOMIC, SOCIAL and CULTURAL RIGHTS on the agenda of EUROPEAN and INTERNATIONAL JURISDICTIONS

Abstract

This chapter is devoted to evolutions with regard to the application of norms of international law concerning economic, social and cultural rights by European and international jurisdictions. Although initially these rights were widely considered not justiceable, the reality of indivisibility of human rights made it necessary that gradually economic, social and cultural rights are brought before jurisdictional and quasi-jurisdictional bodies and protected against violations which would endanger the exercise of civil and political rights. A consistent practice, mainly of the European courts, is presented to prove this evolution.

It became obvious that economic, social and cultural rights can be protected by the judiciary, that the action of States and other actors in this fields can be evaluated according to appropriate rules and criteria, while taking into account their specificity, mainly their closer relationship with the economic development, with the use of resources available and with the economic and social policies followed by different governments.

This evolution finds its new achievement in the Optional Protocol to the Covenant on economic, social and cultural rights, adopted in 2008 and in force since 2013. It is still at its beginning and seen with some lack of confidence by States parties to the Covenant, but its first cases are encouraging. It is mainly its potential to assist States parties, including developing countries, with the support of other international actors, in their efforts to fulfill the commitments taken under the Covenant. One of the objectives followed is to draw the attention on the potential offered by this Protocol to raise the level of the exercise of economic, social and cultural rights.

Key Words: indivisibility, different treatment, justiceable, inhuman treatment, presomption of serious violation, social rights, non-discrimination, cultural rights, fundamental rights, freedom of enterprise, procedural rights, effective remedy, personal data, access to documents, right to work, right to property, collective complaints, use of languages, forced labour, good officies, investigation, internal remedies, international assistance and cooperation

Introduction

Economic, social and cultural rights are recognized as human rights by international law, taking into account both their direct importance for each human being and the need to respect them in order to ensure the exercise of civil and political rights themselves, due to the close relationship between the two categories of rights as an expression of the complexity of human life and personality.

The Universal Declaration of Human Rights adopted in 1948 solemnly proclaimed as human rights both civil and political and economic, social and cultural rights, in identical form (everyone has the right…to social security, to work, to rest and leisure, to an adequate living standard, to education, as well as the right to take part in cultural life, at the same time with the right to life, to personal security, to freedom of thought, conscience and belief, to participate in public affairs). The only difference in the text of the Declaration figures in article 22 on the right to social security, according to which ,,Everyone, as a member of the society…is entitled to realization, through national effort and international cooperation and in accordance with the organization and resources of each State, of the economic, social and cultural rights indispensable for his dignity and the free development of his personality". As other provisions of the Declaration state also in a direct expression (everyone has the right …) the main economic, social and cultural rights, this formulation should be understood as indicating the methods and the framework for the implementation of these rights, and not for placing them in a category of rights of restricted application.

However, the Covenant on economic, social and cultural rights adopted in 1966, at the same time with the Covenant on civil and political rights, does not enunciate directly individual rights of each person, but the obligation of States parties to recognize these rights and to adopt measures, individually and with international assistance and cooperation, using at the maximum their available resources, in order to progressively obtain the full realization of the rights recognized through all adequate means, including through legislative measures. Adopted 20 years after the Universal Declaration, the Covenant places the emphasis on the action of States, not on the existence of individual rights of persons.

Documents were also adopted at the regional level in order to protect economic, social and cultural rights, following as a rule the structure adopted by the two Covenants. In Europe, in 1950 the Council of Europe adopted the Convention on human fundamental rights and freedoms (civil and political rights), completed by 16 additional protocols to date, which established the European Court of Human Rights competent to consider individual petitions concerning violations of its provisions and to adopt decisions compulsory for the States parties. It was followed by the European Social Charter, revised in 1996, completed by protocols concerning the right to work and a system of collective petitions. A Committee of independent experts was created to examine periodic reports of States parties as well as individual and collective petitions received. In the Latin-American area, the Protocol of San Salvador of 1988 follows generally the provisions of the Covenant on economic, social and cultural rights and provides for the right of persons to present individual petitions concerning the right to organize in trade unions and the right to education. The Inter-American Convention of human rights of 1969 recognized the competence of the Inter-American Commission on human rights to consider reports and information from States parties, as well as petitions of persons, groups of persons and non-governmental organizations, if the State concerned accepted this procedure. The Inter-American Court of human rights is competent to consider petitions submitted by a State party alleging the violation by another State party of the 1969 Convention (provided that the two States explicitly accepted this procedure).

In Africa, the African Charter of human rights and the rights of peoples of 1981 covers both civil and political and social and economic rights. An African Commission for human rights and the rights of peoples is competent to consider petitions from individuals and from States. If these petitions reveal serious or mass violations of human rights, the Commission brings the situation to the attention of the Assembly of heads of State and government of the States members of the African Union. The Assembly may ask the Commission to consider thoroughly such cases and present reports, including conclusions and recommendations[276]. An African Court was also created more recently, been competent to consider petitions concerning States which accept this procedure.

This evolution led to a thorough debate on the nature of the economic, social and cultural rights, as well as with regard to the capacity of individuals to claim these rights before judicial institutions, that is whether these rights are justiceable. As for the nature of economic, social and cultural rights, we note that the right to education and the right to property were added by an additional protocol to the European Convention on human rights of 1950 (containing initially civil and political rights). Similarly, the Covenant on civil and political rights of 1966 contains article 27, concerning the rights of persons belonging to ethnic, linguistic or religious minorities to enjoy their own culture, to use their language and to practice and profess their own religion. As these rights were included in international legal documents on civil and political rights, are they also economic, social and cultural? It means that States adopted norms on human rights not on the basis of the different nature of these rights, but having in view the

---

[276] The classical magister work on this subject by Asbjorne Eide, C. Krause and A. Rosas, Economic, Social and Cultural Rights, a textbook, 1995. Extensively presented also by Ion Diaconu, Treatise of international law, vol. II, 2003, Lumina Lex, pp. 424-427 and Human Rights in the Contemporary International Law, theory and practice, 2010, Lumina Lex (in Romanian), pp. 133-141).

importance they granted to such rights at the respective historic moment.

Traditionally, a distinction was also made between negative and positive rights; negative rights were considered those asking States to refrain from acting against and from impeding the exercise of human rights, while the positive rights were meant to engage States to act for ensuring the exercise of the respective rights, including by financial and other measures. This distinction was contested, as the exercise of many of the civil and political rights requires also action from the States, such as the interdiction of torture, the exercise of the right to vote, the right to a fair trial, the functioning of an efficient system of courts[277]. On the other side, many civil and political rights, such as the right to private life, have an important social dimension inherently related to the right to housing, the right to health and to decent food.

Obviously, we have to note that human rights are separated in two treaties, that they have now (after more than 50 years) comparable bodies to monitor their application at international and regional levels, with notable differences concerning the examination of communications about violations of human rights; that means they have different sources, they cover different aspects of human life, they have as correspondent different obligations and sanctions, and of course they are subject to different policies and interests in many States. At the same time, the entirety of human rights has to be covered by obligations of the State in favour of the individual; a reductionist or fragmented approach of rights in

---

[277] Christina Binder and Thomas Shobesberger, The European Court of Human Rights and Social Rights-Emerging Trends in Jurisprudence? in Hungarian Yearbook of International Law and European Law, 2015, p. 53.

different fields of human life cannot respond adequately to the essential needs of people. The issue is not about weakening the application of civil and political rights in order to underline the importance of economic, social and cultural rights, as well as the unity and indivisibility of human rights. On the contrary, progress is needed in both directions, but it is not acceptable to treat one category of rights as less important.

The different treatment of the two categories of rights is a historic fact, resulting from the attitude of States and from the different nature attributed to the obligations under the respective treaties, and not from the objective importance of the respective rights for the individual. The Tehran Conference on human rights of 1968 affirmed in the Declaration adopted that „nowadays political rights without social rights, justice according to the law without social justice and political democracy without economic democracy have no more a true meaning". Even if during the cold war period discussions on this subject were dominated by an ideological approach, the World Conference of Vienna on human rights of 1993 affirmed the principles of the relationship among human rights, according to which these rights are universal, indivisible, interdependent and closely related.

In its general comments, the Committee on Economic, Social and Cultural Rights (CESCR) asked States to consider economic, social and cultural rights as justiceable. The Committee identified some of them as being of direct application at the national level, such as the right to primary education and other aspects of the right to education, the freedom of scientific research and the freedom to perform creative activities. The Committee also recommended that States stipulate in their legislation some rights, in order to ensure their direct applicability and consequently the possibility to invoke them before the national courts (like for instance the rights to sufficient food, to health and to water)[278]. The Committee insists, in its General Comment nr. 9/1998 concerning the application of the Covenant at the national level, that its provisions are recognized in the national legal order and that any person or group injured in their rights have access to adequate means of remedy and reparation[279].

Of course, in as much as these rights are provided for by the national laws they can be claimed before internal judicial bodies, according to the internal legislation[280], that is they are justiceable. As for the international jurisdictions, if the economic, social and cultural rights are provided for by the treaties which establish such jurisdictions, they are subject to the respective jurisdictions similarly with rights considered civil and political (the right to education at the European and Inter-American levels). At the same time, the social needs resulting from the interconnection between economic and social and some political rights led to the trend to consider in the existent judicial and quasi-judicial bodies petitions concerning violations of several economic and social rights which endanger the exercise of some political and civil rights. The international practice progressed towards the examination by these judicial and quasi-judicial bodies of cases concerning the exercise of such rights in connection with other

---

[278] General Comments nr. 3/1990, 9/1998, 14/2000 and 15/2002, in Compilation of general comments and general recommendations adopted by human rights treaty bodies, doc. HRI/GEN/1/Rev. 8, pp. 15, 55, 63, 86 and 105.

[279] Compilation, doc. HRI/GEN/1/Rev. 8, pp. 55-59.

[280] In this respect Selection de jurisprudence relative aux droits économiques, sociaux et culturels, Document d'information soumis par le Secrétariat, E/CN.4/WG. 23/CRP.1.

human rights or on the basis of documents concerning vulnerable groups such as indigenous and tribal people, minorities, migrants, asylum seekers, internally displaced persons, disabled or refugees. The Additional Protocol to the Covenant provided the attributions of the Committee of experts (which is still at the beginning of its activity) and opened the way to the examination of communications with regard to violations of all the provisions of the Covenant concerning economic, social and cultural rights. This evolution proves that economic, social and cultural rights can be subject to the jurisdiction of international bodies. The following sections refer to the practice of such international bodies in considering cases concerning economic, social and cultural rights.

SECTION I - Regional courts of human rights

European Court of Human Rights (ECHR)

Many of the provisions of the European Convention of 1950 have a social dimension, which is recognized by the ECHR. The Court considered cases regarding:

-rights related to the right to life[281], in extreme cases when the right to life was invoked and it was alleged that States did not

---

[281] Cases Budayeva and others v. Russia, ECHR, petitions nr. 15339/02, 11673/02, 15343/02, 20058/02 and 21166/02, decision of 28 March 2008; Omeryildiz v. Turkey, ECHR, petition nr. 48939/99, decision of 30 November 2004; Oyal v. Turkey, ECHR, petition nr. 4865/05, decision of 23 March 2010; Calveli and Ciglio v. Italy, ECHR, petition nr. 32967/96, decision of 12 June 2003; Birzykowski v. Poland, ECHR, petition nr. 11562/05, decision of 27 June 2006.

take measures in the social and administrative fields to protect this right;

-rights related to the interdiction of the inhuman and degrading treatment, like the right to health, the right to adequate medical treatment, the rights to adequate conditions of detention and to hygiene and sanitation services for persons who are in the State's custody (overcrowded prisons). The Court applied the presumption of serious violation for persons in prison or detention and considered that the State is responsible to ensure respect of their economic and social rights[282]; special attention was given to vulnerable groups, mainly those discriminated on grounds of ethnic origin and of sex[283].

-social rights invoked in connection with the right of everyone to the respect of private and family life, of his home and

---

[282] Cases Ananyev and others v. Russia, ECHR, petitions nr. 42525/07 and 60800/08, decision of 10 January 2012; Iacov Stanciu v. Romania, ECHR, petition nr. 35972/05, decision of 24 July 2012; Torreggiani and others v. Italy, ECHR, petitions nr. 43517/09, 46882/09, 55400/09, 57875/09, 35315/10, 37818/10 and 61535/09, decision of 8 January 2013; Mouisel v. France, ECHR, petition nr. 67263/01, decision of 14 November 2002; McGlinchey and others v. UK, ECHR, petition nr. 50390/99, decision of 29 April 2003; Khudobin v. Russia, ECHR, petition nr. 59696/00, decision of 26 October 2006; Vladimir Vassilyev v. Russia, ECHR, petition nr. 28370/05, decision of 10 January 2012, Moldovan and others v. Romania, ECHR, petitions nr. 41138/98 and 64320/01, decision of 12 July 2005; Mublianzila Mayeka and Kaniki Mitunga v. Belgium, decision of 12 October 2006.

[283] Beatrice Pastre-Belda, La protection à géométrie variable de l'article 3 de la Convention européenne des droits de l'homme, in Revue trimestrielle des droits de l'homme, nr. 107/2016, pp. 595-596 and 609.

correspondence[284]; the Court recognized that the right to private life includes also the right to be protected against serious cases of pollution of the environment, as well as in cases of lack of information about risks of pollution, lack of evaluation of dangerous consequences of industrial processes, as well as cases of forced eviction of persons and groups traditionally living in caravans or without offering them any alternative housing.

-economic and social rights related to the right to property[285]; mainly the right to housing was treated in connection with the right to property and interpreted extensively, so as to include also persons who are not owners; the Court considered also cases when the houses were destroyed by the State for security reasons as violations of this right.

-cases concerning the right to health recognized in connection with civil and political rights[286]; although States enjoy a large margin of appreciation concerning aspects of the system of

---

[284] Cases Lopez Ostra v. Spain, ECHR, petition nr. 16798/90, decision of 9 December 1994; Guerra and others v. Italy, ECHR, petition nr. 14967/89, decision of 19 February 1998, Tatar v. Romania, ECHR, petition nr. 67021/01, decision of 27 January 2009; Jane Smith, Thomas and Gesica Coster and Chapman v. UK, ECHR, petitions nr. 25154/94, 24876/94 and 27238/95, decision of 18 January 2001; Iordanova and others. v. Bulgaria, ECHR, petition nr. 25446/06, decision of 24 April 2012.

[285] Cases Omeryildiz v. Turkey, ECHR, petition nr. 48939/99, decision of 30 November 2004; Selcuk and Asker v. Turkey, petitions nr. 23184/94 and 23185/94, decision of 24 April 1998; Khamzayev and Kerimova v. Russia, petitions nr. 1503/02, 17170/04 and 20792/04, decision of 3 May 2011; O'Rourke v. UK, petition nr. 39022/97, decision of 26 June 2001.

[286] Cases Burdov v. Russia, ECHR, petition nr. 59498/00, decision of 7 May 2002; Passannante v. Italy, ECHR, petition nr. 32647/96, decision of admissibility of 12 June 2003.

welfare and medical assistance, the Court considered cases when a State has the direct responsibility to ensure medical services (in case of natural disasters) and considered that an excessive delay in granting a medical service in a public hospital is unjustified and amounts to a violation of the right to private life.

-the Court also considered cases concerning some economic and social rights in connection with the right to a fair trial[287]; it considered that an excessive duration of the procedure for obtaining a social benefit is a violation of the right to a fair process, as well as restraining the right to appeal for such services or not disclosing the documents relevant for such a procedure; in cases of forced eviction also, the Court underlined the need to respect the procedural guarantees, mainly in cases concerning the housing.

-the interdiction of discrimination with regard to the exercise of economic, social and cultural rights is often invoked before the Court[288]; the State has a direct obligation to protect against discrimination with regard to social benefits; if a social benefit is granted, the State has the obligation to ensure its exercise

---

[287] Cases Salesi v. Italy, ECHR, petition nr. 13023/87, decision of 26 February 1993; Feldbrugge v. Netherlands, ECHR, petition nr. 8562/79, decision of 29 May 1986; Kerojarvi v. Finland, ECHR, petition nr. 17506/90, decision of 19 July 1995; cases Burdov v. Russia, Oyal v. Turkey, Khudobin v. Russia, cited above; Saghinadze and others v. Georgia, ECHR, petition nr. 18768/05, decision of 27 May 2010; Connors v. UK, ECHR, petition nr. 66746/01, decision of 27 May 2004; Buckland v. UK, ECHR, petition nr. 40060/08, decision of 18 September 2012.

[288] Cases Gaygusus v. Austria, ECHR, petition nr. 17372/90, decision of 16 September 1996; Van Kuck v. Germany, ECHR, petition nr. 35968/97, decision of 12 June 2005.

without discrimination on grounds provided for by the Convention (sex, race, national or ethnic origin and any other status).

-cultural rights in connection with civil and political rights[289]; the Court adopted an open position with regard to group rights, mainly in the fields of culture and identity; it accepted the concept of cultural pluralism based on diversity, as well as the rights to culture and education (including in mother tongue) as part of the cultural identity; the Court considered cases of cultural expression to be protected, except when there is a need to protect other legitimate values; the Court also pronounced itself for the protection of cultural traditions and of the way of life of some communities, for the freedom to affirm and to promote cultural concepts, for the religious freedoms as elements of culture which can be subject to restrictions only to protect other human rights.

---

[289] Cases Chapman v. UK, ECHR, petition nr. 27238/95, decision of 18 January 2001; Gorzelik and others v. Poland, ECHR, decision of 17 February 2004; Kalderas Gypsis v. Germany and Netherlands, ECHR, petitions nr. 7823/77 and 7824/77, decision of 7 July 1977; Cyprus v. Turkey, ECHR, decision of 10 May 2001; Handisyde v. UK, decision of 6 September 1978; Otto Preminger v. Austria, ECHR, decision of 20 September 1994; Wingrouve v. UK, ECHR, decision of 25 November 1996; I. A. v. Turkey, ECHR, decision of 13 September 2005; Ulusoy and others v. Turkey, decision of 3 May 2007; Chapman v. UK, decision of 18 January 2001; Connors v. UK, decision of 27 May 2004; G. and E. v. Norway, decision of the Commission of 3 October 1983; Noack and others v. Germany, decision of 25 May 2000; Sidiropoulos and others v. Greece, decision of 10 July 1998; cases Larissis and others v. Greece, X v. UK, Dahlab v. Switzerland, Leyla Savin v. Turkey(cited by Ion Diaconu, in Culture and human rights, 2012, Prouniversitaria(in Romanian), pp. 132-134); Kokkinakis v. Greece, decision of 23 May 1993; the use of languages in education in Belgium, decision of 1968, ECHR Serie A, nr. 6; Mentzen alias Mencena v. Latvia, decision of 7 December 2004.

According to its General Comment nr. 21 of 2009[290] concerning the right of everyone to take part in cultural life, CESC places the right to cultural diversity as part of respect for human rights, considering it as an ethical imperative, inseparable from the respect of human dignity.

-the Court had also to consider cases where petitioners complained about the inadequate use of State resources for protecting some of their social rights related to civil and political rights[291]; usually, ECHR avoided to take a definite stand, considering that the distribution of resources is better treated by governments. In cases of health problems in a prison, or of discrimination on grounds of disability, the Court accepted that the State has an extended margin of appreciation as to how to distribute resources. Authors consider that the problem of distribution of limited resources is better treated by governments individually[292].

To conclude, ECHR identified carefully reasons for which it retains violations of human rights provided for in the Convention of 1950 giving them a social dimension, among which: when the action or inaction of the State leads to the violation of an economic, social or cultural right; when the persons victims of the violation are under the direct responsibility of the State (in prisons,

---

[290] Doc. E/C.12/GC/21 of 21 December 2010.

[291] Cases Penticova v. Moldova, ECHR, petition nr. 11462/03, decision on admissibility of 4 January 2005; Sentegs v. Netherlands, ECHR, petition nr. 2767/02, decision on admissibility of 8 July 2003; Cyprus v. Turkey, cited supra, note 60.

[292] L. Clements and A. Simmons, European Court of Human Rights Sympathetic Unease, in M. Langford, Social Rights Jurisprudence-Emerging Trends in International and Comparative Law, 2008, pp. 408-409(cited by C. Binder and Th. Schobesberger), art. cit, p. 55).

in detention); when it applies the principle of non-discrimination, according to which social benefits have to be granted without arbitrary differences; when it takes in consideration additional means to evaluate the conduct of the State, that is procedural obligations to inform the public or to apply the norms about a fair process of law; the Court gives a special attention to the protection of social rights of vulnerable groups.

European Court of Justice of the European Union (CJEU)

The CJEU solved also many cases concerning economic and social rights[293], *beginning with the freedom of circulation of labour and cases of discrimination, the interdiction of an economic activity in order to protect fundamental values of the Union and the restriction to the freedom of circulation of goods in order to protect the freedom of assembly and expression.*

During the last years, CJEU develops an important jurisprudence with regard to economic and social rights provided for in the Charter of fundamental rights, in force since 2009[294]. The Court retained that the radical and immediate reduction of the age of retreat for the personnel of the judiciary in a member State was contrary to an EU Directive and to the principle of non-discrimination provided for in the Charter. The Court also retained

---

[293] Cases Angonese c. Cassa di Risparmio di Bolzano SPA, nr. C-281/98, 2000, ECR-I4139; Garcia Ayelo, nr. 148/02, decision of 2003; Omega 3, nr. 36/02, 2004, ECR-I, 09609; Schroder, nr. C-50/96, 2000, ECR-I, 743 and Cabalero, nr. C-142/00ECR-I-11945; Schmidberger, nr. C-112/00, 2003, ECR-I-5659.

[294] Cases C-286/2, decision of 6 November 2012; Puid, nr. 4/15, decision of 14 November 2013; Abdida, nr. 562/13, decision of the Grand Chamber of 18 December 2014.

that the transfer of an asylum seeker to a country where there is the risk to be subject to an inhuman treatment, as well as the refoulement of a foreigner in a medical critical situation to a country where he cannot receive an adequate medical treatment, are in contradiction to some provisions of the Charter.

The Court considered also cases concerning the freedom of enterprise and the right of property[295]. The Court upheld decisions of the European Commission to refuse to grant rights of emission of dangerous substances to a company, affirming that the objective pursued is the protection of the environment and that the decision does not affect the right to property and corresponds to the principle of proportionality. The same reasoning was made by the Court with regard to the decision of the Commission to accept an emergency measure to forbid some modalities for fishing, in order to protect the respective marine resource.

Some cases solved by CJEU refer to the application of the principle of non-discrimination[296]. The Court invalidated a discriminatory provision which derogated from the EU legislation on equality between men and women by allowing the insurers to make a difference based on sex, with regard to primes and contributions; it also upheld a difference of treatment between conditions for obtaining driving permits for personal cars and for trucks and retained as discrimination on ethnic grounds the

---

[295] Case Arctic Paper Mochenwangen, nr. T-634/13, decision of the EU Tribunal of 26 September 2014; case Giordano, nr. 611/12 P, decision of the Grand Chamber of 14 October 2014.

[296] Cases Test-Achats (2011), nr. C-236/09, decision of 30 April 2011; Glatzel, nr. C-356/12, decision of the Court of 22 May 2014; Chez Raspredelenie, nr. C-83/14, decision f the Court of 2014.

installation of electric manometers at an inaccessible height, in a district inhabited by Roma, different from other districts.

Other cases considered by CJEU refer to the right to a fair trial, to the duration of a procedure and in general to the procedural rights before an EU jurisdiction[297]. The Court clarified the procedural rights of persons suspected to be associated with terrorism. This include the rights of such persons to a good administration of justice, to an effective remedy and to a fair trial. The Court decided that in the absence of any proof that the respective person was involved in activities related to international terrorism, restrictive measures adopted were not justified. In a case where the procedure for recovering a debt took almost 12 years, the Court retained that this represented a violation of the reasonable timeline provided for by the Charter (art. 41.1 concerning the right to a good administration).

The right to an effective remedy[298] was also considered by the Court in a case concerning a refusal of a subvention which could not be contested because a regional program prohibited the judicial control in such cases. The Court retained that the European Regulation which provided for the granting of the subvention did not allow the lack of the judicial control of a decision to refuse

---

[297] Case nr. 584/10 P, Commission and others v. Kadi (appeal to the decision T/85/09), as well as in many similar cases cited in the Report of the Commission concerning the application of fundamental rights during 2013, doc. COM (2013), final, p. 14; case of the Commune Millau, nr. C-531-12 P, decision of the Court of 19 June 2014.

[298] Case Liivimaa Liharets, nr. C-562/12, decision of the Court of 17 September 2014; case FLS Plast AIS, nr. C-243/12 P, decision of the Court of 19 June 2014; case Deltafina SpA, nr C-578/11 P, decision of 12 June 2014.

such a subvention. The Court also retained a violation of the right to be judged in a reasonable timeline according to art. 47 of the Charter, applying the classical criteria of ECHR in this field.

In a case concerning the protection of personal data (art. 8 of the Charter)[299], the Court decided to invalidate the Decision of the Commission nr. 2000 (Safe Harbour) which authorized the transfer of personal data to USA, claiming that this Decision did not contain sufficient proof from the Commission concerning the limitation of access by the US public authorities to the data transferred and with regard to the existence of an effective protection against such an interference. The Court decided that a legislation which gives general access of public authorities to the contents of electronic communications compromises the essence of the right to the respect of private life. Following this decision of the Court, the EU Commission adopted a new Guide concerning the possibility of transfer of data according to the Decision 2000 (Safe Harbour).

In a case concerning access to documents of the EU institutions (art. 42 of the Charter)[300], the Court cancelled in part a decision of the Council of the Union which refused access of the public to a document concerning the adhesion of the Union to the European Convention on human rights of 1950. The Court retained an error of evaluation of the Council, refusing access to one of its directives concerning the negotiation of the adhesion, noting that the position in this document was also conveyed to the participants in the negotiations.

---

[299] Case Schrems, nr. C-362/14, Report of the Commission, doc. COM (2015), final.
[300] Case Besselnik, presented in the Report of the Commission, doc. COM (2016), final.

Inter-American and African courts on human rights

The Inter-American Court of Human Rights was created in 1979, in accordance with the American Convention of human rights of 1969, in order to promote the application of this Convention and of other instruments on human rights adopted within the Americas. The jurisdiction of the Court was accepted by most of the Latin American States, but applications can be submitted to the Court only by States and by the Inter-American Commission on human rights.

The Court considered cases concerning the rights to work, to property, to education, the rights of indigenous peoples to their land and to their cultural expression and identity, the right to benefit from the scientific progress[301].

The African Court of Human Rights and the Rights of Peoples was created by the Protocol of 2004 to the African Charter of the human rights and the rights of peoples. Applications can be submitted to the Court by the African Commission on human rights and rights of peoples, by intergovernmental African organizations, by a State whose citizen is a victim of a violation of human rights and by individual citizens of States which made a declaration

---

[301] Cases Lagos del Campo v. Peru, nr. 12795, decision of 31 August 2017; Five Pensioners v. Peru, decision of 28 February 2003; Sawhoyamaka Indigenous Community v. Paraguay, decision of 29 March 2006; Girls Yean and Bosico, v. Dominican Republic, decision of 8 September 2005; Kichwa Indigenous people of Sarayaku v. Ecuador, decision of 27 June 2012; Artavia Murillo a. o. v. Costa Rica (In Vitro Fertilisation), decision of 28 November 2012.

accepting the competence of the Court to consider such applications.

The African Court considered cases concerning the right to mental and physical health, right to work, right to work under equitable and satisfactory conditions and to equal pay for equal work, right to equality and non-discrimination, right to property, right to land of indigenous peoples having a particular status and deserving special protection[302].

SECTION II - Opinions of quasi-jurisdictional bodies concerning economic, social and cultural rights

1.*The European Social Charter* was concluded within the Council of Europe in 1961, revised in 1996 and was ratified by 43 States. This Charter is based on the option of States which have to accept 6 of the 9 articles considered the most important (concerning the right to work, the right to organize, the right to collective negotiation, the right of children and young people to protection, the right to social security, the right to social and medical assistance, the right of the family to social, juridical and

---

[302] Cases George Maili Kemboge v. Tanzania, nr. 002/2016, decision of 11 May 2018; Rutabingwa Chrysante v. Rwanda, nr. 022/2015, decision of 11May 2018; Fidele Mulindahabi v. Rwanda, nr. 008/2017, order of 28 September 2017; African Commission v. Kenya, nr. 006/2012 (the Ogiek case), decision of 26 May 2017; Sindicat des anciens travailleurs du groupe du laboratoire Australian laboratory Services, ALS-Bamako v. Mali, nr. 002/2005, decision of 5 September 2016; Urban Mkandawire v. Malawi, nr. 003/2011, decision of 21 June 2013.

economic protection, the right of migrant workers and of their families to protection and assistance, as well as the right to equal opportunities and equal treatment with regard to employment and occupation without discrimination on ground of sex), as well as other provisions concerning social and economic rights, so as to reach a total of 16 articles or 63 paragraphs. The application of the Charter is monitored on the basis of reports from States parties, by a *Committee of independent experts*. This Committee presents its reports to an Intergovernmental Committee formed of representatives of States parties which is entitled to adopt recommendations, submitted thereafter to the Committee of ministers of the Council of Europe and conveyed to the respective States. The Committee of experts examines also collective complaints concerning violation of economic or social rights, presented by organizations of employers, by trade unions, by European and international non-governmental organizations having a consultative status to the Council of Europe or by national bodies representing trade unions or employers from the country concerned by the complaint.

Collective complaints presented to the Committee during the last years referred, for instance, to work beyond the time regularly established, presented by the European Council of Police Trade-Unions or by national organizations of trade-unions[303]; numerous petitions aimed at the protection of children and families[304], presented by the International Federation of Human Rights or by Defense for Children International. Many individual

---

[303] Reclamations nr. 68/2011 and nr. 84/2012 concerning France, nr. 60/2010 concerning Portugal.
[304] Reclamations nr. 62/2010 and 98/2013 concerning Belgium; reclamations nr. 92, 93, 94 and 95, all in 2013, concerning France, Ireland, Italy and Slovenia.

complaints refer to the protection of the social rights of homeless[305], to the protection of the rights to association and to collective negotiation[306], to the protection of the right to housing[307], to the protection of Roma[308]. Other petitions requested immediate measures in favour of homeless and for ensuring the medicine necessary[309], or measures in the field of social security[310], for the protection of health[311], or of the right to medical assistance[312], or for the elimination of discrimination and ensuring juridical and economic assistance and the protection of the family[313].

According to analysts, the efficacy of the procedure of examination of collective complaints within the Council of Europe presents limits resulting from the small number of States which accepted it, from the fact that the same body examines the periodic reports of States and collective complaints, as well as from the

---

[305] Reclamations nr. 86/2012 and 90/2013 concerning Netherlands.
[306] Reclamations nr. 83/2012 concerning Ireland, 85/2013 concerning Sweden, nr. 101/2013 concerning France, 103/2013 concerning Norway.
[307] Reclamation nr. 62/2010 concerning Belgium.
[308] Reclamations nr. 103/2014 concerning France, 104/2014 concerning the Czech Republic, nr. 61/2010 concerning Portugal, nr. 27/2005 concerning Italy.
[309] Reclamations nr. 86/2012 and 90/2013 concerning Netherlands, reclamations nr. 93/2013 and 98/2013 concerning Ireland, respectively Belgium.
[310] Reclamations nr. 102/2014 concerning Italy and nr. 108/2014 concerning Finland.
[311] Reclamations nr. 87/2012 concerning Italy and nr. 92/2013 concerning Sweden.
[312] Reclamation nr.14/2003 concerning France.
[313] Petitions nr. 62/2010 concerning Belgium and 60/2010 concerning Portugal.

submission of the recommendations adopted by the Committee of experts to political bodies of the Council[314].

Numerous complaints were submitted to the Committee in the beginning against Greece for restriction to the social and economic rights, the State party trying to justify them by the measures imposed by the European Union and by the International Monetary Fund in the framework of the so-called "plan to save the country"[315].

2.The Human Rights Committee, created by the Covenant on civil and political rights, considered first of all cases concerning the exercise of economic and cultural rights according to art. 27 of the Covenant, mainly by indigenous peoples. The Committee retained the right of an ethnic community to perform an economic activity which represents an essential element of its culture, more precisely the reindeer-breeding by members of the Sami community[316]; it also retained, in a different case, that

---

[314] An analysis of the functioning of this mechanism by Robin R. Churchill and Urfan Khaliq, System of the European Social Charter: An Effective Mechanism for Ensuring Compliance with Economic, Social and Cultural Rights? in EJIL, 2004, vol. 15 no. 3, pp. 417-456.

[315] Cases cited by Peggy Ducoulombier, La liberté des Etats parties à la Charte sociale européenne dans le choix de leur engagement : une liberté surveillée, in Revue trimestrielle des droits de l'homme, no. 26, 2013, p. 858.

[316] Cases Kitok v. Sweden, nr. 197/1995, decision on 27 July 1998, RUDH 1989, p. 84; Ilmari Lansman and others v. Finland, nr. 511/1992, Selected decisions of the Human Rights Committee under the Optional Protocol, vol. 5/2005, pp. 150-156; Jouni Lansman and others v. Finland, nr. 671/1995, Selected decisions, vol. 6/2006, pp. 167-176; Paader and others v. Finland, nr. 2102/2011, opinion

activities of prospection of energetic resources, envisaged by the State party, were threatening the traditional way of life and the culture of the indigenous people[317]; similar opinions were retained by the Committee in other cases concerning the rights of the Sami. In a different case, the Committee retained an arbitrary interference in the family and private life of petitioners, by the construction of a hotel above an old cemetery of an indigenous group[318].

The Human Rights Committee considered also cases concerning other violations of some human rights provided for by the Covenant, mainly cultural rights. To respond to a communication concerning discrimination by forbidding the use of a language in exterior commercial advertising, the Committee retained that a State can choose one or several official languages, but cannot exclude, beyond the spheres of public life, the freedom of an individual to expression in a language of his choice and retained a violation of the Covenant[319]. In a more recent case concerning the right to education, the Committee retained that the refusal to enroll ethnic Roma children in primary school and their enrolling in special classes represented a violation of their right to

---

adopted on 26 March 2014, doc. A/69/40(vol. II, part One, pp. 455-467.

[317] Cases Banda of the Laque Lubicon v. Canada, decision of 26 March 1990, Selected decisions, 2002, vol. 3, pp. 62-79; George Howard v. Canada, nr. 879/1999, Selected decisions, vol. 8/2007, pp. 126-136.

[318] Case Francis Hopu and Tepoaitu Bessert v. France, no. 549/1993, Selected decisions, vol. 7/2005, pp. 68-74.

[319] Cases Allan Singer v. Canada, nr. 455/1991, Selected decisions, vol.5/2005, pp. 76-83; Walter Hoffman and Gwen Simpson v. Canada, nr. 1220/2003, Selected decisions, vol. 8/2007, pp. 45-50.

education and of the principle of non-discrimination[320]. Other cases referred to the right of the individual to his name, as an important element of his identity, to the absence of an alternative to the military service and the obligation to perform it, as a violation of the religious freedoms[321].

In more recent cases, the Committee approached more directly situations of violation of civil and political rights caused as a result of conditions of inhuman or degrading treatment, caused by violations of the rights to health or to housing[322], as well as concerning demolition of the housing of Roma communities[323].

3. *The Committee for the Elimination of Racial Discrimination (CERD) also considered communications concerning economic, social and cultural rights.* CERD considered a communication concerning application by the postal services of a higher tax for treating correspondence in a language different from the official one, as well as communications about discrimination with regard to the protection of the right to work[324], the equal

---

[320] Case Raihon Hudoyberganova v. Uzbekistan, nr. 931/2000, Selected decisions, vol. 8, 2007, pp. 176-179.

[321] Cases A. R. Coerial and M. A. R. Aurik v. Netherlands, nr 453/1991, Selected decisions, vol. 5/2005, pp. 72-76; Yeo Bum Yoon and Myung Jin Choi v. Republic of Korea, Selected decisions, vol. 9/2008, pp. 2018-225.

[322] Cases Hudoybergenov v. Turkmenistan, nr. 2221/2012; Mellet v. Ireland, nr. 2324/2013.

[323] Case Yordanova v. Bulgaria, cited supra, p.169, where the Committee referred to the general Comments of CESC nr. 4/1991 concerning the right to housing and 7/1997 concerning forced evacuation.

[324] Cases Nikolas Regerat and others v. France, no. 24/2002, doc CERD/C/62/D/24/2000 of 16 April 2003; Jilmaz Dogan v. The

access to banking services, to education and to housing for Roma individuals[325]. The Committee sent recommendations to the State parties to eliminate discriminations and sometimes to grant compensations for the prejudice suffered.

4. The Inter-American and African commissions for human rights also considered cases of violations of economic, social and cultural rights of persons belonging to indigenous people from these regions. *The Inter-American Commission for human rights* examined in 1985 a petition against Brazil concerning activities of developers and companies engaged in exploiting minerals and wood in the area of Amazons, inhabited by the Yanomani Indians. The Commission found that the intrusion of these companies, which included also the construction of a highway through the territories inhabited by Yanomani brought trouble on their social life and illnesses which decimated the population. The Commission retained that, by granting the license and authorizing these activities, the State violated the provisions of the American Declaration of human rights, including mainly the rights to life and to health[326]. In a different case, the Inter-American Commission retained that by granting concessions to build on

---

Netherlands, no. 4/1991, presented in Ion Diaconu, Racial Discrimination, 2011, Eleven International Publishing, p. 333.

[325] Cases Z. B. Ahmed Habassi v. Denmark, nr. 10/1997, Murat Er v. Denmark, nr. 40/2007, presented in Ion Diaconu, Racial Discrimination, pp. 334 and 336; L.R. and other Slovak citizens of Roma origin v. Slovakia, nr. 31/2003, ibidem, p. 335; I. G. v. Republic of Korea, nr. 5/2012, doc. CERD/C/86/D/51/2012.

[326] Resolution no. 12/85, Case no.7615, Annual Report of the Inter-American Commission on Human Rights, 1984-1985; similarly, in the case Comunitat Indigena Yakye Aksa c. Paraguay, decision of 13 June 2005(where the Court upheld the right to water of indigenous populations), Serie C, nr. 125.

territories used by the Maya community in Belize, there is a threat to produce irreversible long-term damages to the natural environment of this community. The Commission underlined the fundamental rights of indigenous people corresponding to a right to a life project which includes essential elements, such as the right to education, to physical, cultural and spiritual welfare[327].

The IACHR considered also other communications concerning economic, social and cultural rights such as the right to the protection of children and families, the right to medical treatment, the right to physical and mental health of disabled people, the rights related to the treatment and condition of foreigners, the rights to work, to social security and property, the prohibition of forced labor and others[328].

The *African Commission of human rights and the rights of peoples* refers mainly to the rights of indigenous and tribal people affected by the deterioration of the environment in the region, as a result of extractive activities and of forced displacement of populations from their ancestral territories. The Commission

---

[327] Case Maya Indigenous Community of Toledo c. Belize, communication no. 12053, Report no. 40/04, IACHR, OEA, Serie I/VIII, Doc. 5, Rev. 1, p. 727, 2004.

[328] Cases Rochak & others v. El Salvador, communication nr. 12577, opinion of 7 November 2012; People of Quishque-Tapayrihua v. Peru, communication nr. 1216/03, opinion of 24 July 2014; Eulogia and son Sergio v. Peru, communication nr. 1334/09, opinion of 4 April 2014; Haitian and Dominican of Haitian Descent v. Dominican Republic (deportation, conditions of living), communication nr. 12189 of November 1999, opinion of 14 September 2000; Jose Pereira v. Brazil, communication no. 11289/03, friendly settlement of 18 September 2003; Baena Ricardo and others v. Panama, communication nr 11325/1999, opinion of 2 February 2001.

underlined the importance of the right to a healthy environment, provided for in the African Charter of 1981, as well as of an impact study and an independent scientific evaluation before the starting of such activities. The Commission affirmed the right of the respective populations to benefit of their natural resources, as well as their right to development, underlining the importance of their free, previous and well-informed consent for such activities[329]. In the case Ogoniland, the African Commission affirmed that article 24 of the African Charter creates for the States the obligation to adopt reasonable measures for preventing environmental pollution and deterioration, for promoting preservation, sustainable development and ecological use of natural resources. It asked the State concerned to ensure the full cleaning of the land and waters damaged by the operations with oil and to prepare an impact study on the effects of the respective activity on the environment[330].

The African Commission also considered other cases concerning economic and social rights, such as the right to physical and mental health of disable people, protection of the family, the right to health and to water resources, the right to education, the right to work[331].

---

[329] Presented in the document of the UN Human Rights Council, nr. A/HRC/19/34, paragr. 39.
[330] Case CERAC and CESR v. Nigeria, no. 155/96, decision of 27 May 2002. A similar solution in the case Endorois Welfare Council v. Kenya, no. 276/2003, decision of 4 February 2010.
[331] Amnesty International v. Zambia, communication nr. 212/98, opinion of 5 May 1999; Sudan Human Rights Organization & Center on Housing Rights and Evictions v. Sudan, communication nr.179/03-296/05, opinion of 2009; Free Legal Assistance Group a.o. v. Zaire, communication nr. 25/89-47/90-56/91, opinion of 4 April 1996; Urban Mkandawire v. Malawi, communication nr.

SECTION III - Additional Protocol to the Covenant on economic, social and cultural rights

The Declaration adopted by the World Conference on human rights of Vienna encouraged the UN Commission for human rights to continue the consideration of an optional protocol to the Covenant of 1966, which should create a system of protection of economic, social and cultural rights similar to that concerning civil and political rights. This subject received a real progress only after the decision of the Human Rights Council of 2006 to create an open-ended group in order to prepare a draft of a treaty containing a mechanism of complaints with regard to economic, social and cultural rights. After two years of negotiations, the Additional Protocol was adopted by the Resolution of the General Assembly nr. A/Res. 63/117 of 19 December 2008 and open to signature by the States which were parties to the Covenant. The Protocol is in force since the 5 May 2013, when 10 ratifications were received. Until now, 45 States have signed and 22 have ratified it (situation on 6 November 2017). The Protocol opens the way to promote the application of the Covenant also through the system of individual communications. Individual persons (citizens of States parties) have now the possibility to present communications about violations by their States of their rights provided for by the Covenant.

003/2011, opinion of 21 June 2013; Parohit and Moore v. Gambia, communication nr. 241/2001, opinion of 15-29 May 2003.

According to the Protocol, the Committee for economic, social and cultural rights (CESC) is competent to examine individual communications concerning alleged violations of articles 6(concerning the right to work, which includes the right of everyone to the opportunity to gain his living by work which he freely chooses or accepts), article 7 (the right of everyone to the enjoyment of just and favourable conditions of work), article 8 (the right of everyone to form trade unions and to join them), article 9 (the right of everyone to social security, including social insurance), article 11 (the right of everyone to an adequate standard of living for him and his family, including adequate food, closing and housing), article 12 (the right of everyone to the enjoyment of the highest attainable standard of physical and mental health), article 13 (the right of everyone to education), article 14 (the right to education for populations from territories under the jurisdiction of a State) and article 15 (the right to take part in cultural life and to benefit from the scientific progress). The Protocol does not include under the competence of the Committee to receive communications with regard to article 10 (protection of family, of mothers and children and young persons who are covered by other similar bodies under the respective Conventions).

These rights, proclaimed in terms sometimes sufficiently precise, sometimes in general terms, have to be translated in specific rights of persons and obligations of States. The Covenant contains also general principles and provisions to be taken into account when the Committee will evaluate the application of operative articles, that is the situation with regard to human rights. According to article 2, States parties committed themselves to take measures to the maximum of their available resources, in order to achieving progressively the full realization of the rights recognized by the Covenant by all appropriate means. That means, measures taken have to be conceived within the available resources and to aim at ensuring the progressive realization of the rights, because economic, social and cultural rights cannot be guaranteed without a positive intervention, mainly financial, by States. This raises three issues: to recognize/identify the rights to which the State party is obliged by the Covenant; to apply such measures meant to progressively realize those rights; to ensure the observance of these rights. If the recognition of rights is the lowest level, the other two steps are of crucial importance in order to transform the rights recognized into reality.

With regard to measures which can be taken, in its General Comment nr. 3 CESC recognized in 1999 that legislative measures are preferable in many cases and sometimes indispensable; but then the Committee states that legislation is not sufficient; administrative, economic, financial, educational and social measures can be necessary, as well as programmes of action, organisms and procedures (judicial and extra-judicial). With regard to the allocation of the maximum of available resources, the Committee underlines the obligation of the State to demonstrate that all efforts were made to use all available resources in the effort to satisfy on a basis of priority the minimum of its obligations[332].

According to the Principles of Limburg on the application of the Covenant, the realization of the economic, social and cultural rights can be achieved through a variety of political arrangements; nevertheless, States have to act in good faith for the fulfillment of their obligations. After 10 years, the Maastricht Guide concerning the violations of these rights brings more precise elements about the obligations of States, affirming that the

---

[332] Compilation..., General Comment nr. 3/1999, doc. HRI/GEN/1/Rev. 8, p. 15.

obligation to respect, to protect and to fulfill each of these rights contains elements of obligations of conduct and of result; the obligation of conduct requests action calculated reasonably to achieve the benefit of the respective right; the obligation of result requests that the State achieves precise targets to satisfy a higher standard of substance in the exercise of the right.

In order to ensure that these rights are respected, it is necessary that governments intervene in the economic and social life; this is what States do also in order to ensure that some civil and political rights are observed, in order to avoid violations, to protect individuals against them, to create a political, legal and institutional system adequate to the requirements of respecting these rights.

According to the same article 2 of the Covenant, States parties are committed to guarantee that the rights enunciated will be exercised without discrimination of any kind on grounds of race, colour, sex, language, religion, political or other opinion, national or social origin, property, birth or other status. The text adds that developing countries, with due regard to human rights and their national economy, may determine to what extent they would guarantee to foreigners the economic rights recognized in the Covenant.

Of an equal importance and of general application is also the provision of article 3, according to which States are committed to ensure equal rights to men and women to benefit of all economic, social and cultural rights enunciated in the Covenant. On the other side, according to article 4 of the Covenant, economic, social and cultural rights may be subject to limitations determined by law only in so far as this may be compatible with the nature of the right and solely for the purpose of promoting the general welfare in a democratic society.

Another disposition of principle that CESC has to have in view refers to the relationship between the provisions of the Covenant and the situation of human rights in the States parties. According to article 5, nothing in the Covenant may be interpreted as implying for any State, group or person any right to engage in any activity or to perform any act aimed at the destruction of any rights or freedoms recognized therein or at their limitation to a greater extent than is provided by the Covenant. At the same time, it stipulates that no restriction or derogation from any of the rights recognized or existing in a State party in virtue of the law, regulations or custom, shall be admitted under the pretext that the Covenant does not recognize them or that it recognizes them to a lesser extent.

These are principles of a general application with regard to all human rights, and their application is an integral part of the competence of CESC for the examination of individual communications concerning human rights enunciated in articles 6-15 mentioned.

According to the Protocol there are three mechanisms of monitoring the application of the Covenant: individual petitions; petitions between States; the procedure of investigation. The States have to declare when they ratify the Protocol whether they accept petitions between States and the procedure of investigation. According to article 2 of the Protocol, an individual communication can be presented by or on behalf of the person or the group whose rights provided for in the Covenant were allegedly seriously and systematically violated by the State party.

Communications between States can be submitted when a State pretends that another State did not fulfill its obligations. It is imperative that before a communication is sent to CESC the internal remedies available are exhausted.

As a first step, the Committee offers its good offices to the person/group and the State concerned, seeking an agreed solution. If it is not successful, the Committee considers thoroughly the situation in closed meetings on the basis of the pretentions presented by the parties and can consult relevant bodies (depending on the substance of the right, such as ILO with regard to the right to trade unions and labour organization, WHO with regard to the right to health). According to the Protocol, the Committee takes into account to what extent measures taken by the State are reasonable and the fact that the State can take various policy measures to implement its undertakings. Then, it adopts recommendations motivated and conveys its point of view and opinions to the State. The State is requested to inform in written form about measures taken and the Committee follows the evolution of the situation.

A new element refers to the presentation of communications on behalf of a group, concerning serious and systematic violation of rights of a group; this results from the nature of economic, social and cultural rights, which concern as a rule important segments of the population of States. The newest procedure is that of investigation, where the Committee invites the State to cooperate in the examination of the communication and to submit written observations. The investigation can be made by one or several members of the Committee who have to consider all information received. The Committee conveys its comments and recommendations to the State, including with regard to modalities to implement its obligations; the State presents its observations and then the Committee can publish a summary of the procedure. The Committee can also establish a time table for the follow-up, asking the State to inform about the application of the recommendations. States are obliged to take measures so that petitioners are not submitted to bad treatment or pressure because of presenting a communication.

The Protocol provides also the requirement of international assistance and cooperation (including through the establishment of a fund for promoting human rights). The Committee can also include reommendations to that effect.

The adoption and the entry in force of the Protocol can be an important achievement, creating the instrument which allows the presentation and the consideration of communications concerning alleged violations of economic, social and cultural rights attributed to States. The mechanism created is similar to the Human Rights Committee, created to monitor the implementation of civil and political rights, with some specific elements concerning the violation of rights of a group, the offer of good offices and the procedure of investigation. Moreover, CESC is competent not only to address recommendations, but also to propose to States ways and means to fulfill their obligations and to respect individual rights which might have been violated.

An obvious advantage in the activity of CESC for examining individual communications consists in the general comments adopted by the Committee during its more than 30 years of existence. These general comments describe the basic obligations of States under the Covenant and offer criteria and interpretations of crucial importance concerning the meaning of the rights and the corresponding obligations, as well as the level of respect required for different rights. The Maastricht Guide also offers clarifications about the obligations of respect, of protection and fulfillment, of conduct and of result, as well as about the margin of discretion, the minimum basic obligations and the issue of available resources. The consideration of individual and group communications may further clarify the meaning of the rights in question in the current practice of fulfillment of the obligations of States.

The Additional Protocol opens the possibility of a dialogue between the Committee and the parties in dispute in each case, through the procedure of good offices; already at this stage CESC can offer to the parties solutions for the implementation of the provisions of the Covenant invoked in the communications. Accepting such solutions is already a positive step in promoting the economic, social and cultural rights according to the Covenant. The Committee is competent to convey to the States concerned recommendations concerning ways and means to follow in order to respect its obligations. The Committee is not satisfied with ascertaining that some obligations are not fulfilled but can adopt a positive roll indicating ways and means, having in mind the experience and good practices of other States, in order to assist the State to take adequate measures. Finally, the Protocol provides for the requirement of international assistance and cooperation, including by the establishment of a fund for promoting economic, social and cultural rights. This means that the Committee can recommend to international relevant organizations and other bodies, as well as to other States where appropriate, to offer to the respective State the assistance necessary, to initiate programmes or plans of action aimed at the gradual fulfilment by the respective

State of its obligations, or to apply other necessary measures allowing the State to concentrate its efforts for that purpose.

Therefore, the Protocol looks beyond ascertaining violations of human rights and addressing adequate recommendations; CESC can propose solutions and initiate measures of international assistance meant to offer to the State the necessary support and means for respecting economic, social and cultural human rights. Thus, CESC has the mission to promote directly respect for these rights in different States parties and to be involved in the efforts of the international community to promote the fulfillment of these rights, including through the economic and social development.

The mechanism of individual communications represents an impulse to create the essential conditions and fulfill the requirements for respecting the rights enunciated by the Covenant. For that, a bigger number of States parties to the Covenant should ratify the Additional Protocol and more communications of substance about these rights should be submitted to the Committee. A serious limitation of the application of the Protocol is presently the small number of African States(Cape Verde, Central African Republic, Gabon and Niger) and Asian States(Mongolia) which ratified it. Although many of the States in the respective regions tend to achieve a sustainable development, including in the economic and cultural fields, the level of application of the provisions of the Covenant at the national level is reduced in many of these countries and the mechanisms of protection are absent or often not used. Moreover, the regional protection of these rights is still weak or lacking in these regions, with the exception of indigenous rights. government or if a State accepts expressly this procedure). Therefore, the Protocol may fulfill an important roll in this field.

The Committee received a number of 22 communications, of which 12 were found inadmissible mainly on the ground that the facts alleged occurred before the entry into force of the Protocol (*ratione temporis*). Three cases were solved and 5 others are pending. In the first case solved concerning Spain, a house of a home owner was repossessed by a bank for the non-payment of the mortgage. The communicant complained that he did not receive an adequate notice of the enforcement procedure and this prevented a proper defense of his rights. The Committee found a violation of the Covenant and emphasized that an effective remedy was a fundamental aspect of the right to housing. In the second case solved concerning also Spain, the communication (a person in prison) complained about the reduction of his disability pension during the time served in prison with the amount spent for him. The Committee found that the measure taken was reasonable and proportionate and had no disproportionate effect on the rights of the communicant. In the third case, also on the right to housing, the communicant, a low-income tenant of Madrid, complained of eviction from a private rental accommodation and that the authorities did not offer an alternative and did not demonstrate that they had taken all reasonable measures, up to the maximum of their available resources, to satisfy his right. The communicant invoked the rights to social security, to adequate housing, to health, to non-discrimination, broadly aiming at austerity measures on social security and housing taken in Spain.

Concerning Ecuador, communications refer to discrimination against a foreign minor with regard to participation in football tours (articles 2, 4, 10.3, 13 and 15), to access to compensation established by a collective work contract (articles 2. 6.7 and 12) and to discrimination against a woman domestic worker with regard to access to the national system of social security (articles 3 and 9). Two more recent communications were received against Luxembourg (on the dismissal of the representative of a trade union) and against Italy (on the donation of embryos produced in vitro fertilization for scientific research).

The beginning of the activity of the Committee on the basis of the Protocol shows the use of good practices, like the list of pending cases with description, third party interventions with interest in the proceedings, a follow-up procedure and 1-2 years for solving each case. The opinions adopted seem to be careful, well founded and reasonable. The Committee stated that it will not use the practice of a „grading system" (of qualifying the violations) but will elaborate a conclusion tailored on the particular circumstances of each case and appropriate recommendations.

It is obvious that States have hesitations with regard to ratifying and applying this Protocol, probably having in mind the economic situation of many of them and the difficulties to fulfill the commitments under the Covenant as well as the uncertainties with regard to the results and the efficiency of the mechanism created. The existence and the activity of the European, Latin-American and African systems, as well as the Protocol itself, although at the beginning, and the internal jurisdiction of States, show that economic, social and cultural rights can be subject to judiciary and quasi-judiciary procedures. The jurisprudence of the Committee is very important to define the extent of the application of these rights, to offer the victims the necessary remedies and to States adequate and reasonable solutions. The mechanism created by the Protocol started to function; in as much as States will see that it is useful, it will gain confidence and will be acceded increasingly. Economic, social and cultural rights will be thus brought closer to the principle of indivisibility of human rights.

*   *   *

There are considerable differences at national level of guarantee of economic, social and cultural rights. The principle of progressive realization of this rights provided for in the Covenant and the procedures of the mechanism created by the Additional Protocol leave sufficient space for a different application at the national level. Ways and means used for ensuring recognition, respect, protection and fulfilment of these rights are diverse and difficult to compare. Nevertheless, the Covenant requests, according to article 2, that States parties take measures for the progressive realization of these rights and to establish and respect a timetable for their realization. This general provision cannot be interpreted as depriving the obligations under the operative provisions of the Covenant of real contents.

There are at present several forums which are competent to receive petitions concerning economic, social and cultural rights: ECHR and the Committee on Economic and Social Rights in Europe, the Inter-American Commission on human rights and the Inter-American Court of human rights, the African Commission and the African Court of human rights and the rights of peoples, as well as the human rights treaty bodies created under the treaties concluded within the UN; all of them can create precedents for a uniform practice in the application of the international Covenant, which will support the activity of a forum to consider individual communications in this field . These regional forums and human rights treaty bodies could also extend their activity and preoccupations in promoting economic, social and cultural rights and can certainly benefit of a sustained activity of CESC in this field.

The financial crises, the recession, as well as in some cases the absence of the political will of State, are real; economic, social and cultural rights are costly and only a few States can ensure their full realization through a normal process of economic and social development. The request according to the Covenant to allocate the minimum of resources available supposes respect for these rights, but the extent of respect will depend of the level of economic development of States. CESC made it clear in its general comments that even in periods of severe restrictions on resources, caused by recession, processes of restructuring or others, the vulnerable members of the population have to be protected by adopting programmes at reduced costs.

During the global financial crisis in 2009, the UN General Assembly adopted a resolution about the economic and financial world crisis, underlining explicitly the need for the global cooperation among States through a prompt and responsible action, giving due attention to human and social aspects. The resolution does not mention economic and social rights and refers to reducing the negative effects of the crisis by safeguarding the economic gains, as well as those of development and social; it does not make a distinction between human rights, but it is obvious that it has in view a system of protection of economic, social and cultural rights.

Important competences are recognized to the Committee on economic, social and cultural rights, both for ascertaining violations of the rights enunciated by the Covenant and for promoting adequate solutions through the procedure of good offices and through the recommendations made, as well as for promoting international assistance and cooperation in adequate modalities and forms depending on the nature and the extent of difficulties encountered by the State concerned.

The Human Rights Council, which took in 2006 the decision leading to the elaboration of the Protocol to the Covenant, should continue to recommend that States parties to the Covenant ratify the Optional Protocol and by this to contribute to raising the level of implementation of economic, social and cultural rights, including by developing countries, taking into account the opportunities offered to the Committee of experts of the Covenant when it considers communications according to the Protocol.

The Human Rights Council should also recommend to all regional human rights bodies and to human rights bodies created by international instruments, as well as to other United Nations bodies, specialized agencies, funds, programmes and mechanisms, to support the Committee on economic, social and cultural rights in the exercise of its competences under the Optional Protocol with regard to the consideration of communications submitted and to promoting the follow up of the views and recommendations of the Committee that indicate the need for a technical advice or assistance.

The Human Rights Council could, moreover, recommend to regional human rights bodies and to human rights bodies created by international instruments to give increased attention within their mandates to economic, social and cultural rights as set forth in international human rights law.

CHAPTER VI - EUROPE, MIGRATION and the RIGHT to ASYLUM

Abstract

International instruments on human rights contain many norms for the protection of asylum seekers and migrants, it is true in several documents which are not accepted by all States. Such norms were not respected always and everywhere. The reasons of migrations evoluated as a result of international events and developments from wars and political persecution to underdevelopment and poverty. Similarly, the dimensions of the phenomenon of migration were different and thus raised specific problems for the receiving States.

The crisis that Europe faced during the last 5-10 years, which continue to torment the European States and institutions, raised unprecedented human, social and political difficulties that are not yet overcome. A combination of factors-armed conflicts and the increase of extreme poverty in the areas neighbouring the continent, while the European Union was itself facing economic difficulties -have largely contributed to the dimensions of the flow of migration and to the difficulties to absorb it.

It is thus necessary to consider the solutions used in Europe to respond to these problems, from the point of view of the commitments of European States and institutions to respect human rights and fundamental freedoms for all, including migrants and asylum seekers.

Key Words: migrants, refugees, Dublin regulations, border control, non-refoulement, non-discrimination, State responsible, exclusion, subsidiary protection, collective expulsion, detention, procedural guarantees

Introduction

Migration of populations and of individuals is accounted since centuries and issues raised by it were treated differently, function of situations, of events and by the States concerned.

It was after the First World War that the problems appeared, since States introduced formalities for foreigners entering their territory through a regime of passports. The war produced an important number of persons deprived of citizenship, who had thus difficulties to travel to other countries. The League of Nations created in 1921 a High Commission for refugees and convened in 1922 an Intergovernmental Conference where it was decided to create a certificate of identity and of travel, called Nansen passport, at the initiative of the Norwegian polar explorer Fridtjof Nansen who became the first high commissioner for refugees of the League of Nations and received the Nobel prix for peace in 1922. This passport was created initially for the Russian refugees and stateless, then in 1924 was extended to Armenians and since 1928 to Assyro-Chaldeens. The Nansen passport was recognized between 1922 and 1945 as a document of identity and travel by numerous States.

Events during and after the Second World War led to an exponential increase of the phenomenon of migration mainly for political reasons, which determined the adoption of the 1951 Convention relating to the status of refugees. As this Convention referred only to refugees of Europe, the Protocol to the Convention adopted in 1966 extended the application of the Convention to the whole world. Since 1951 the Office of the High Commissioner for Refugees was created within the United Nations.

During the second half of the XX-eth century a migration for economic purposes took place, without precedent in the history of mankind, in the developed countries of Western Europe and of North America, responding to the request of labour force due to the intense process of development. Millions of people moved to these countries from less developed countries and regions, mainly from areas neighbouring Europe and North America (Turkey, Iraq, Iran, Northern Africa, Latin American countries, South-East Europe, partly due to ethnic conflicts in the area); an intra-European migration also took place after the creation of the European communities from Southern countries (Italy, Spain and Portugal) to more developed States of the center and the North of Europe. This was a migration wanted and encouraged by the receiving States, which led to the establishment of large numbers of migrants on the territory of these States. This evolution continues presently with the migration of labour force of Eastern and South European countries to other States of Europe.

Many of the fundamental human rights and freedoms, recognized by the basic instruments in this field (the two covenants on economic, social and cultural rights, respectively on civil and political rights, the conventions on the elimination of racial discrimination and of discrimination against women, the convention against torture and inhuman and degrading treatment and punishment, the convention on the rights of the child) concern everyone, that is also refugees and migrants. This should be supplemented by the Convention relating to the status of refugees adopted in 1951 and modified by the Protocol of 1966. General documents adopted in Europe are the Convention of 1950 concerning fundamental human rights and freedoms (Convention of 1950), amended by several additional protocols and, more recently, within the European Union, the Charter of fundamental rights adopted in 2007, which form together the basic norms adopted and applied on the continent.

In parallel with the increased migrations, a concern developed for recognizing and respecting some specific rights of the persons migrating to other countries, which led more recently to international norms concerning the rights of migrants. In 1990 the General Assembly adopted the International Convention on the Protection of the Rights of All Migrant Workers and Members of their Families and since 2004 a Committee of experts for the protection of the rights of migrant workers and of the members of their families functions within the United Nations.

According to norms of the general international law, States have the right to control and to regulate the entrance and the stay of foreigners on their territory, including the right to decide to expel them. As mentioned above, other norms of international law concerning the protection of fundamental human rights and freedoms have to be respected also when the States exercise their sovereign attributions concerning the regulation and the control of entry and stay of foreigners on their territory, which represent limits for the discretionary exercise of these attributions.

The conflicts which took place around Europe at the beginning of the 21st century (in Northern Africa, in Syria and

Iraq), as well as the increased level of poverty in some countries of Africa and South America, led to an emigration without precedent. Europe was confronted with the attempts to reach the continent through the sea using improvised means, which led to the sad record of 3000 lives lost in the Mediterranean at the beginning of 2014[333]. With 42.673 km of maritime external borders and 7721 km of terrestrial external borders, the Schengen space which includes 26-member States (among them 4 States non-EU members) faces each year more than 700 million crossings of these borders[334].

In order to face this phenomenon, which presents considerably different dimensions[335] and is attributed different consequences from those of the migrations of the second half of XX-eth century, the European Union adopted a series of specific norms, some concerning the right to free movement of citizens of member States and of associated States (with some limits and restrictions), and others in order to ensure a uniform control of entry and stay of other individuals in the Union's space, according to the agreement Schengen. According to its competences as an organization of integration, the Union adopted, beyond the Treaties on the Union and on the functioning of the Union and the Charter of fundamental rights, numerous internal legal instruments in order to regulate in a uniform way the policies of member States in this

---

333 Figures presented by Mrs. Anne Brasseur, president of the Parliamentary Assembly of the Council of Europe, on the occasion of its session of 3 October 2014.
334 European Commission. Third Report on Immigration and Asylum (2011), Brussels, 30.5.2012, COM 2012, 250 final.
335 More than 1 million during the year 2015, evaluation by UNHCR, over 1 Million Refugees and Migrant Arrive in Europe, 22 December 2015.

field, among which the Regulation concerning the Dublin Convention with its subsequent modifications(Dublin II and III), Eurodac, Border Code and Frontex, as well as successive directives concerning the Conditions of Reception, the Asylum Procedure, the Qualification, the Facilities, the Return and others. These documents concern the control, the procedures of the examination of asylum applications and the return of those whose requests are rejected, but provide also the obligation to respect human rights according to the EU treaties, to the Charter of fundamental rights and to the jurisprudence of the European Court of Human Rights in this field.

Although the system created by the Dublin agreement and the subsequent regulations appears as a procedural one, specifying how to determine the State which is responsible to consider the request of asylum and procedures to follow, it imposed considerable tasks to the States of first entry on the EU territory, mainly Greece and Italy, while the clause of sovereignty which allowed other States to consider themselves such requests did not attenuate too much these tasks.

With regard to immigration and border control, the Regulation (EU) nr. 1052/2013 of the European Parliament and the Council of 22 October 2013 established two main objectives of the system to survey the borders[336]: to prevent and combat illegal immigration and to contribute to the protection of and to save the life of migrants. At the same time, the European Council recommended the conclusion of agreements of readmission with a

---

[336] JO, L 295 of 6 November 2013, p. 11.

number of neighbouring States, as well as to consolidate the existing norms in the field of the return[337].

Analysts appreciated that the increased emphasis by the EU on these regulations and the practice of member States of surveying the borders radically transformed the management of migration and had as a result the violation of fundamental rights of migrants not only in the border States members of the EU, which are the key entrance points, but also in the States situated at the external borders of the Union, which have conditional agreements with EU[338]. First of all, the external control at the borders was qualified as a primary problem of security and became a central element of the EU policy in the field of migration and asylum. EU institutions which had as their initial mission to combat the trafficking of persons and the organized crime (Interpol) were mobilized to deal also with the control of migration, which included in their preoccupations an amalgam of populations and persons who wanted to travel to other countries for different purposes.

Although the Border Code Schengen provides for making the border control with full respect of human dignity(art. 6), so as to avoid discrimination, in many cases such discrimination was retained[339]. Interceptions on the sea and the return of the

---

[337] Conseil Européen, Conclusions sur la politique de l'UE en matière de retour, Conseil JAI (Luxembourg, 5 et 6 juin 2014).
[338] Idil Atak, Francois Crépeau, Managing migrations at the external borders of the European Union: Meeting the Human Rights Challenges, in European Journal of Human Rights, no. 5, December 2014, p. 593.
[339] In 2004, the Chamber of Lords of the United Kingdom (further UK) retained that the scheme of control of immigration acting at the airport of Prague, which was instituted on the basis of an agreement

individuals concerned would also be contrary to the Convention on the status of refugees, because they violate the principle of non-refoulement (art. 53 of the Convention) and do not ensure the right of access to an effective procedure for examination of a request of asylum.

It is underlined that important documents of the EU law enunciate the basic principles to be respected in this field: art. 78 of TFEU (according to which the EU policy in the field of asylum has to be in conformity with the Convention on the status of refugees) and art. 18 of the Charter of fundamental rights (which sets forth the right to asylum and the interdiction of refoulement). These engagements would be contradicted by the Directive Recast concerning the procedure of asylum (2013/32/EU of 26 June 2013), which limits the application of the asylum procedure to requests formulated on the territory or in the transit areas of member States[340]. The interview which takes place sometimes with migrants is focused on knowing the routes of migrations and of traffickers, and not on the personal situation of the respective migrants, nor on the analysis of the policies which affect their rights or of persecutions they suffer. The combination of the personal data with those from other data bases (those concerning systems of alert SIS) also leads to rejecting requests of asylum in all Schengen States for persons who have an interdiction of entrance for up to 5 years in one of the member States, although each member State has its own regulations with regard to the recognition of the status of refugee. At the same time, the collecting, processing and the transmission of personal data of

---

with the Czech Republic, in order to prevent Czech citizens of Roma origin to travel to UK, represented racial discrimination. Case cited by I. Atak and F. Crepeau, art. cit., p. 599.

[340] I. Atak and F. Crépeau, art. cit., p. 601.

migrants to security agencies and to third States may lead to interference in the private life and to the violation of norms concerning the protection of personal data, which is not in conformity with norms of EU on this subject[341]. As we will see, the European Court of Justice of the European Union pursued to eliminate many of these violations of human rights, adopting decisions within its procedure of preliminary questions, sometimes following decisions of the European Court of Human Rights, which determined changes of the regulations adopted by the EU institutions.

It has been advocated that these measures have in common a collective and summary character. In order to spend less time and resources and to convince other migrants to come legally instead of following the procedures of evaluation from case to case of asylum requests, they resorted to quick procedures and to collective criteria in order to differentiate those who need international protection from the others. Doubts are expressed with regard to the presumption that the exceptional situation offers full freedom to adopt any emergency measures and to choose among the obligations concerning human rights those which are respected and those which are not[342].

At the same time, EU attempted to externalize its border policies to neighbouring States, in order to reduce pressure on Greece and Italy as countries of the first arrival which should take up the examination of asylum requests according to the Dublin

---

[341] Ibidem, pp. 603-604.
[342] Mikaela Heikkila and Maija Mustaniemi-Laakso, Seeing the Individual in the Midst of Large-Scale Phenomena: Some Remarks on the European Approach to the Refugee Situation, in European Yearbook on Human Rights, 2016, Intersentia, p 188.

Regulation. For that purpose, immigration officers were detached in neighbouring countries, in order to reduce the flow of migration in cooperation with local authorities. It is appreciated that this has negative consequences for human rights, due to measures adopted in neighbouring countries such as stricter measures of security mainly against foreigners who are in transit, including measures to incriminate illegal immigration in third States. Such actions did not stop migrations but diverted them to other directions and intensified the activity of traffickers, making the situation of immigrants even more vulnerable. A Progress Report of the European Commission of 2013 concerning Turkey focused on preventing illegal migration to Europe, ignoring the rights of migrants and their protection against abuses[343].

It is considered that agreements of readmission (concluded for instance in exchange of eliminating entry visas for Turkish or Tunisian citizens) do not take into account human rights. Some of these agreements led to creating centers of detention in neighbouring States or to an expeditious return of migrants in their countries of origin or of transit; they contain no reference to respect for human rights of these persons and to principles such as non-refoulement or the superior interest of the child. Such agreements also ignore the absence in the partner States of a system of examining asylum requests, the lack of the necessary resources or infrastructure in order to receive significant numbers of immigrants and to ensure respect for their elementary rights[344].

---

[343] I. Atak and F. Crépeau, art. cit., pp. 608-610.
[344] European Commission, 2013, Progress Report, SWD (2013) 417 final, Brussels, 16 October 2013, pp. 64-66.

Measures of harmonization adopted by EU, mainly the directives Return and Conditions of Reception[345] led to create centers of detention, financed by EU (in Italy, Greece and then Turkey), which contributed to a long-term detention of individuals concerned as illegal migrants, without the examination of their individual situation. Moreover, the detention in such centers is not offering the guarantees provided for by the instruments on human rights related to detention, such as the right to be informed about the reasons for being detained, access to a counsel, services of interpretation, medical assistance when necessary, means to contact the family or consular representatives, access to remedies to challenge the detention, although the two directives contain provisions of this kind[346]. The document adopted by the Council of the Union in May 2012, entitled Global Approach concerning Migration and Mobility (GAMM), which reflected an agenda closer to respecting human rights, mainly for the protection of vulnerable immigrants, such as unaccompanied children, asylum seekers, stateless persons and the victims of trafficking, show that these regulations did not lead to changes in the situation, as the priority remains to survey the borders in order to combat illegal immigration[347].

This situation led to a series of cases before the national courts and then before the European courts, which tried to give some solutions in accordance with obligations to respect human rights of the individuals concerned.

---

[345] Return Directive, 2008/115/EC; Reception Conditions Directive, 2013/33/EU.
[346] I. Atak, F. Crépeau, art. cit, pp. 613-615.
[347] I, Atak, Fr. Crépeau, art. cit., pp. 618-619.

SECTION I - The Court of Justice of EU

The Court of Justice of the European Union (CJEU) gave, according to its traditional roll, continuous input for the regulations of the Union in the field of migration and the right to asylum. It is worth noting that in the cases submitted to CJEU by Hungary and Slovakia in 2015 against the Council (C-643 and C-647/15) with regard to migrants quota established in charge of member States following the relocation of migrants from Greece and Italy, the Court retained that the principle of solidarity among member States can be a source of obligations likely to be applied by constraint.

The Court considered different aspects of the application of the EU norms concerning migration and asylum, under the procedure of examination of preliminary questions received from the judiciary of member States.

The State responsible to consider the request of asylum

The first step to make in order to apply the rules of the Dublin system on this matter was to determine what member State has to examine the request of asylum.

According to the Dublin system, the State of the first entry on the Shengen territory is responsible to consider the request of asylum, even if the asylum seeker makes a request in another State. Nevertheless, in the case *Puid, concerning Germany*[348], CJEU recalls the obligation not to transfer an asylum seeker to the State

---

[348] Case Puid, C-4/11, decision of 14 November 2013.

responsible to consider the request if in the latter there are systemic deficiencies in the procedure of asylum and with regard to the conditions of reception. The Court aimed at maintaining the global functioning of the Dublin system, requesting the member State to apply some criteria to identify another member State as responsible to examine the request of asylum. The EU institutions integrated this jurisprudence in the EU Regulation nr. 604/2013 of the European Parliament and the Council of 20 June 2013 which sets forth some criteria and mechanisms to determine the State member responsible to examine a request of international protection introduced in a member State by a citizen of a neutral State or by a stateless individual[349].

This Regulation was modified following the decision of CJEU in the case *M. A. and others v. Secretary of State for Home Department (concerns Ireland)*[350] with regard to the situation of an unaccompanied minor; according to the Court, when such a minor has no member of family legally staying on the territory of a member State and made a request for asylum in several member States, the Dublin Regulation designates as responsible to examine his request the member State where he is situated after deposing the request. The Court took into account also the situation when the minor is situated in a State where he did not make such a request; it indicated that the respective State informs the applicant that he can introduce a request and offers him an effective possibility to do it. If he does not make such a request in the State where he is situated, the responsibility for the examination of the request for asylum rests with the State where he presented the last request, except the

---

[349] J O, L. 180 du 29 Juillet 2013.
[350] Case C-648/11, decision of 6 June 2013.

situation when this does not correspond to the superior interest of the child.

In the cases *N. S. v. UK*[351] and *M. E. v. Ireland*[352], CJEU retained that transfers according to the Dublin systems are forbidden when authorities know that there are systemic deficiencies in the asylum system and in the conditions of reception in the State of first entry. The Court did not question the basic principles of the Dublin system, according to which the conditions in member States could be considered equal in the absence of a proof to the contrary. The reasoning in the two decisions was incorporated in amendments to the Dublin rules, but the application of the decision on inadequate conditions was limited to Greece and the courts of member States did not consider that conditions in other member States would represent systemic deficiencies, so as to impose an extended suspension of transfer of asylum seekers.

The case *Abdulahi*[353] *concerning Hungary* brought before the Court the situation of a person who entered in Greece, then in Macedonia, Serbia, Hungary and requested asylum in Austria. The applicant contested the return to Hungary and then to Greece, alleging the existence of systemic deficiencies and of conditions which generate the risk of inhuman treatment. As Hungary accepted to examine the asylum request, the CJEU retained that it could not contest this decision unless the applicant demonstrate that such deficiencies exist in the respective State and underlined that the objective of the EU norms is to define a method which is

---

[351] Case C-411/10, decision of 21 December 2011.
[352] Case 493/10, decision of 21 December 2011.
[353] Case Abdulahi, C-349/12, decision of 10 December 2013.

clear and efficient to establish rapidly the State responsible to examine the asylum request.

The case *Mirza* (C-695/15, judgment of 17 March 2016, concerns Hungary), raised the issue of transfer of an applicant to a State which is not a member of the EU. Hungary asked the Court to interpret the Regulation Dublin III with regard to the possibility of transfer to a State non-member of the EU, even if that State is not responsible to process the application of asylum. The issue concerned a Pakistani citizen, who entered Hungary from Serbia, then the Czech Republic. The latter asked the Hungarian authorities to treat his request. The applicant requested again international protection in Hungary, which was refused. The Hungarian authorities maintained that Serbia is a safe country and asked the Court if the transfer to Serbia would be in accordance with EU law. The Court confirmed it[354].

Cases of exclusion of the consideration of requests of asylum from some individuals

According to EU norms, it is excluded to examine requests of asylum in cases of: individuals who committed crimes against peace, crimes against humanity, crimes of war, non-political crimes committed outside of the country of reception before the request (acts of terrorism) and acts contrary to the purposes and principles of the UN Charter. These individuals cannot obtain the status of refugee, nor the regime of subsidiary protection.

---

[354] Annual Report of CJEU, 2016, p. 34.

CJEU justified these causes of exclusion, in cases *B and D (v. Germany)*[355], in order to maintain the credibility of the system of protection, as a punishment for facts committed in the past, and in order to refuse protection to persons who do not deserve it. With regard to non-political serious crimes, the Court refers to acts of terrorism, even motivated by political objectives, and refers to the resolutions of the Security Council nr. 1373 and 1377 (2002), adding that such acts are contrary to the purposes and objectives of the UN Charter. Nevertheless, the Court affirmed that an individual evaluation is necessary before deciding to exclude the examination of a request of an individual.

Indirectly, CJEU expressed itself also with regard to measures adopted by some member States in order to stop immigration in the maritime areas, beyond their maritime borders, in the application of the recommendations related to the Regulation Frontex. In the case *European Parliament v. EU Council*, the Court cancelled the Guidelines adopted by the Council (decision 2018/252/EU)[356] concerning operations Frontex at sea, because they were adopted without the participation of the Parliament. At the same time, the Court allowed the application of these recommendations until their replacement but underlined that the new measures should contain elements of maritime external control which should include political choices and be executed according to the legal ordinary procedures, because they can affect individual freedoms and fundamental rights. Thus, the Court did not accept as being in conformity with human rights the way it was proceeded in a first stage, by returning the asylum seekers with military ships in one of the countries supposed of origin, without receiving and

---

[355] Cases C-57/09 and C-101/09, decision of 9 November 2010.
[356] Case 355/10, decision of 5 September 2012.

examining requests of asylum from the respective individuals. Still, the Court allowed the application of the Guidelines until new measures were adopted and did not refer to collective expulsion, although this is forbidden by art. 19.1 of the Charter of fundamental rights of the European Union.

Subsidiary protection

The secondary legislation of the Union introduced the concept of subsidiary protection, along with that of status of refugee, for the cases where the latter is not granted, but nevertheless it is considered necessary to ensure a certain degree of protection to the persons persecuted.

The Court underlined, with regard to the Directive Qualification, the reasons which make necessary this type of protection. In the case *X, Y and Z*[357], the Court confirmed that homosexuals represent a certain social group as they are explicitly protected by the penal legislation. Thereby, the Court accepted the definition of the Directive, according to which two criteria have to be fulfilled, namely that the qualification of the person has to be inherited or essential and to have been perceived as such by the society. It was noted that this definition does not correspond to international practice, mainly that of High Commissioner for Refugees, where these criteria are used alternatively, not cumulatively[358].

---

[357] Case X and others, C-199/12, decision of 7 November 2013, paras. 45,48.
[358] Vincent Chetail et Géraldine Ruiz, Asyle et immigration, Chroniques/Columns, in Journal européen des droits de l'homme, no. 5, 2014, pp. 623-650.

As for the definition of persecution, CJEU has in view that according to the European Convention of 1950 the right to private life is not a fundamental right from which no derogation would be allowed. Consequently, only the lack of sanction for acts of persecution would not be sufficient to consider persecution as existent. This has to be proved by a series of diverse measures such as acts of physical or mental violence, discriminatory measures according to the law, by the administration or by the police, judicial proceedings or disproportionate sanctions and refusal of a judicial remedy.

In the case *A, B and C (C-148, 149 and 150/13, decision of 2 December 2014, concerns Netherlands)*, the Court was asked whether the EU law limits the action of member States when they evaluate an application for asylum by somebody who has a fear of being persecuted in his country of origin on account of his sexual orientation. The Court answered that the statement of the applicant may require confirmation, because an established fact cannot be based only on his statement. The method a State uses to assess that statement should be consistent with the Process Directive and with the human rights as set forth in the Charter of fundamental rights (mainly the rights to human dignity and to respect for family life). This precludes, in the opinion of the Court, questions about his sexual practices, evidence of such practices and tests of any kind[359].

The Court also referred, in the case *Elgafaji (concerning Netherlands)*[360] about returning an Iraqi citizen to his country of origin, to the subsidiary protection as different from the status of refugee and asked that States examine whether the applicant is

---

[359] Annual Report of the Court of Justice of EU, 2014, p. 34.
[360] Case C-465/07, decision of 17 February 2009.

affected by factors specific to his personal circumstances or by general non-discriminated violence. CJEU tried to justify the application of the clauses of the Directive Qualification as being in conformity with the interpretation of the art. 3 of the European Convention of human rights, given by the ECHR, according to which the return of an individual in a situation of generalized violence of serious intensity would represent a violation of this article, similarly to the situation where a person is exposed to a risk of inhuman treatment as a member of a group perceived as such due to its specific features. It has to be noted that ECHR gave this interpretation for the cases where States were asked to grant the status of refugee, not that of subsidiary protection.

In the cases *Ibrahim Alo and Amira Osso*[361] *concerning Germany*, CJEU decided that the Directive Qualification is not giving the right to impose restrictions to the movement of beneficiaries of the subsidiary protection and that such a restriction is not justified for reasons related to territorial competences regarding social assistance charges, but left to the discretion of German authorities to decide whether this can be justified for reasons of migration and integration policy.

Protection of private and family life as a ground to prevent refoulement

In the case *Diakite (concerns Belgium)*[362], CJEU examined the request of subsidiary protection of a citizen of Guinea, taking into account „serious threats to life... as a result of blind violence

---

[361] Cases C-443/14 and 444/14, decision of 1 March 2016.
[362] Case Diakite, C-285/12, decision of 30 January 2014

in case of an internal or international conflict". As issues raised concerned both international humanitarian law and the protection of refugees, the Court chose an autonomous interpretation of the notion of internal conflict, according to the Directive Procedures, retaining only the criterion of blind and non-discriminated violence of such a level of intensity which creates for the applicant a real risk to be submitted to a serious indivudual threat to his life or his personality, only by his presence. In substance, the Court evaluated that there was not in Guinea an internal armed conflict of such an intensity. The Court ignored some of the criteria of the jurisprudence of the International Criminal Tribunal for Yugoslavia (case Tadic) concerning armed conflicts, as well as that given by the Protocol of 1967 concerning armed conflicts without international character.

CJEU had also to solve many questions with regard to the application of the Directive Return. The decision in the case *Filev and Osmani (concerns Germany)* pointed out that a measure of interdiction of entry on the territory of a member State for an unlimited duration is not compatible with that Directive, which sets forth the obligation that States limit the effects of this interdiction to maximum 5 years[363]. In a different case (*Mahdi, C-146/14, concerns Bulgaria*) the Court underlined that it was necessary that, when a judicial authority examines a request to prolong the detention of a citizen of a third State, the control it makes should allow to decide on merits whether the detention is prolonged, or whether it can replace it by a less coercive measure, or whether it can set the individual free on the basis of all facts and proof at its disposal; that means that a new hearing of the individual can be

---

[363] Case Filev and Osmani, C-297/12, decision of 19 September 2013, para. 27.

necessary. In this case the Court decided that the administrative authority cannot prolong the detention waiting for the decision to return the individual to the country of origin only based on the reason of lack of identity papers, and that the authority has to reevaluate the circumstances which justified initially the detention. It decided also that, both for the initial decision of detention and for any extension, the authority has to present to the individual detained in a written form the reasons for the detention referring to facts and to the applicable law. Moreover, it underlined that the risk to hide has to be evaluated function of the situation of the person, and that the detention is justified only if that risk continues to exist[364].

In a different case concerning the right to be heard of the applicant (*case Mukarubega, C-166/13, concerns France*), the Court was asked whether after the interview with the asylum seeker with regard to the illegal stay, a new audience has to take place before adopting the decision of return. Although it clarified the separate contents and purpose of the audition in the two stages (one with regard to the legality of the initial presence in the territory and the other one about reasons for which he requests international protection before the adoption of the decision of return), the Court did not give a clear answer, leaving at the appreciation of authorities whether with the occasion of the first audience the applicant had the opportunity to present all the reasons which would entitle him to remain on the territory of the State. In the end the Court refers to a balance between the fundamental right of the applicant to be heard before the adoption of a decision affecting him and the obligation of the State to

---

[364] Case Mahdi, C-146/14(PPU), para. 64, decision of 5 June 2014; Annual Report, CJEU, 2014, p. 37.

combat illegal immigration[365]. This last consideration seems disputable; it is difficult to accept that the two preoccupations are in absolute contradiction and that they have to be opposed to each other; they are protected by different rights which according to international law are not exclusive-respect for a fundamental human right and exercise of an attribute of sovereignty.

In the case *K. v. Bundesasylamt (concerns Austria)*[366], CJEU decided that art. 6 and 8 of the Regulation Dublin II contain compulsory provisions concerning the preservation of the unity of the family. Although another member State was responsible to examine the request of asylum, the Court decided that for humanitarian reasons Austria has to adopt the respective decision. The notion of family was understood as having a larger meaning, including not only members of the family, but also family relations.

In the case *Commission v. Netherlands*[367], the Court retained that the State did not respect the obligation provided for in the Directive concerning longtime residents, imposing excessive and disproportionate taxes to those who requested the respective status (to which they were entitled) and to members of the family who requested the family reunification. The Court affirmed that member States are not entitled to establish taxes which create an obstacle to the exercise of the rights provided for by the Directive.

The issue of family reunification was submitted to CJEU also in connection with the right to the free movement of labour force. The Court stressed the right of permanent stay of the

---

[365] Annual Report, CJEU, 2014, p. 38.
[366] Case C-245/11, decision of 6 November 2012.
[367] Case C-508/10, decision of 26 April 2012.

husband of the European citizen who exercised his right to free movement, even in case of subsequent separation[368]. The EU law confirmed the relationship between the right to free movement and the derivative right to stay of citizens of third States members of the family of a European citizen[369]. In the case *Noorzia (concerns Austria)*, the Court clarified that the minimum age which can determine the right to a family reunification is established at the moment of the request of reunification[370].

Health reasons to prevent expulsion

In terms of law, medical cases are not the object of the EU asylum law, both with regard to refugees and to the subsidiary protection.

Nevertheless, if an individual is exposed to a risk of expulsion, the Directive Return concerning the return of illegal migrants, in the interpretation given by the CJEU in the case *Abdida (concerns Belgium)*[371], contains provisions according to which the principle of non-refoulement has to be respected with regard to asylum seekers exposed to the risk of inhuman treatment according to art. 3 of the Convention of human rights of 1950, as defined in the jurisprudence of the European Court of Human Rights. At the same time, CJEU accepted that the challenge of the return must have suspending effect and that during the respective laps of time the individual concerned should receive the necessary health care and the social benefits.

---

[368] Case Ogieriakhi, C-244/13, decision of 10 July 2014.
[369] Free Movement Directive, 2004/32/EC, OJ 2oo4L 158/77.
[370] Case Noorzia, C-338/13, decision of 17 July 2014.
[371] Case Abdida, C-562/13, decision of 18 December 2014, Annual Report, 2014, p. 38.

This raises, in case of transfer to another member State according to the Dublin system, the problem of the evaluation by a member State of health conditions, in general of conditions offered to asylum seekers, in another member State, which would be in contradiction with the principle of mutual confidence that all member States respect human rights[372].

Equally, in the case *M'Bodj (C-542/13, concerns Belgium)*, where an applicant suffering from a serious illness asked for international protection, the Court was asked whether the granting of a permission to reside represents a form of international protection, conferring entitlement to economic and social benefits, according to the Directive Procedure. The answer of the Court was that the Directive does not require a State to grant social welfare and health care benefits to a foreign national, unless in the State of origin there is no appropriate treatment, or the applicant is intentionally deprived of health care. At the same time, the risk of deterioration of health in that country warrants that subsidiary protection is granted to the applicant. The Court also noted that, according to the Directive, international protection has to be granted for the reasons which would justify such a protection, not on compassionate or humanitarian grounds[373].

Respect for the procedural rights during the asylum procedure

---

[372] Issue treated by Dr. Lourdes Peroni, in EU Law Analysis, Expert insight into EU law developments, 10 January 2017, in Google, Barnard & Peers, European Union Law.
[373] Annual Report of CJEU, 2014, p. 35, decision of 18 December 2014.

The asylum procedure within the member States of the Union was initially foreseen as a relationship between member States, of transfer from the State which received a request of asylum to the State which was the first to register the entry of the of asylum seeker; the first State had to examine the transfer according to its rules without an explicit requirement of an audience of the individual concerned. Then it was accepted, within Dublin II, that the individual could challenge the transfer to the first receiving State only if he invokes systemic deficiencies of the asylum procedure and conditions of reception which generate the real risk of inhuman treatment in that State.

As the European Court of Human Rights insisted in its decisions concerning cases of asylum on the respect of procedural rights of the applicants (the right to be heard, to have access to documents and to a counsel), CJEU considers it necessary to take into account in the application of EU norms on asylum the connection established by ECHR between aspects of substance and the procedural aspects of human rights[374]. Consequently, in the cases *M. G. and N. R.* (*concern Netherlands*) CJEU answered a preliminary question, stating that it was necessary to respect the right of the applicant to be heard also when the decision of his detention is prolonged, in conformity with norms concerning the right to defense, even if this is not explicitly provided for in the directives on asylum, because the lack of that audience would deprive the person of a better defense and may lead to an incorrect administrative procedure[375].

---

[374] Case Moussa Abdida (concerns Belgium), C-562/13, decision of 18 December 2014.
[375] Cases C-383/13 PPU, decision of 10 September 2013.

In the case *Al Chodors (concerns the Czech Republic)*[376], the asylum seeker who travelled from Hungary to the Czech Republic in order to reach Germany, was detained in the Czech Republic waiting for the transfer, for the reason that there was the risk of hiding. The Czech law does not contain objective criteria for the risk of hiding and such an evaluation was not made. After a decision of a Czech court that the detention order was illegal, a preliminary question of CJEU on this subject was asked. In virtue of the provisions of Dublin III, according to which it is explicitly required that the national law establish objective criteria for the risk of hiding, the Court decided that the authorization of detention, without evaluating the respective risk on the basis of objective criteria, would limit the exercise of fundamental rights provided for in art. 6 of the Charter. Any such limit has to be provided for in the law, has to respect the essential aspects of the rights in question and the principle of proportionality. It is appreciated that this position of CJEU represents an alignment to the jurisdiction of ECHR (*case Del Rio Prada*), according to which a decision to deprive an individual of his freedom has to be not only legal, but also should be based on a national law accessible, precise and predictable enough, in order to avoid its arbitrary character.

Detention in case of asylum procedures

The norms adopted by EU provide for relatively strict terms for the detention of individuals found illegally on the territory of member States and who request asylum. The maximum duration of detention of such persons is of 18 months, with the

---

[376] Case presented and analyzed by Tommaso Poli, Immigration detention and the rule of law: The ECJ's first ruling on detaining asylum seekers in the Dublin system, in EU Law Analysis, 5 May 2017.

possibility to prolong it with 12 months, if the return did not take place due to the lack of cooperation of the asylum seeker or of third States.

A clear distinction is made between detention related to the examination of requests of asylum and condemnation to imprisonment. According to the Directive Dublin III, "asylum seekers can be detained when they are subject to the Dublin process, but the only reason for detention is the existence of a significant risk that the person would be hiding". In that case the individual can be detained in order to ensure the process of transfer according to the Dublin system, on the basis of an individual evaluation, if the detention is proportional and if other alternative less coercive measures cannot be effectively applied. In the cases M.G. *and N. R. v. Netherlands* mentioned above, where the petitioners requested asylum, CJEU retained that the sanction by imprisonment only for illegal stay would undermine the efficacy of the Directive Return and would not contribute to return.

In the case *Achugbabian (concerns France)*[377], CJEU stressed that the Directive Return is applicable as soon as an individual is found staying illegally in a member State. The measures adopted are established by the internal law, but without undermining the objective of the Directive, namely the return of the individual. For that, the State has to be able to prevent that the individual hides; the State needs time to identify the person under constraint, to search for information and to establish the illegality of the stay. The Court admitted that this verification may take time and asked States to act diligently and to take position on the legality of the stay of the individual. Obviously, even if it does not

---

[377] Case C-329/11, decision of 6 December 2011.

say it openly, the Court justifies measures of constraint, including detention of the asylum seeker in view of the return. Moreover, the duration of the detention of 18 months, plus possibly other 12 months, seems too long.

In the case *Kadzoev (concerns Bulgaria)*[378], the CJEU considered that an individual can be detained if there are reasonable prospects for return. The Court mentioned decisions of the ECHR according to which the principle of proportionality requests that detention has a duration which corresponds to the purpose followed, as well as the Guidelines elaborated by the Council of ministers of the Council of Europe which contained the recommendation that the detention of asylum seekers should be as short as possible.

In the case *Hassen El-Dridi (concerns Italy)*[379], CJEU affirms that detention in accordance with the Directive Return should observe the principle of proportionality in order to ensure respect for human fundamental rights, as it is the most serious form of constraint provided for the Directive in connection with the procedure of return. Other solutions mentioned by the Court would be: voluntary return accepted by the individual, for which authorities may grant a period of 7-30 days; regular reporting to authorities; financial guarantee; to render the personal documents; to establish the residence in an accepted place.

In the case *Arslan (concerning the Czech Republic)*, CJEU recalled that an asylum seeker should not be detained only because he requested asylum; he should be able to move freely on the territory of a State or within an area of the latter, although he can

---

[378] Case C-357/09PPU, decision of 30 November 2009.
[379] Case C-61/11, decision of 28 April 2011.

be placed in a center for legal or public order reasons. He cannot be detained as long as he remains in the respective State for the asylum procedure. Nevertheless, if he is detained in order to be transferred to another State, the detention on the basis of the national law is not forbidden if it appears that the respective individual formulates requests with the aim to delay the return, that is on the basis of the conduct of the person before and during the examination of the asylum request[380].

The Court was asked also questions about specialized detention centers for asylum applicants in federal States. In the cases *Pham (*C-474/13 and *Bero and Buzalmate* (C-473/13 and C-514/13, concerning Germany), the Court was asked to determine whether a member State is required to detain illegally- staying third country nationals in a specialized detention center in a situation when the federated State competent to decide upon such a detention center does not have such a facility.

The Court affirmed that the national authorities must be in a position to implement the detention measures in specialized centers, regardless of the administrative or constitutional structure of the State. Although it is not obliged to set up a specialized detention center in each federated State, it has to ensure that those federated States without such centers can provide accommodation to third country nationals in specialized centers located in other federated States. In *Pham*, the Court also said that there is the obligation of the State to keep such nationals separated from the ordinary prisoners, without any exception and that this is a substantive condition for detention, not a procedural one. Furthermore, in this respect the Court said that a member State

---

[380] Case C-534/11, decision of 30 May 2013.

cannot take account of the willingness of a third country national to be detained in an ordinary prison[381].

In the case *Celaj* (C-290/14, decision of 1 October 2015, concerns Italy), the Court was asked to interpret the provisions of the Directive Return with regard to the situation of an Albanian citizen, arrested in Italy after being returned with a ban of entry for 3 years. Then, he reentered in Italy in violation of the ban, which is punished by the Italian law with imprisonment. The Court noted that the Directive Return does not preclude criminal penalties for being imposed following national rules of criminal procedure. Nonetheless, the Court underlined that the imposition of criminal penalties is subject to the conditions that the ban issued complies with the provisions of the Directive on entry bans and with fundamental human rights and with the provisions of the Convention on the status of refugees if appropriate[382].

Respect of human rights during the examination of asylum requests

According to the norms of the European Union, human rights should be respected during the examination of the applications for asylum, in particular during the detention. Numerous decisions of CJEU recalled this obligation and referred to the need to ensure such conditions which should not lead to violations of human rights, in particular not to an inhuman and degrading treatment (under the impulse of the decisions adopted by ECHR on the basis of art. 3 of the European Convention of 1950).

---

[381] Annual Report, CJEU, 2014, pp. 36-37, decision of 17 July 2014.
[382] Annual Report, CJEU, 2015, pp. 34.

In the case *Cimade and GISTI (concerns France)*[383], CJEU underlined that the Directive Conditions has the objective to ensure full respect of human rights and the application of the provisions of the Charter of fundamental rights and that the individuals concerned have to enjoy protection till they are transferred. In the case Al *Chodors*, mentioned above, the Court affirmed the primacy of human rights over the right to asylum, underlining that the development of the law of asylum of the EU depends on the respect of human rights.

In the case *Alo and Osso, decision* of 1 March 2016, mentioned above, the CJEU was asked whether the German law is in conformity with the EU law, because in Germany beneficiaries of subsidiary protection have access to benefits of social security, but the authorization of residence is given provided that the residence is situated in a certain place. The Court answered that it considers the law compatible with the EU law, affirming that a State can subject the subsidiary protection to a condition of residence in order to promote integration, if the applicants have more difficulties of integration than other foreign citizens who reside legally in the member State[384].

SECTION II - The European Court of Human Rights

In numerous cases the European Court of Human Rights (further ECHR) adopted decisions concerning respect of human rights of migrants, in response to applications submitted by

---

[383] Case C-179/11, decision of 27 September 2012.
[384] Annual Report, CJEU, 1916, p. 20.

individuals. The Court judged on the basis of the 1950 Convention of fundamental human rights and freedoms, concluded within the Council of Europe, with modifications brought by additional protocols. All member States of the European Union are parties to the 1950 Convention and, according to the Treaty of Lisbon of 2007, the European Union itself has to adhere to this Convention. Related to this subject, ECHR referred mainly to the provisions of art. 2 (right to life), art. 3 (interdiction of torture and of inhuman and degrading treatment), art.5 (right to liberty), art.6 (right to a hearing by an independent tribunal), art. 8 (right to private and family life), art. 13 (right to an effective remedy), art. 4 of the Protocol nr. 4 (concerning the interdiction of collective expulsion), as well as art. 1 of the Protocol nr.13 on the prohibition of capital punishment, whose application can also raise problems within the procedure of examination of requests of asylum when it leads to expulsion or extradition[385].

In one of the cases concerning migration, ECHR formulated the principle according to which if the States have the right to establish as sovereign subjects of international law their policies of immigration, the „difficulties in managing the flows of migration cannot justify resorting to practices which would be contrary to their conventional obligations"[386].

Collective expulsion and discrimination

---

[385] Presentations of a general character on this subject by Linos-Alexandre Sicilianos, La Cour Européenne des droits de l'homme face à l'Europe en crise, in Revue trimestrielle des droits de l'homme, no. 105/2016, pp. 15-30.
[386] Decision in the case Georgia v. Russia, petition nr. 13255/07, decision of 3 July 2014.

The Protocol nr. 4 of 1963 to the 1950 Convention prohibits the collective expulsion of aliens by the States parties. The Court examined several cases on this subject.

In the case *Hirsi Jamaa and others v. Italy*[387], concerning the embarkment on ships under Italian flag serviced by military personnel of a number of migrants coming from the African states, the Court reaffirmed the obligations which rest with the State. With regard to the disembarkment of the migrants on the shores of Lybia, the Court underlined that the difficulties to protect Southern borders of EU in the context of the phenomenon of migration cannot absolve the States of obligations according to international law on refugees, including the principle of non-refoulement, enounced also in the Charter of fundamental rights of EU and held that the petitioners were exposed to the real risk to be subject in Lybia to a treatment contrary to art. 3 of the Convention. It retained also that some persons originated from countries like Eritrea and Somalia are exposed to the risk of being transferred to these countries; the disembarkment in Lybia leaves integral responsibility of Italy, which had to ensure that the intermediate country offers sufficient guarantees against arbitrary expulsion to countries where they are exposed to the risk of being subject to inhuman treatment. The Court considered that even if it was executed in the high seas the embarkment of the petitioners was an act of exercise of jurisdiction according to art. 1 of the Convention, which engages the responsibility of the State.

At the same time, the Court retained that the return of the petitioners had a collective character and was executed without individual identification and examination of each situation, thus

---

[387] Petition nr. 27765/09, decision of 23 February 2012.

representing a collective expulsion, with a violation of art.4 of the Protocol nr. 4 to the Convention.

The Court reaffirmed the right of individuals to obtain sufficient information allowing them to have access to internal procedures. In this case they were deprived of any remedy to present a petition and to obtain a rigorous examination of their requests against the return. The Court also retained a violation of art. 13 of the Convention.

The Court also asked the Italian government to obtain assurances from the Lybian authorities that petitioners will not be subject to treatment incompatible with art. 3 of the Convention or repatriated in an arbitrary manner.

The case *Sharifi and others v. Italy and Greece*[388] brought to the Court a petition of a number of 32 Afghans, 2 Sudanese and 1 Eritrean who entered Italy coming from Greece, where they were immediately transferred. They invoked the fear of deportation to their countries of origin and the risk to be killed, tortured and subject to inhuman treatment. The Court retained the violation by Greece of art. 13, in conjunction with art. 3, for being deprived of access to the asylum procedure and exposed to the risk of return in the countries of origin. The Court retained the violation by Italy of art. 4 of the Protocol nr. 4 of the Convention, which prohibits collective expulsion, because by the transfer to Greece asylum seekers were exposed to the risks resulting from the deficient asylum procedures existing in Greece, as well as of art. 13 in conjunction with art. 3 and art. 4 of the Protocol because asylum seekers had no access to the asylum procedures nor to any other remedy.

---

[388] Petition nr. 16643/09, decision of 21 October 2014.

The Court requested that the Dublin system be applied so as to be compatible with the Convention on human rights, emphasizing that no form of collective expulsion and of discrimination can be justified under that system and that the State which transfers asylum seekers should be ensured that the State of destination offers sufficient guarantees that its policy of asylum respects human rights and prevents the return of asylum seekers to countries of origin without evaluating the risk to be subject to inhuman treatment.

The Court also took a decision on the violation by the Russian Federation of provisions of the Convention concerning arrest, detention and expulsion from Russia of *thousands of Georgian citizens*, by an administrative procedure. The Court retained the violation of human rights by the collective expulsion, arbitrary detention, inhuman and degrading treatment, as well as of the right to an effective remedy[389].

In the case *M. A. v. Cyprus*[390], the issue of collective expulsion was also raised with regard to a group of migrants taken during a night to be heard and then returned in the countries of origin. The petitioners complained also that a remedy with automatic suspending effect against the return was not granted to them, invoking the violation of art. 13, in conjunction with art. 2 and 3 of the Convention. The Court retained other violations of the Convention, but did not accept the accusation of collective expulsion, because orders of individual expulsion were adopted after completing the asylum procedure for each individual. Similarly, in the case *Khlaifia and others v. Italy*[391], the Court

---
[389] Case Georgia v. Russia cited above, p. 233.
[390] Petition nr. 41872/10, decision of 23 July 2013.
[391] Petition nr. 16483/12, decision of 15 December 2016.

reaffirmed that it was necessary to proceed to a sufficient individual examination of each person. At the same time, it retained that art. 4 of Protocol nr. 4 does not guarantee the right of individual interview in all circumstances, but requests that each person has the real and effective possibility to present arguments against its expulsion and that they are adequately considered by authorities. The Court noted that in this case the petitioners were identified twice and had the possibility to present such arguments; it did not retain that a collective expulsion took place, even if the individuals were expelled at the same time. It retained that, if the individual does not claim the risk of inhuman treatment in case of return, the absence of the suspending effect of challenging the return does not represent a violation of art. 13 of the Convention. In several decisions on this subject, ECHR clarified some elements to be taken into account in order to retain whether a collective expulsion took place: the existence of identical decrees of expulsion, without referring to the specific situation of each migrant; absence of the individual interview; the impossibility to consult a counsel; the application of the same measure to a significant number of individuals (retained from the cases Khlaifia, Hirsi Jamaa, Sharifi and others, mentioned above).

Refusal of excluding de plano the examination of asylum requests, on grounds of the previous conduct of the applicant

The 1950 Convention and its interpretation and application according to the jurisprudence of ECHR does not allow to restrict the right to asylum and the rights relating to it in any circumstance.

In the case *Chahal v. UK*[392], ECHR retained that activities of a person, however undesirable, cannot represent a material

---
[392] Petition nr. 22414/93, decision of 15 November 1996.

consideration to justify a refusal of the protection offered by the European Convention of 1950 and that this Convention offers no margin of discretion to balance the risk of inhuman treatment with reasons to refuse protection and to expel the persons concerned. Similarly, in the case *Saadi v. Italy*, the Court retained that, because the prohibition of torture and of inhuman treatment is absolute, the conduct of an individual or his previous punishment are irrelevant for the evaluation of the risk of violation of art. 3 in another State[393].

In the case *Khan v. Germany*[394], a Pakistani citizen received a permanent residence in 2001, then was condemned for unintentional homicide. After his liberation, his authorization of residence was not prolonged, and the authorities tried to expel him. He claimed the illegality of the refusal to prolong his stay in the country. The Court took into account that there was no risk of expulsion for a considerable period of time, that an order of expulsion can be contested before the courts and that the German government gave assurances to that extent. The Court discontinued the examination of the petition.

There seems to be necessary to refer also in this framework to decisions of the Court where it held that extradition of some asylum seekers to States where they were exposed to death penalty represented a violation of art. 2 and 3 of the Convention, as indicated above. The classical case *Soering v. UK*[395], concerning the extradition of a German citizen to USA, where he was accused of a crime leading to capital punishment, was followed with regard to asylum seekers in similar situations.

---

[393] Petition nr. 37201/06, decision of 28 February 2008.
[394] Petition nr. 38030/12, decision of 21 September 2016.
[395] Petition nr. 14038/88, decision of 7 July 1989.

In the case *Saadoon and Mufdhi v. UK*[396], the Court held that the provision of art. 1 of the Protocol nr. 13 on the prohibition of death penalty, which is applied without possibility of derogation, as well as the provisions of art. 2 and 3, have to be strictly interpreted. Consequently, it is forbidden to extradite or to deport individuals in a State where there are substantial reasons to believe that they would be exposed to the real risk of death penalty.

In the case *Aswat v. UK*[397], ECHR also decided that the extradition of Haroon Aswat to USA would represent a real risk of inhuman treatment, on grounds of the mental illness he suffered from. He was condemned in USA for conspiracy to establish a jihadiste training campus. Taking into account that in USA he could have an uncertain future and could be subject to a very strict regime, the Court retained a violation of art. 3.

The case *El Masri v. the Former Yugoslav Republic of Macedonia*[398] referred to a foreigner suspected of terrorist acts, kept in solitary detention for 23 days, outside of any judicial framework and subsequently transferred without a judiciary procedure in another State to be detained and interrogated. The State's authorities surrendered in the custody of CIA agents the respective German citizen suspected of terrorist attacks, who was then detained in Afghanistan, although they had to know that he was exposed to a real risk to be subject to a flagrant violation of his rights, according to art. 5 of the Convention.

The Court affirms that the national penal authorities had to strive to investigate the allegations concerning the violation of art.

---

[396] Petition nr. 61498/08, decision of 2 March 2010.
[397] Petition nr. 17299/12, decision of 16 April 2013.
[398] Petition nr. 39630/09, decision of 13 December 2012.

5, in order to prevent any impunity to appear. Therefore, there is responsibility of the State for the transfer of the individual to US authorities, in spite of the existence of a real risk that he could be subject to an inhuman treatment. The State was found responsible for the violation of art.5 for arbitrarily depriving the petitioner of liberty after being taken up from its territory and for the whole period of his captivity in Afghanistan. The Court also affirmed that keeping the individual in solitary detention without any intervention of the judiciary and without registering him as a detained person, in complete violation of art. 5, represents a very serious violation of the right to liberty and security. This case does not seem to be directly related to migration or to an asylum procedure; similar cases were submitted to the Court by *Al-Nashiri v. Poland and v. Romania, Hussain v. Poland, Abu Zurbaydah v. Lithuania*.

In a more complicated case, concerning the extrajudicial transfer with the cooperation of Italian officials to CIA agents of the Egyptian imam *Abu Omar (Osama Mustafa Hassan Nasr),* who had been granted political asylum in Italy and married an Italian, the Court found that the transfer and the detention for several months in Italy had been undertaken with the awareness of the Italian authorities. The Court retained that his extrajudicial transfer and the detention represented a violation of arts. 3, 5, 8 and 13 of the Convention[399].

In the case *Othman (Abu Qatada) v. UK*[400], although it is not a classic case of a request for asylum, the Court reviewed its jurisprudence in connection with diplomatic assurances given in

---

[399] Nasr and Ghali v. Italy, petition 4483/09, decision of 23 February 2016.
[400] Petition nr. 8139/09, decision of 17 January 2012.

cases of measures to expel foreigners pursued for terrorist attacks in the countries of origin. The Court examined the contents of assurances received from Jordan in order to establish whether they were sufficient to protect the petitioner from the real risk of inhuman treatment. The Court established that the State would violate art. 5 of the Convention if it would expel the individual to a State where he would be exposed to the risk of flagrant violation of his right to liberty. The Court applied a high degree of evaluation of a possible violation if the respective individual would be arbitrarily detained for many years without a judgment. It also appreciated that in case of expulsion there would be a clear denial of justice if a real risk would exist that proof obtained by torture is admitted in the proceedings against the individual in the country of destination. In that case, nevertheless, the Court retained that the expulsion of the petitioner to Jordan would not represent a violation of art. 3 of the Convention.

Interdiction of refoulement in countries where there is the real risk of torture or of inhuman treatment and dangers for the right to life

It is the most frequent subject in the decisions of ECHR concerning individual petitions for alleged violations of human rights in the States parties in the framework of the procedures of examination of asylum requests. The Court developed a substantial jurisprudence in order to establish the situation of a real risk that an individual is subject to an inhuman or degrading treatment. Recognizing the specific vulnerability of asylum seekers, the Court stressed that, in order to evaluate whether there are substantial reasons to consider that such a real risk exists, the State has to examine all material at its disposal, including that obtained *proprio motu*, such proof brought by the petitioner (which can be contested by the State), as well as information received from reports of independent organizations acting in the field of human rights concerning facts known by the State at the moment of expulsion or of the examination of the asylum request. A situation of tension in the respective country is not *per se* generating violations of art. 3 unless it has a general character confirmed by other sources, while if the petitioner affirms that he is exposed to a real risk as a member of a group systematically exposed, the protection under art.3 is applied if he proves that there are serious reasons to believe that he is personally concerned.

In the case *Singh and others v. Belgium*[401], the Court noted that the authorities rejected documentary proof on which the request of asylum was based, without taking any measure to verify their authenticity. This was not considered a thorough and rigorous evaluation of the request. The Court retained a violation of art. 3 of the Convention.

In the case *Vinter and others v. UK*[402], where the issue was the extradition to USA of the petitioners, the Court retained that if the internal law of a State does not provide for a mechanism or a possibility to review a punishment of life imprisonment, this situation is incompatible with art. 3 at the moment of application of the punishment. As the US law does not provide for the possibility of taking into account changes and progress towards the rehabilitation of the individual, the punishment to life imprisonment and consequently the extradition to USA cannot be justified.

---

[401] Petition nr. 33210/11, decision of 2 October 2012.
[402] Petitions nr. 66069/09, 130/10 and 3896/10, decision of 9 July 2013.

The case *Trabelsi v. Belgium*[403], concerning an accusation of terrorism, refers also to extradition to States which apply incompressible punishment of imprisonment for life. The Court considers that extradition to a State where there is the risk of being in prison for life represents a violation of art. 3 of the Convention if in the respective State there is no mechanism to reexamine the situation in order to take into account, on the basis of objective and previously established criteria known by the detainee when the punishment was established, whether during the execution of the punishment he did progress so that there is no reason according to the penal law to maintain him in detention. In the absence of such a mechanism, the punishment would not be compressible and consequently the extradition would be contrary to art. 3 of the Convention.

In the case *R. D. v. France*, a Guinean national married to a Christian and alleging that she faced violent reprisals from her Muslim father and brothers if returned in the country of origin, sought asylum in France. She was arrested and received an order of immediate return to Guinea. Her application for asylum was rejected. ECHR requested the French Government not to deport her for the duration of the Court's proceedings. Finally, the Court decided that there would be a violation of art. 3 (concerning the prohibition of torture and inhuman and degrading treatment) in the event of her return to Guinea, but did nor retain a violation of art. 13 (lack of remedy before the national courts)[404].

In the case *MSS v. Belgium and Greece*[405], the Court examined the petition of an Afghan asylum seeker who had to be

---

[403] Petition nr. 140/10, decision of 4 September 2014.
[404] R. D. v. France, petition 34648/14, decision of 16 June 2016.
[405] Petition nr. 30696/09, decision of 21 January 2011.

returned to Greece as decided by the Belgian authorities according to the regulations Dublin II. The Court examined the compatibility of these regulations with the provisions of the 1950 Convention with regard to the transfer of the asylum seeker to Greece. The Court retained violations by Greece of art. 3 because of the conditions of detention and of life, and of art. 13 in conjunction with art. 3 due to deficiencies in the procedure of asylum which followed in his case, to the risk of expulsion to Afghanistan without a serious examination of the reasons of the asylum request and without access to an effective remedy. As for Belgium, the Court retained a violation of art. 3 by the transfer of the asylum seeker to Greece exposing him to risks related to the deficiencies of the asylum procedure, as well as by exposing him to conditions of detention and of life which represent a violation of art. 3. It also retained that the Belgian authorities violated art. 13, in conjunction with art. 3, because they did not examine the situation in Greece before deciding the transfer of the asylum seeker. It seems that the Court took in consideration his state of vulnerability, the traumatic experiences suffered, his feelings of arbitrary, of inferiority and anxiety and their effects on his dignity as inhuman treatment contrary to art. 3. After this decision, Belgium ceased to transfer asylum seekers to Greece, applying the sovereign clause which allows to examining itself such cases; it also asked by law that its courts also examine cases of inhuman treatment, representing violations of art. 3 of the Convention, to which a transfer to another State of an asylum seeker would lead.

ECHR also referred again to the structural deficiencies in the asylum procedure, which determined the modifications introduced by EU institutions in the regulations Dublin III.

In the case *Tarakhel and others v. Switzerland*[406], 8 Afghan citizens, coming from Iran, then through Italy reached Austria and then Switzerland, requested asylum in the last two countries. The Swiss authorities ordered the transfer to Italy, as country which has to examine the request according to the Dublin system. The petitioners contested the transfer, affirming that in the absence of individual guarantees of protection they will be submitted to an inhuman treatment having in view the systemic deficiencies in the arrangements of asylum in Italy, that is a violation of art. 3; they added complaints concerning art. 8 and 13 of the Convention. The Court referred to a report of the Commissioner for human rights of the Council of Europe concerning the situation in Italy, including the difficult conditions in the reception centers, and underlined that these asylum seekers are a particularly vulnerable group and need protection according to art. 3. The Court considered that the Swiss authorities did not have sufficient guarantees that if transferred petitioners will be treated adequately, and that it would be a violation of art. 3 if they would be returned without obtaining such guarantees. Therefore, it established an obligation for national authorities to ensure that in other States there are facilities of reception before the return.

In the case *F. G. v. Sweden*[407], the Court considered mainly the obligation of the State to investigate a risk factor to which the petitioner did not refer in his asylum request. The petitioner referred to his activity as dissident to the regime of Iran, mentioning also that he converted to Christianity. His request to stop the deportation was refused and the fact that he converted to another religion was not considered a circumstance to justify to

---

[406] Petition nr. 29217/12, decision of 4 November 2014.
[407] Decision of 15 October 2015.

reexamine the situation. The Court considered that his expulsion to Iran would represent a violation of art. 2 and 3, because it was not accompanied by an evaluation of the risk associated with his choice of another religion. Although the order of expulsion expired, the Court continued to examining the case, considering that it raised serious questions of interpretation of the Convention and referred to obligations of the State party which have an impact on the situation of the petitioner. Essentially, the Court retained that, when an asylum request is based on a risk widely known and when there is accessible information from many sources about such a risk, art. 2 and 3 of the Convention require that the State undertake *ex officio* the evaluation of that risk. The Court considered necessary an evaluation *ex nunc* of the consequences of the risk of the applicant's choice of another religion, even if he did not plead initially this cause.

A similar case, *F.G. and others v. Sweden*[408], raised the issue of the activity of migrants in the country of reception, where they could continue to promote dissident causes concerning their country of origin. They expressed the fear that if they were deported in Iran they would be subject to an inhuman treatment because of the activity they deployed in Sweden, reporting about violations of human rights in Iran. The Court took into account the political visibility and their activity for the protection of human rights and the risk to be identified by Iranian authorities in case of expulsion. Therefore, their expulsion was considered a violation of art. 3 of the Convention on the interdiction of inhuman treatment.

---

[408] F.G. v. Sweden, petition nr. 43611/11, decision of 23 March 2016.

In the case *L. M. and others v. Russian Federation*[409], the Court considered that having in view the situation of humanitarian crisis in Syria, the magnitude of the sufferings of the civilian population and the massive violations of human rights and of humanitarian law by all parties, the expulsion of petitioners to Syria would represent a violation of art. 3 of the Convention.

In several other cases against the Russian Federation, the applicants were Uzbek nationals who were persecuted in their country for religious extremism and terrorism or for belonging to an Islamic organization which was banned. They applied for asylum and argued that if returned to their country they will be subject to torture and inhuman treatment. The Court ruled that their return to Uzbekistan would amount to a violation of art. 10 of the Convention[410].

In a similar case, *Chinese nationals of a Uighur origin* fled their country for reasons related to alleged pressure on the Muslim population, sought asylum in Turkey and their request was rejected. The Court ruled that deporting the applicants would be a violation of arts. 2 and 3 in conjunction with art. 13 of the Convention. The Court also retained that there had been a violation of art. 5 in regard to the length of their detention[411].

---

[409] Petition nr. 52077/10, decision of 15 May 2012.
[410] Fozil Nazarov v. Russia, petition nr. 74759/13, decision of 11 December 2014; Rakhimov v. Russian Federation, petition nr. 50552/13, decision of 10 July 2014; Egamberdiyev v. Russian Federation, petition nr. 34742/13, decision of 26 June 2014.
[411] A. D. and others v. Turkey, petition nr. 22681/09, decision of 22 July 2014.

In a different case *J. K. v. Sweden*[412], the Court approached the issue of sharing the task of the proof of the real risk to which asylum seekers can be exposed in the country of origin. Among the three Iraqi asylum seekers, the wife worked for the American forces in Iraq and was threatened by Al-Qaeda, their daughter was killed, the husband was subject to several attacks and seriously wounded, while his brother was kidnapped. Petitioners maintained that their return to Iraq would represent a violation of art. 3. Their request was rejected, the Swedish tribunal considering that they were not submitted to new personal threats after 2008, when the wife ceased to work for American clients and the threat from Al-Qaeda was no more as present and specific. The European Court recalled its previous jurisprudence, mainly concerning the risk of inhuman treatment from private groups and the quality of member of a target group, affirming that if the petitioner offers a substantial presentation of the real individual risk in case he is deported, this is different from a situation of general danger in the country of origin, and the authorities of immigration have to ascertain and to evaluate *ex officio* all facts relevant for the evaluation of the real risk. The treatment suffered in the past, contrary to art. 3, is considered a powerful indication of the real risk if it is confirmed by information from objective and credible sources about the situation in the respective country. The Swedish government did not make the effort to eliminate any doubt about this risk. The Court retained that petitioners were exposed to a real risk of persecution when returned and the Iraqi authorities could not protect them, and therefore their deportation would generate a violation of art. 3 of the Convention.

---

[412] Petition nr. 59166/12, decision of 23 August 2016.

The Court also followed the evolution of the situation of internal conflict in some countries concerning the degree or real risk of inhuman treatment in case of expulsion and decided consequently. After deciding in the case *Sufi and Elmi v. UK*[413] that the level of violence in Mogadishu was of such intensity that everyone in town could be exposed to the risk of inhuman treatment contrary to art. 3, in the case *K. A. B v. Sweden*[414] the Court noted that the situation in the capital of Somalia improved and the level of violence decreased. It took into account also the personal situation of the petitioner, who did not belong to a group persecuted by a violent group and had a housing in town, where his wife lived, and retained that he did not demonstrate that he would be subject to a real risk of inhuman treatment in case of expulsion.

The prohibition of arbitrary detention in the context of migration

In the case *Musa v. Malta*[415], the petitioner complained against detention after formulating the asylum request and being present before the immigration authorities. The Court did not accept that the surrender of an individual to immigration authorities to examine his asylum request would have as an effect the authorized entry in the respective country, unless if the national law authorizes his stay in the territory during the examination of the asylum request (which was the case for the Maltese law). Nevertheless, the Court retained that the detention was arbitrary due to its duration of 6 months for the authorities to decide whether they accept the request, namely an unreasonable duration, and consequently retained a violation of art. 5.1 concerning the right to liberty and security of person.

---

[413] Petitions nr. 8319 and 11449/07, decision of 28 June 2011.
[414] Petition nr. 886/11, decision of 5 September 2013.
[415] Petition nr. 42337/12, decision of 23 July 2013.

In another case concerning the application of art. 5, *Vassis and others v. France*[416], the petitioners arrested at sea in a area of high sea, complained of being illegally deprived of liberty. The Court reaffirmed that, after bringing asylum seekers on the territory of the State, a prompt examination of their situation is necessary more than in usual cases of depriving of liberty. In this case, the period of 48 hours in the custody of police, after 18 days of escort on sea was considered contrary to the obligation of prompt examination, in order to protect the individuals concerned from inhuman treatment and to avoid an unjustified interference with their individual freedom. The Court retained a violation of art. 5.3 of the Convention concerning the right to a trial within a reasonable time.

Conditions of detention

In the case *Mohammadi v. Austria*[417], an Afghan asylum seeker contested the transfer to Hungary, affirming that there asylum seekers were systematically detained, with the risk of being imprisoned in deplorable conditions. He also claimed the risk of refoulement to a third country, Serbia, where he did come from, without the examination of his asylum request by Hungary. The Court retained that the transfer to Hungary does not represent a violation of art. 3, because reports do not indicate systemic deficiencies in the asylum procedure and in the system of detention in Hungary.

In the case *AME v. Netherlands*[418], an asylum seeker from Somalia complained that his transfer to Italy would expose him to

---

[416] Petition nr. 62736/09, decision din 27 June 2013.
[417] Petition nr. 71932/12, decision of 7 May2014.
[418] Petition nr. 51428/10, decision of 13 January 2015.

bad conditions and expressed the fear that Italian authorities would expel him directly to Somalia, without examining his asylum request. The Court declared the petition inadmissible, because the petitioner did not establish that when returned to Italy there would exist the real and imminent risk of difficult conditions, which would fall below the threshold of art. 3. The Court took into account the personal situation of the asylum seeker and the fact that the situation in Italy was different from that in Greece.

In a similar case, *AS v. Switzerland*[419], a Syrian asylum seeker of Kurdish origin invoked systemic deficiencies of the system of reception in Italy, where there would not exist good conditions of housing and of health care for him and his family. The Court retained that the transfer to Italy would not represent a violation of arts. 3 and 8 of the Convention.

In the case *Khlaifia v. Italy*, mentioned above, the petitioner invoked the conditions of detention in the island of Lampedusa while the Italian government invoked the state of necessity as a circumstance exonerating its agents of responsibility. The Court recognized the multiple obligations facing the Italian authorities to adopt measures at sea to save the migrants, to ensure conditions of health and reception of migrants and to maintain public order on an island inhabited by a small community, but did not accept the argument based on the state of necessity. The Court affirmed that these constraints do not exonerate the State from its obligation to guarantee conditions of detention compatible with respect for human dignity[420].

---

[419] Petition nr. 39350/13, decision of 30 June 2015.
[420] Case Khlaifia and others v. Italy, petition nr. 16483/12, decision of 15 December 2016.

Protection of the right to health care in the context of expulsion

The most significant on this issue is the decision of ECHR in the case *Paposhvili v. Belgium*[421], where the Court asked for a more rigorous examination of the risk of inhuman treatment in the case of expulsion of seriously ill migrants. The Georgian migrant lived in Belgium and was seriously ill; he pretended that expulsion to Georgia would expose him to an inhuman treatment and to a premature death, as a result of losing the medical treatment he received in Belgium. He died during the consideration of the case by ECHR. The Court continued its examination and decided that his expulsion without evaluating the risk for his family life would have represented a violation of art. 3 of the European Convention. The Court affirmed that such exceptional situations, when there is proof that the individual concerned, even without the imminent risk of death, would be exposed to the risk of inhuman treatment due to the lack of adequate medicine in the country of origin or to lack of access to them, and would be exposed to a serious, rapid and irreversible decline of its health situation, leading to intense suffering or to significant reduction of his life hope, would correspond to a higher threshold of application of art. 3 of the Convention. The Court underlined the duty of authorities to evaluate more rigorously the risk required by the absolute nature of art. 3, namely to verify whether the health care available in the receiving State is sufficient and adequate for the treatment of the petitioner and to consider to what extent the individual concerned will have access to it. Another option enounced by the Court is to obtain individual and sufficient guarantees from the authorities of

---

[421] Petition nr. 41738/10, decision of 13 December 2016.

the State that the adequate treatment is available and accessible to the person, as a precondition for transfer.

In a different case, *Sow v. Belgium*[422], a citizen of Guinea invoked initially the forced marriage to which she was submitted in her country of origin as a reason of her asylum request, then she expressed fear that she would be subject to sexual mutilation when returned to Guinea. Her request was rejected because the fear was not presented initially and was not sufficiently motivated. The Court did not retain a violation of art. 3 if the petitioner was returned to her country of origin.

The protection of the right to family life and the protection of the child in the context of the asylum procedure

In the case *Tarakhel v. Switzerland*, mentioned above, the Court retained that the right to family life of the asylum seeker would be violated if individual preliminary guarantees are not obtained; the Court established the requirement that the State which transfers an asylum seeker obtain individual guarantees from the State of reception that basic rights and needs of the petitioner will be respected particularly when there are doubts with regard to the ability of the State of reception to ensure conditions of life for asylum seekers. In that case, the Swiss State received assurances that the family will not be separated and will have adequate conditions of living for the children.

Analysts consider that this decision of the Court showed that the Dublin system does not correspond to the requirements of respect for human rights. This is why the Court stressed the duty of the State to evaluate the circumstances specific to vulnerable

---

[422] Petition nr. 27081/13, decision of 19 January 2016.

petitioners before transferring them to other States where they could be exposed to a risk of inadequate treatment and the need to obtain guarantees. It also showed that the Dublin system creates risks for asylum seekers, because it delays the examination of asylum requests, leads very often to the separation of children from the family and delays the possibility for the asylum seekers to work legally or to have access to basic social services. It would encourage the transfer to States which do not ensure conditions of protection (Greece, Italy and Bulgaria). As a result, Belgium, Germany and Netherlands introduced the procedure of requesting individual guarantees for transfers to Italy. The essence of the Tarakhel decision would be that arrangements among States, such as the Regulation Dublin, cannot be applied when they expose asylum seekers to violations of human rights[423]. The Court rejected the automaticity inherent to the Dublin system, emphasizing the principle of the superior interest of the child in the context of art. 3 of the Convention[424].

In a case also related to the protection of the right to private and family life, but more unusual *(Gelleri v. Romania)*[425], a Turkish citizen received political asylum in Romania in 1998, married a Romanian citizen and was involved in business activities in the country. In 2005, the prosecutor of the Court of Appeal of Bucharest declared him *persona non grata* and gave an order of expulsion and of prohibition for 10 years to enter Romania. The justification given was that this person engaged in activities which

---

[423] Petition nr.29217/12, decision of ECHR of 4 November 2014. Presentation and analyses of this case by Madeleine Garlick and Suzan Fratzke, Dublin Asylum System Faces Uncertain Future after Ruling in Afghan Family's Case, Google, on line, April 2015.
[424] The same idea maintained by L. A. Sicilianos, art. cit., p. 18.
[425] ECHR, petition nr. 33118/05, decision of 15 September 2011.

threatened national security, without other explanations. Mr. Gelleri contested the order of expulsion to the Court of Appeal; his appeal was rejected, and the court mentioned that the reasons of expulsion cannot be communicated, because they are state secret. The Romanian Office for Refugees also withdrew his status of refugee and he was expelled.

ECHR held that the Court of Appeal made only a purely formal examination of the order of expulsion and did not try to find whether the individual posed a threat to national security. Consequently, the measures taken did not guarantee him a minimum degree of protection against the arbitrary. The Court retained that the interference in his private and family life was not in conformity to a law corresponding to the requirements of the Convention, as well as a violation of art 1 of the Protocol nr. 7, concerning procedural guarantees for aliens in case of procedures of expulsion

With regard to taking into account the right to private and family life, ECHR also developed the conception according to which the request to deliver an entry visa in the context of a procedure of family reunification should be examined so as to ensure a just balance of interests in presence. For instance, in the case *Muzinga and Mugenzi v. France*, the Court underlined the existence of an international and European consensus concerning the need to grant to refugees a procedure of family reunification more favourable than that accorded to other foreigners, taking into account their specific vulnerability, namely a more flexible, rapid and efficient procedure[426].

---

[426] Case Muzinga and Mugenzi, petition nr. 52701/09, decision of 10 July 2014.

In the case *B. A. C. v. Greece*[427], a Turkish citizen who requested asylum in 2002, claimed the violation of his right to family life, in violation of art. 8 of the Convention, because he lived in Greece for 12 years with an uncertain status. He also invoked the violation of art. 3 of the Convention, alleging that he was exposed to a real risk of inhuman treatment in Turkey if he was expelled, as well as the absence of an effective remedy to challenge expulsion. The Court retained that the authorities did not respect their positive obligation according to art. 8 of the Convention to offer effective and accessible means for the protection of his family life, by not examining his asylum request in a reasonable period of time, so as to reduce to a minimum his uncertain situation. It retained also the violation of art. 13, in conjunction with art. 8. The Court also affirmed that the return of the petitioner to Turkey without taking into account his personal circumstances (bad treatment suffered previously and his unclear situation which exposed him any time to the risk to be returned without examining his asylum request) would represent a violation of art. 3 of the Convention.

In the case *Rahimi v. Greece*[428], a child Afghan citizen unaccompanied was detained in a detention center for adults and then liberated without any assistance or accommodation. According to the Court, the conditions of detention and the lack of attention to his request of asylum after liberation represent inhuman and degrading treatment according to art. 3 of the Convention.

---

[427] Petition nr. 11981/15, decision of 13 October 2016.
[428] Petition nr. 8687/08, decision of 5 April 2011.

The case *Popov and others v. France*[429] referred to the detention for 15 days of two very young children together with their parents in a center for adults till they were returned.

The Court underlined that the extreme vulnerability of children is a decisive factor and has precedence over the status of illegal immigrant. In this case the long period and the conditions of detention were considered as having a very damaging effect on the children. It was also considered that they were placed in the situation to see that their parents could not exercise for them any remedy, were detained illegally without an order to be placed in the center, and consequently were deprived of the protection required by the Convention, in violation of art. 5.4. The Court retained also a violation of art. 8 and underlined again the superior interest of the child.

In the same order of ideas, in the case *A. B. and others v. France*[430], concerning the placement of a child of 4 years in detention for 18 days together with his parents, the Court retained a violation of art. 3 towards the child, because even if the material conditions did not raise any problem, the center of detention represented a source of anxiety and of stress due to the atmosphere of constraint, to the presence of armed police and of the loud megaphone calls, as well as due to the moral and psychological stress to which his parents were submitted. The duration for which the child was subject to these conditions was the determining factor in the Court's decision. Similarly, in the case *R. M. and others against France*[431] the Court retained a violation of art. 3 because a child of 7 months was kept in

---

[429] Petitions nr. 39472 and 39474/07, decision of 19 January 2012.
[430] Petition nr. 11593/12, decision of 12 July 2016.
[431] Petition nr. 33291/11, decision of 12 July 2016.

administrative detention for 7 days waiting for the decision to return his parents to another country. The Court also retained violations of art. 5.1 and 5.4 with regard to the child and of art. 8 for all three persons.

In the case *Bio v. Denmark*[432], an individual of African origin, Danish citizen since 2002, married a woman from Ghana and asked for the permit of residence for his wife. The request was refused, because according to the Danish law only those attached to Denmark can have this right, respectively after 28 years since they received the citizenship. The petitioner invoked a violation of art. 8 of the Convention concerning the right to family life and of art. 14, as a discrimination against those who are citizens for a shorter period of time. In practical terms, a measure concerning the control of immigration, regulating the reunification of families, has also a discriminatory effect on grounds of ethnic origin or on citizenship as compared to citizens of Danish origin.

The Court retained that although art. 8 does not impose obligations with regard to the reunification of the family, a measure of control of immigration can represent a discrimination and a violation of art.14 of the Convention. The authorities of the State have to ensure that such a measure has no prejudicial and disproportionate effect on a group and if such a measure has an objective and reasonable justification, even if it is not directly aimed at that group. The government of Denmark did not present compulsory or very powerful reasons, which are not related to ethnic origin of individuals, in order to justify the indirect discrimination. The Court recalled that European documents, of the Council of Europe and of the EU, show the trend not to accept

---

[432] Petition nr. 38590/10, decision of 24 May 2016.

discrimination among citizens on grounds of birth or other status with regard to the reunification of families.

In connection also with a request of a permit of residence, the Court examined the case *Jeunesse v. Netherlands*[433], where the authorities refused a permit of residence to a Surinamese citizen who lived in Netherlands with the Dutch husband and their three children. Successive requests were rejected because they were not presented through the Dutch mission in Suriname. The petitioner invoked the violation of art. 8 concerning respect of the right to family life. The Court accepted the right of the State to request that applications of this kind are presented abroad, but retained that the return of the individual in this case would be incompatible with art. 8, because there are exceptional circumstances and the authorities did not establish a just balance between the interests of the petitioner, of the husband and of the children to maintain their family life in Netherlands and the interest of the public order of the State to control immigration. The Court underlined that national authorities have to take into account and to evaluate the practicability and the proportionality of any return of a foreign parent, in order to ensure effective protection and to give due importance to the superior interest of the child who is affected. The Court clarified thereby the extent of the State's obligation according to art. 8 to protect the right to family life in cases of immigration, which is the margin of discretion of the State and what are the elements it has to take into account in order to ensure the effective protection of the superior interest of the child.

In the case *Udeh and others v. Switzerland*[434], Nigerian petitioners complained about the violation of their right to family

---

[433] Petition nr. 12738/10, decision of 3 October 2014.
[434] Petition nr. 12020/09, decision of 16 April 2013.

life. A Nigerian citizen requested asylum in Switzerland and was refused. Then he married in Switzerland and obtained a permit of residence. In 2007 the authorities withdrew his permit of residence, because he was missing from the country more than 6 months being condemned in Germany for drug trafficking. Although it was recognized that he had a family in Switzerland, had good relations with his family and could integrate in the society, the permit of residence was refused. The Court retained that in this case the State went beyond his margin of discretion and that the expulsion of the petitioner would represent a violation of art. 8 of the Convention.

In one case the Court was confronted with the recognition of a religious marriage, concluded in another State. Two *Iranian citizens ZH and RH*[435] requested asylum in Switzerland after being registered in Italy. They presented themselves as a couple married in Iran, although one was 18 and the other one only 14 years old. Their request of asylum was rejected and the first one was transferred to Italy. The petitioners pretended that the transfer of one of them to Italy would represent a violation of art. 8 concerning the right to family life. The Swiss court considered that the marriage was incompatible with public order, because sexual relation with a minor below 16 years is an offense according to the Swiss law; consequently, it did not recognize the right to family life according to art. 8. ECHR retained that art. 8 cannot be interpreted so as to impose to a State to recognize a religious marriage concluded by a child of 14 years. It considered that it was better that national courts examine and decide on the issues raised in this case.

Procedural guarantees, suspending effect of the remedy

---

[435] Petition nr. 60119/12, decision of 8 December 2015.

In the case *Mohmmed v. Austria*[436], that Sudanese national exposed to a transfer from Austria to Hungary, according to Dublin II, maintained that this transfer would expose him to similar conditions of an inhuman treatment and that his asylum request in Austria did not have a suspending effect on the order of transfer. The Court retained that there was a violation of art. 13, in conjunction with art. 3, namely due to the absence of an effective remedy, as the petitioner was deprived of the right of protection against the transfer in the framework of asylum procedures. At the same time, the Court did not accept that the transfer to Hungary would violate art. 3 of the Convention, having in mind the recent amendments to the Hungarian legislation which improved the situation of asylum seekers. In the case *I. M. v. France* also, the Court retained that the detention of individuals may diminish their ability to allege the grounds of their case and that an effective remedy requires an appeal with suspending effect in order to prevent refoulement, sufficient time to prepare the appeal and effective legal assistance and interpretation[437].

The case *Souza Ribeiro v. France*[438] referred to the expulsion of a foreigner one hour after he addressed to the court, requesting the annulation of the order of expulsion, which deprived him of an effective remedy. The Court held that, although States have the right to combat illegal immigration, art. 13 of the Convention does not allow them to deny the practical access to a minimum of procedural guarantees to protect them against the illegal expulsion. The Court retained the violation of art. 13, in conjunction with art. 8 and reaffirmed that an effective remedy

---

[436] Petition nr. 2283/12, decision of 6 June 2013.
[437] Case I. M. v. France, petition nr. 9152/09, decision of 2 February 2012.
[438] Petition nr. 22689/07, decision of 13 December 2012.

should include a suspending effect, if expulsion would lead to a real risk of violation of arts. 2 or 3 of the Convention, or of art. 1 of the Protocol 4 to the Convention.

In the case *Dhahbi v. Italy*[439], the Court examined also to what extent the migrants concerned suffered a different treatment with regard to social benefits. The Court underlined the need to take into account also the requirement of proportionality, considering that the application of the reason of budgetary constraints on the exclusive ground of citizenship is not reasonable, representing discrimination. The Court held that it is not legitimate to differentiate between citizens and some foreigners who were granted the right to residence and who contributed from their salary to the social benefit concerned.

The Court also referred to the relationship between the application of the Convention and the law of the European Union; in the same case *Dhabhi*, the Tunisian citizen invoked also the agreement of association between the Union and Tunisia and asked to send to CJEU a prejudicial question, which was refused by Italian courts. ECHR retained that according to art. 6.1 of the Convention the refusal to send such a prejudicial question should be motivated, indicating the reasons for which it would not be relevant, or the existence of a previous interpretation of CJEU. Because the decision of the internal courts does not refer to the jurisprudence of CJEU, showing that they did not consider the request to address to CJEU or did not present reasons for the refusal to do it, the Court retained the violation of art. 6.1 of the Convention on the right to a fair trial.

---

[439] Case Dhahbi v. Italy, petition nr. 17210/09, decision of 8 April 2014.

In a different case which is not directly related to an asylum request, two Belgian citizens *Ullens de Schootten and Rezabeck*[440] requested the Belgian courts to ask CJEU to take a stand on the conformity with the Union's law of a Belgian royal decree on the basis of which they were sanctioned. Their request was rejected. They addressed to ECHR, maintaining that this refusal represented a violation of their right of access to justice. Although it affirms that the national judge is called to decide on the prejudicial request, ECHR considers that when there is such a possibility, the refusal of the judge to use it may in some circumstances affect the equitable character of the procedure and thereby the right of access to justice can be violated by the arbitrary refusal to allow a procedure of prejudicial question. According to ECHR, art. 6.1 of the European Convention makes it compulsory for internal jurisdictions to present reasons of their decision to refuse a prejudicial question, mainly if the applicable law admits such a refusal only in exceptional circumstances. ECHR considers that it has the right to control whether this obligation of giving reasons is respected in this case and whether there is no manifest error in the reasoning.

ECHR examined also the admission of a *petition against Portugal*[441], where the petitioner asked previously the European Commission to ascertain a violation by Portugal of his rights and was not satisfied with the conclusion of the Commission. The State invoked the inadmissibility of the petition, maintaining that the case was already submitted to another international forum. The Court rejected the exception of the State and declared the petition

---

[440] Petitions nr. 3989/07 and 38353/07, decision of 23 September 2011.
[441] Case Karoussiotis v. Portugal, petition nr. 23205/08, decision of 1 February 2012.

admissible. The Court maintained that the referral to another forum means a judiciary or quasi judiciary procedure similar to its procedure. With regard to the procedure before the European Commission, the Court noted that it refers to a pre-contentious procedure which has the purpose to obtain a voluntary respect of the obligation and then to a contentious stage, which has no effect on the rights of the petitioner as it is not regulating individual situations; the Court considers that it cannot be assimilated with a remedy according to art. 34 of the Convention (concerning the individual applications to ECHR) neither from the procedural point of view, nor by its effects. Therefore, the Commission, when it takes position on a petition by an individual, does not act as an international instance of inquiry or of regulation in the meaning of art. 35 of the European Convention (as another jurisdictional international procedure).

In the case *AM v. France*[442], the petitioner, detained and waiting to be returned to Tunisia, contested the detention and the return before the judgment of his appeal. He claimed the violation of art. 5.4 of the Convention, because the deportation had to be suspended in order to judge his contestation, as well as because the courts did not take a decision on the merits of his contestation concerning detention. The Court did not accept that the procedure of contesting the detention while waiting for the deportation has a suspending effect on the order of deportation, but retained that art. 5.4 was violated because the short time elapsed did not allow the authority to control the legality of his arrest, that is whether this was in conformity with the requirements of the law and with the objective of art. 5.

---

[442] Petition nr. 56324/13, decision of 12 July 2016.

* * *

It is obvious that the European Union and member States were not prepared to face the unprecedent flow of refugees and that the Dublin system as it was defined was not adequate to respond in this situation to States' concerns and to requirements to protect human rights of individuals. The changes brought to the regulations adopted during the crisis did not solve the main issues of their application.

Both at the level of political factors, of the applicable norms and of the jurisprudence of the two courts of justice, there is a preoccupation for maintaining a certain coherence in the application of the legal norms and principles concerning the status of refugee or of the subsidiary protection on the continent, in view of the fact that the 28 member States of the Union are parties to the European Convention on human rights and are subject to the jurisdiction of ECHR on the basis of individual petitions submitted by individual complaining for alleged violations of the Convention by these States. The jurisprudence of the two courts offers numerous cases where each of them referred to conventional norms applied or to the jurisprudence of the other in the reasoning of its decisions. It is admitted that there is a dialogue between the two courts concerning the protection of human rights[443], which is partially noted also with regard to issues concerning asylum and migration.

---

[443] Aurora Ciucă, The dialogue between ECHR and the Court of Justice of EU concerning the protection of human rights, in the book Regulations of the European Union of a particular interest, sui generis, for Romania, 2017, pp. 51 and foll.

At the same time, it is obvious that in the field of the right to asylum ECHR exercised both a substantial and a procedural indirect and sometimes direct control on the application of the European Union's law in conformity with the European Convention on fundamental rights and freedoms of 1950. In its decision concerning one of the cases of transfer[444], the Court affirmed that „when States create international organizations or international arrangements in order to cooperate in different fields this may have implications for the respect of human rights. It would be incompatible with the object and the purpose of the Convention (concerning human rights of 1950) that thereby States are exempt of their responsibility according to the Convention in the respective field of activity". The Court referred to the comments of the High Commissioner for human rights of the Council of Europe according to which, leaving aside the commendable objectives of the Dublin system, its efficiency could be undermined in practice by different approaches of member States.

In the conception of the two courts there are mainly differences of approach with regard to the evaluation of asylum requests, which lead to different practices of protection of human rights. The EU law provides for the exclusion of examination of asylum requests from individuals who committed some offences, even if the respective persons are exposed to the risk to be subject to inhuman treatment; the ECHR does not accept this conception and gives an absolute value to the norms on the protection of the right to life, on the prohibition of torture and of inhuman and degrading treatment and on the interdiction of collective expulsion

---

[444] Case T. I. v. UK, petition nr. 43844/98, decision of 7 March 2000.

from the 1950 Convention over any other considerations. Although the Charter of fundamental rights of the Union contains an explicit interdiction of collective expulsions, CJEU did not receive any prejudicial question with regard to this issue from the national courts.

Although the documents adopted by the EU institutions prove a certain progress with regard to the protection of human rights of legal migrants and included also provisions aiming at ensuring respect for some rights of those considered illegal, the EU policies concerning migration and asylum continue to focus on concerns for security, on the border control and on increasing the capacity of neighbouring countries to stop migration on their territories and less on respect of human rights of migrants called illegal. Analysts appreciate that there is a disproportionate concern on the border control, while the number of those reaching the EU space illegally on sea or on the terrestrial way represents a small percentage of those residing illegally in the member States or as compared to the number of residents established by the entry visa already granted[445].

The insufficient protection for the respect of human rights during the border controls led to the absence of protection of the migrants, to loss of human life on sea, to serious violations of human rights by the border authorities and in detention centers and to a lack of responsibility for such violations, in the absence of the remedies provided for by generally accepted norms of international law.

There are differences in the jurisprudence of the two courts with regard to the procedural guarantees to be observed in the

---

[445] As maintained by I. Atak & Fr. Crepeau, art. cit., Conclusion.

examination of asylum requests. ECHR applies more strict criteria with regard to respecting the right to an efficient remedy, according to art. 13 of the Convention of 1950. ECHR starts from the conception that imprisonment should not be applied as a sanction to persons requesting asylum in other States, that the detention of the petitioner does not have to be the answer to an asylum request except in cases well determined, and that the measure of detention can be preceded by less severe forms of control.

The European Court on Human Rights received many petitions from the migrants and asylum seekers and on their belalf and adopted decisions on the basis of its Convention on human rights and fundamental freedoms, sometimes refering directly to the structural deficiencies of the Dublin regulations, underlying the responsibility of States parties to the Convention to respect human rights in spite of their commitments and arrangements within other international frameworks, and consequently the need to make the necessary changes. The ECHR could not accept the exclusion of some persons from the consideration of their asylum request because of previous conduct, the presumption of respect for human rights by all States members of the EU, the collective refoulement of migrants, as well as the return without following the procedural requirements of the examination of asylum requests. ECHR decided in many cases that the transfer of individuals to countries where they would be subject to inhuman treatment, to imprisonment for life or to the death penalty would represent a violation of the Convention. ECHR also developed a substantial jurisprudence containing criteria to follow in order to establish whether in a country there is a real risk of inhuman treatment.

CJEU adopted also several decisions, mainly in response to preliminary questions from the national courts of member States, explaining and clarifying its regulations concerning immigration and asylum, sometimes adopting new rules which were subsequently introduced in the secondary legislation. The Court of EU also tried, without departing from the conceptions and the policies of the Union in this field, to keep the application of the Dublin system as close as possible to the jurisprudence of the European Court of Human Rights in cases where measures taken in the application of EU rules were challenged. That made the practice of the Court not always coherent and not following a systematic approach, but responding to questions as they came.

Although the flow of migrants to Europe decreased, the difficulties persist and the system of consideration of asylum requests and of treatment of migration is the same. Some political developments in several European States tend to create more difficulties.

It is generally recognized that it is impossible to close the borders of member States of the EU; the attempts to do it contribute to extend the clandestine forms of illegal immigration and to the intensification of the activity of traffickers, accompanied by the worst violations of human rights. On the other side, the rapprochement of policies of immigration and asylum from those to increase security and combat criminality is of the nature to legitimate the prolonged detention and the forceful return of asylum seekers irrespective of the individual reasons of those trying to exercise their human right to request asylum in other countries.

As migrations will continue whatever may be the restrictions applied, European States have to find ways and means to develop, in cooperation with the countries of origin, policies and solutions on a long term basis in order to treat and control migrations with full respect for human rights. Taking into account the potential of Europe, the starting points could be probably a stronger contribution to solving existing conflicts and to promoting rapid and massive projects of development in the areas neighbouring Europe which are the source of migration.

CHAPTER VII – JURISDICTIONAL IMMUNITY of STATES before EUROPEAN JURISDICTIONS

Abstract

The jurisdictional immunity of States is a subject which comes again on the agenda of jurisdictional bodies with regard to acts or omissions in which States are involved as such. It is well known that States are not subject to criminal international law. Norms of criminal international law are applicable to individuals who, mainly in their functions as high officials or persons having the competence to take decisions in this field, commit crimes of war, crimes against humanity, acts of aggression, of genocide or other serious violations of norms of criminal international law, as recognized in international instruments and in the jurisprudence of international criminal courts, some of which are functioning presently, mainly the International Criminal Court created in 1998 by the Rome Statute.

This chapter refers to immunity of States from the jurisdiction of the courts of other States in civil law cases, as an exception from the principle of territorial competence of the national courts, which derives from the principles of sovereignty and equal rights of States. The main difficulty appeared when the jurisdictional immunity of States was opposed to imperative norms of international law, recognized and accepted by the international community of States as norms from which no derogation is admissible.

Although no doubt was expressed to the existence of such imperative norms (such as the prohibition of torture, of genocide or of norms of humanitarian law), jurisdictional immunity of States was invoked not to contest the existence or the application of the respective imperative norm, but as a procedural preliminary exception. Does it not mean impunity of States for such violations of international law? Do we have to make a choice between immunity and impunity? It is through this angle that we intend to consider the cases submitted to different jurisdictions with regard to State immunity of jurisdiction.

Key Words: jurisdictional immunity, imperative norms, derogation, procedural exception, *acta jure imperii, acta gestionis,* remedies, state responsibility, *ratione personae,* access to justice, reparation, denial of justice, crimes against humanity, torture, civil claims

Introduction

In principle, the courts of a State exercise their competence of jurisdiction under the national law according to criteria of territorial or personnel connection, sometimes of universal jurisdiction. This principle is confirmed by international law, deriving from the State sovereignty and equal rights of States. At the same time, following the same principle, according to a generally accepted customary rule, a State cannot be subject to the jurisdiction of another State, that means enjoys immunity from the jurisdiction of the courts of another State in civil law cases. Nevertheless, international law developed a restrictive approach to State immunity, mainly through the distinction between acts of the exercise of State authority *(acta jure imperii)* and acts of a commercial nature *(acta gestionis)*. The difficulty in examining some cases of acts of State authority comes mainly from the fact that petitioners or claiming States invoke imperative norms *(jus cogens)*, form which States cannot derogate in their mutual relations by agreements with other States, by unilateral statements or by reservations to multilateral treaties[446], mainly from norms concerning the prohibition of serious violations of human rights and of humanitarian law, in order to challenge State immunity.

In other terms, are the norms of jus cogens, which are substantial norms of the general international law and which should protect important values for the community of States, prevailing over the immunity of jurisdiction of States, which is a procedural norm that prevents the exercise of the competence of the courts of another State? If the immunity of jurisdiction is recognised even in such cases, what are the remedies available to victims of serious violations of human rights, in order to avoid impunity? There is thus a need that international law remains coherent and protects all legitimate interests, those of States and those of victims of serious violations of human rights. It should be the golden rule that no serious violation of human rights remains without a proper sanction under international law; in any case, the issue should be pursued by other means under the State responsibility for unlawful acts.

---

[446] As presented above, chapter I, pp.20-28.

SECTION I – Applicable law

1. International law contains some customary norms in this field, as developed in the United Nations Convention on Jurisdictional Immunities of States and their Property[447], adopted by the General Assembly on 2 December 2004 by the resolution A/59/508, on the basis of the draft submitted by the International Law Commission in the exercise of its mission of codification and progressive development of international law.

According to this Convention, a State enjoys immunity, in respect of itself and its property, from the jurisdictions of the courts of another State. A State has to give effect to State immunity by refraining from exercising jurisdiction in a proceeding before its courts against another State and to that end shall ensure that its courts determine on their own initiative that the immunity of that other State is respected. A proceeding before a court of a State is

---

[447] According to data available on 4 December 2017 the Convention was ratified by 21 States and it needs 30 ratifications to be in force. Germany did not ratify it and Italy ratified it after the dispute with Germany, considered herewith. In the case Jones v. Ministry of Interior of the Kingdom of Saudi Arabia, commented herewith, a member of the Chamber of Lords characterized this Convention, while not yet in force, „as the most authoritative statement available on the current international understanding on the limits of State sovereignty in civil cases" (cited by Elina Steinerte and Rebeca M. M. Wallace, in AJIL, vol. 100/2006, International Decisions, p. 902). Is also retained that the Working Group of the International Law Commission noted the current interest in the interaction between the issue of State immunity and jus cogens, but concluded that the issue was not ripe enough to engage in a codification exercise over it (the Chairmen's report, doc. A/C.6/54/L.12, para. 47).

considered to have been instituted against another State if that other State is named as a party to the proceedings or, even if it is not named, if the proceeding in effect seeks to affect the property, rights, interests or activities of that other State. According to the Convention, some privileges and immunities of States are reserved from the start and are not affected by the Convention. This concerns the exercise of the functions of diplomatic missions, consular posts, special missions, missions or delegations to international organizations or to international conferences and persons connected with them, privileges and immunities accorded to heads of State *ratione personae* and the immunities enjoyed with respect to aircraft or space objects owned or operated by a State.

A State cannot invoke immunity from jurisdiction if it has expressly consented to the exercise of jurisdiction by the court of another State with regard to a matter or a case, by an international agreement, in a written contract, or by a declaration before the court or a written communication in a specific proceeding. A State also cannot invoke immunity of jurisdiction if it instituted itself the proceeding before the court of the other State or intervened in the proceedings relating to the merits, unless it intervenes for invoking immunity or asserting its rights or interests in property at issue. Furthermore, a States cannot invoke immunity of jurisdiction in a proceeding concerning a dispute arising out of a commercial transaction in which it is engaged with a foreign natural or juridical person, if according to private international law such a dispute falls within the jurisdiction of the court of another State, as well, as under some conditions, with regard to contracts of employment.

In an article entitled „Personal injuries and damage to property", the Convention stipulates that a State cannot invoke immunity from jurisdiction before a court of another State which is otherwise competent in a proceeding which relates to pecuniary compensation for death or injury to the person, or damage to or loss of tangible property, caused by an act or omission which is alleged to be attributable to the State, if the act or the omission occurred in whole or in part in the territory of this other State and if the author of the act or omission was present in that territory at the time of the act or omission. The comment of the International Law Commission to this text, proposed in its report to the General Assembly, says explicitly that this provision does not apply to situations involving armed conflicts[448].The text is interpreted as referring to isolated acts, to incidents which are not frequent in international life[449].

2. The European Convention on State Immunity was adopted within the Council of Europe on 16 May 1972 and is in force since 1976[450]. According to article 11 of this Convention, a State cannot claim immunity from the jurisdiction of another State in proceedings to redress for injuries to persons (including bodily harm, negligent bodily harm, and manslaughter) or damage to property, irrespective of whether the tort was carried out by the State *jure imperii* or *jure gestionis*. The conditions to apply this rule are that the act or omission took place in the territory of the forum and that the person who committed the act or omission was present in the territory of the forum at the time of the act or omission.

---

[448] Yearbook of the International Law Commission, 1991, vol. II, part II, p. 45(the last comment on this article).

[449] . According to Christian Tomuschat, L'immunité des Etats en cas de violations graves des droits de l'homme, in RGDIP, 2005. I, p. 69.

[450] The European Convention was ratified by 8 States only. Germany is party to the European Convention, not Italy.

On this subject, after a laborious activity of preparation, the UN General Assembly adopted the resolution nr. 60/147 of 16 December 2005, which proclaimed the Basic Principles and Guidelines on the Right to Remedy and Reparation for Victims of Gross Violations of International Human Rights Law and Serious Violations of International Humanitarian Law. The resolution does not mention immunity of jurisdiction of States in connection with such serious violations of human rights and contains references to norms of international law sanctioning mainly violations committed by individuals. Nevertheless, according to provisions of the resolution concerning the scope of the obligation of States, they have the duty to provide those who claim to be victims of a human rights or humanitarian law violation with equal and effective access to justice irrespective of who may be ultimately the bearer of responsibility for the violation and to provide effective remedies to victims, including reparation. The references to humanitarian law show clearly that situations of military conflicts are not excluded.

Therefore, there is no norm of international conventional law in force on the immunity of jurisdiction of States. It remains to see to what extent norms of international customary law are applicable. For that, different cases of the internal and international jurisdictional bodies are examined in order to see what are the trends and the solutions proposed and what is their effect in international life.

SECTION II - Immunity of jurisdiction for acts committed in connection with the Second World War

1.The first case where the immunity of jurisdiction of States was contested for acts *jure imperii*, as violations of imperative norms (jus cogens) was that of prefecture of *Voiotia v. Germany*, judgment by the Leivadia district court, upheld by the Hellenic Supreme Court. The district court awarded damages of approximately $ 30 million as indemnity for atrocities including willful murder and destruction of private property committed by the German occupation forces on 10 June 1944 in the village of Distomo, a war crime by a massacre among the population of this village[451].

Although according to the Greek Constitution a generally accepted rule of international law constitutes an integral part of the Greek legal order, prevailing over any statutory provision to the contrary, the Greek courts based this decisions mainly on the European Convention on State Immunity adopted within the Council of Europe on 16 May 1972 (to which Germany is a party, but not Greece), considering that it constitutes a codification of pre-existing customary law in continental Europe.

The Greek courts referred to international practice and concluded that there is a customary rule of international law which excludes State immunity in cases of torts committed in the territory of the forum by persons (agents of a foreign State) present in this territory, even if they were *acta jure imperii*. The courts also took into account the fact that the atrocities attributed to the German State were committed during an armed conflict, for which immunity is retained, but they eliminated the application of the exception in that case, referring to a rule of the Regulations

---

[451] As presented by Maria Gavouneli and Ilias Bantekas, in International Decisions, The American Journal of International Law, vol. 95, pp.198-204.

Concerning the Laws and Customs of War on Land attached to the 1907 Hague Fourth Convention, according to which in case of military occupation that is directly derived from an armed conflict, crimes carried out by organs of the occupied power in abuse of their sovereign power do not attract immunity. The courts considered that among the crimes not protected by immunity were reprisals against a specific and limited number of innocent people who were not involved in sabotage acts carried out by underground groups and in the resistance, activity resulting in the death of German soldiers, that such acts were not objectively necessary to maintain the military occupation and were carried out in the territory of the forum in an abuse of sovereign power.

The conclusion was that such acts were in breach of peremptory international law and were not acts *jure imperii*. The main argument is that such acts represent crimes of war and crimes against humanity, violating imperative norms of international law.

Analysts of the Greek court's argumentation note that consideration is given to the nature of the violated norm, in particular if it constitutes a peremptory norm of international law, the violation of which entails personal criminal liability even in cases when these acts would have otherwise been described as *jure imperii*. They also note that this position is not universally accepted and that in most of the cases the courts affirmed State immunity[452].

Later-on, the Constitutional Court of Greece corrected the jurisprudence of the Court of Cassation, declaring that the norm of immunity of jurisdiction of States exists and is applicable even in cases where the courts have to pronounce themselves on serious

---

[452] M. Gavounelli, I. Bantekas, art. cit., pp. 201-202.

crimes committed within the Greek territory. The ministry of justice of Greece refused to give its agreement to the execution of the decisions of the courts on German properties in Greece.

As the Greek petitioners could not obtain the execution in their country of the decisions adopted, they requested an exequatur at the Court of appeal of Florence. The Court of appeal gave the exequatur requested and inscribed a judicial hypothec on a building affected to cultural activities by Germany[453].

2. Another case in this respect (*case Ferrini*[454]) concerns acts committed by German troops after the armistice between Italy and Allies in 1943[455]. German forces who occupied most of the Italian territory were responsible for serious violations of humanitarian law. Victims or their inheritors introduced proceedings against Germany or against individuals involved but requested the condemnation in solidarity of the German State, which is allowed according to the Italian law. This raised the issue of immunity of jurisdiction of Germany, as its military conduct represented an act *jure imperii*. The Italian Court of Cassation adopted 13 ordinances and a decision responding to a series of civil requests submitted to different Italian courts by victims of the crimes of deportation and forced labour, or by their inheritors. The Court affirmed the conclusion to which it arrived in the case Ferrini, according to which a State accused of committing international crimes has no right to immunity of jurisdiction

---

[453] Natalino Ronzitti, La Cour Constitutionnelle italienne et l'immunité juridictionnelle des Etats, in AFDI, vol. LX, 2014, p. 4.

[454] Presented by Carlo Focarelli, Denying Foreign State Immunity for Commission of International Crimes: the Ferrini Decision, in International Comparative Law Quarterly, 2005, vol. 54, pp. 951-958.

[455] Extensive presentation by Natalino Ronzitti, art. cit., pp. 3-15

granted by the international customary law. Following this decision, number of other petitions were introduced, and judgments were pronounced condemning Germany to damages for violation of humanitarian law.

Germany invoked decisions of internal and international courts which recognized immunity even in cases where the defendant State was accused of violation of jus cogens[456]. The Italian Court of Cassation responded to this argument that the respective cases evidenced that there was not a certain and explicit international custom according to which it was possible to derogate from the principle of jurisdictional immunity of States in civil cases for acts *jure imperii* of such a seriousness as crimes against humanity, but these decisions cannot be considered to give expression to a custom which would be contrary. And the Court affirms that a principle limiting the immunity of a State author of crimes against humanity is in the process to take shape.

The Court presented the State immunity of jurisdiction as coexisting in the international legal order with a parallel principle of equal general scope, according to which international crimes threaten the entire humanity and undermine the mere foundations of the coexistence of peoples. After placing the two norms on an equal footing, the Court applies the primacy of the norm of a superior rank, that concerning respect for human fundamental rights. And the Court maintains that international order would not be coherent if it would admit that States are submitted to foreign

---

[456] Cases cited by Carlo Focarelli, Immunité des Etats et Jus Cogens, La dynamique du droit international et la fonction du jus cogens dans le processus de changement de la règle sur l'immunité juridictionnelle de Etats étrangers, in RGDIP, no. 4, 2008, p. 765-766.

jurisdiction in cases of alleged violation of contracts and not in cases of much more serious violations, which are true crimes against humanity and mark a departure of the tolerated exercise of sovereignty. The Court concluded that Germany is not entitled in this dispute to immunity of civil jurisdiction of the Italian judge[457].

Without contesting the norm on the State immunity of jurisdiction for *acta jure imperii*, the Italian Court basis its decision essentially on the primacy of an imperative norm which forbids the crimes against humanity.

Germany introduced an action to the International Court of Justice, on the basis of the jurisdictional clause of the European Convention of 29 April 1957 on peaceful settlement of disputes, to which both States are parties. The ICJ retained[458] that, by submitting Germany to the jurisdiction of its courts, Italy violated the customary law on sovereign immunity of States and rejected the Italian arguments to the contrary. The Court did not accept arguments according to which military activities are justiceable because the unlawful act was committed on the territory of the State of forum, and that the immunity of jurisdiction was not applicable if the State was responsible of crimes of war and crimes against humanity, for violation of norms of jus cogens. The Court ignored also the argument that by admitting the immunity of jurisdiction of Germany, the victims did not have any other alternative remedy available. The Court requested Italy to adopt adequate legislation or use another method of its choice so that decisions of its courts contrary to the immunity of jurisdiction of Germany are deprived of effect.

---

[457] Inconsistencies in the reasoning of the Court are analysed by C. Focarelli, Immunité des Etats et Jus Cogens, art. cit., pp. 768-772.
[458] CIJ, Germany v. Italy, decision of 3 February 2012.

The Italian government followed the decision of the Court, adopting a law to give effect to the 2004 UN Convention mentioned above, ratified by Italy thereafter, setting forth that if the ICJ adopted a decision against Italy declaring that the foreign State could not be judged, the courts should *ex officio* declare their incompetence and that decisions already adopted should be open to a revision and cancelled.

The decision of the ICJ is considered as contradictory: on one side it accepts the immunity of jurisdiction of Germany and considers that Italy violated this customary norm of international law, and on the other side, it considers that Germany violated international law because it refused the status of war prisoners to the Italian military deported by German occupation forces and detained in Germany after the Italian armistice with allies, leaving these persons without juridical protection[459]. The decision of the Court maintains this injustice, because it leaves this issue unsettled. It is true that the Court mentions the possibility of new negotiations between the two governments to find a solution to the problem of claims of Italians resulting from the treatment of Italian military prisoners detained in Germany, but makes no recommendation to Germany to this effect.

The Italian Constitutional Court adopted in 2014 a decision affirming that the judges should not execute the decision of the International Court of Justice[460]. The Constitutional Court started from the point of view that international norms which are contrary to fundamental principles of the Constitution, such as the inviolable rights of human persons and the right of access to a judge, are not part of the internal order and remain outside of the

---

[459] CIJ, decision of 2012, para. 99.
[460] Cour Const., no. 238, decision of 22 October 2014.

Italian legal system. Applying it to this case, this means that the international norm is not applicable in the Italian legal order, because it forbids the judge to consider acts which produced a serious violation of humanitarian law. The Constitutional Court also declared unconstitutional the internal law mentioned, because it obliges the judge to deny its competence to examine such acts and thus represents a serious violation of inviolable human rights. According to the Court, the Italian courts cannot give effect to international judgments which ignore one of the supreme principles of the Italian legal order and foreign governmental powers cannot be protected when this leads to committing crimes of war and crimes against humanity and violate inviolable human rights.

As for the customary law, according to the Italian conception, each customary norm is immediately transposed in the national order with an equal value to a constitutional norm, but if it is contrary to fundamental principles of the Italian Constitution it remains outside the internal legal order. Consequently, the Constitutional Court admitted that the norm of immunity of jurisdiction of States is submitted to the constitutional control[461].

The Italian Constitutional Court is not clarifying whether the norm of jurisdictional immunity has a procedural character, as underlined by the ICJ, or a substantial one. This is particularly important, because if it has only a procedural character, it means it does not prevail over imperative norms of respect for human rights and humanitarian law; its effect is only not to accept the competence of jurisdiction of the courts of foreign States, but it leaves open other possible remedies were the application of the imperative norm can be claimed.

---

[461] As presented by N. Ronzitti, art. cit., p. 9-11.

3. The ICJ decision was followed by the Supreme Court of Poland in the case *Natoniewski*[462], concerning also a request of reparation to victims for damages caused by German occupation during the Second World War. The Polish Court accepted the plea of immunity of jurisdiction of State and rejected the application, declaring that there are insufficient grounds for recognizing an exception to State immunity in cases concerning redress for breaches of human rights, occasioned by unlawful acts committed in the territory of the forum State which come within the category of armed activities.

4. The *Supreme Court of Slovenia*[463], in a case concerning a claim of damages for an activity which took place in the territory belonging now to Slovenia, found that „there was a trend, but no norm of customary international law, which in case of violations of the cogent norms of international law in the area of human rights protection, as a consequence of State activities in the framework of *jure imperii*..., would allow Slovenian courts to try foreign States in such cases".

5. The *Court of Cassation of France* also recognized the immunity of the German State in cases alleging that French

---

[462] Decision of 29 October 2010, text in Polish Yearbook of International Law, vol. XXX (2010), p. 299; extensive presentation and analysis by Marcin Kaldunski, State Immunity and War Crimes; The Polish Supreme Court on the Natoniewski Case, in Polish Yearbook, 2010, pp. 235-241.
[463] The Constitutional Court of Slovenia, judgment of 8 March 2001, Case Up-13/99.

citizens were deported and submitted to forced labour in Germany[464].

As a more general trend, the international law doctrine emphasizes the evolution of conceptions towards recognizing the right of individuals victims of armed conflict, of massive violations of human rights or of humanitarian law to obtain reparation of damages suffered, following the norms of responsibility of States for unlawful acts (restitution, compensation, satisfaction and assurances and guarantees of non-repetition)[465].

6. Another interesting case, partly related to the Second World War, was initiated by *Von Dardel* on his behalf and on behalf of *Raoul Wallenberg v. Soviet Union* before US courts in 1984. Raoul Wallenberg, a Swedish diplomat, was arrested in 1945 in Budapest by Soviet forces and then suffered imprisonment and possible death in Soviet Union. He was acting in Hungary during the war at the initiative of the US government for saving the Jewish population from deportation in Nazi concentration camps. As Soviet Union did not participate in court and invoked jurisdictional immunity only by diplomatic channels, the District Court considered that for several reasons immunity was waived or lost and pronounced a decision condemning Soviet Union by default[466]. The US General Attorney intervened in 1989 and on behalf of the

---

[464] Cases Bucheron, decision of 16 December 2003, nr. 02-45961 and Grosz, decision of 3 January 2006, nr. 04-47504.

[465] Evolution presented by Natalino Ronzitti, art. cit., pp. 12-13, and in particular the resolutions adopted by the International Law Association of 2010 and 2014. See also Theo Van Boven, Basic Principles and Guidance on the right of reparation for victims of (gross) violations of human rights and international humanitarian law, doc. E/CN.4/Sub.2/1997/104, of 13 January 1997.

[466] US District Court of Columbia, 623 F, Suppl. 246(1985)

United States decided that this case be dismissed for lack of subject matter and of personal jurisdiction. The decision taken retained that the absence of presence to the proceedings does not mean losing the State immunity, that the allegation of violation of an international agreement or of the internal legislation of the defendant does not mean losing jurisdictional immunity and that international conventions invoked (on diplomatic privileges and immunities) do not contain an implicit waiver of immunity of jurisdiction[467].

As it is known, some issues were not settled after the Second World War, because a peace treaty with Germany was not concluded. Germany paid for damages caused to some States and to citizens of other States. Germany signed two agreements with Italy, a Treaty concerning compensation for Italian Nationals Subjected to National-Socialist Measures of Persecution and a Treaty on Settlement of Certain Property Related Economy and Financial Questions. There is no information whether the two treaties concerned the Italian military prisoners and these treaties were not invoked during the proceedings. There is also no information in the cases considered whether the alleged victims of violations in Poland, Slovenia and in other States and territories in Europe could receive any compensation from Germany after the war. The peace treaty with Italy as well as those with Bulgaria, Hungary, Italy and Romania could not solve issues concerning individual claims towards Germany.

---

[467] US Attorney, June 29, 1989, US District Court for the District of Columbia, on behalf of USA.

SECTION III - Other cases

1. In the case *Al Adsani v. UK*[468], the European Court on Human Rights considered an application against British courts which denied to the petitioner, who alleged being submitted to torture in the State of Kuwait, the right to submit a request on this issue against the State of Kuwait. The petitioner maintained that a State which violates a norm of jus cogens loses the legal benefit of the jurisdictional immunity, placing itself out of the limits of international legal order and that international law recognizes an exception to the principle of jurisdictional immunity of a State and of its officials in cases of civil law concerning reparation for acts of torture.

The Court found by a narrow majority that there was no breach of article 6.1 of the European Convention, considering that the decision of the House of Lords of 2006 did not amount to an unjustified restriction on the applicant's right to access to justice. It followed the decision of ICJ of 2012, according to which there was no general acceptance in international law of the principle that a peremptory norm creates an exception to State jurisdictional immunity in respect of civil claims for damages for torture.

With regard to the extension of jurisdictional immunity to State officials, ECHR noted that although there was some emerging support in favour of an exception to immunity in cases concerning civil claims for torture against foreign State officials,

---

[468] Application nr. 35763/97, decision of 21 November 2001. Extensive and critical presentation by Xiaodong Yang, State Immunity in ECHR; Reaffirmations and Misconceptions, in BYIL, Issue 1, January 2003, pp. 333-408.

the State's right to immunity could not be circumvented by suing the individual servants. One cannot ignore that the Convention against torture of 1984 established universal jurisdiction in relation to torture; it can be interpreted to obliging only States parties in which the torture occurred to provide for a civil remedy to victims. It seems that one should see also the contribution of this Convention to form a customary norm of international law, after more than 30 years of its adoption and an extensive practice of its application by 162 States parties (situation in August 2017). Also, it seems difficult to follow this conception, while State officials can be pursued under international criminal courts' statutes, including the Rome Statute of the ICC, for crimes of genocide, crimes of war and crimes against humanity. Why not in civil jurisdictions for damages caused by the same crimes? How could be justified a different system for criminal and civil law cases? At the same time, ECHR noted that, in light of developments under way in favour of an exception to immunity in case of State officials, States parties to the European Convention should keep this area of law under review.

In the case *McElthinney v. Ireland*[469], an applicant injured by a shot fired by a British soldier pursued an action against the British government and argued that rules granting State immunity could not infringe the applicant's right to a fair trial under article 6 of the Convention. The Court accepted the plea of State immunity, maintaining that the Convention, including art. 6, should be interpreted in harmony with rules of international law.

The case *Fogarty v. UK*[470] raised the issue of discrimination by a foreign State. The applicant issued proceedings

---

[469] Application nr. 31253/96, decision of 21 November 2002.
[470] Application nr. 37112/97, decision of 21 November 2001.

claiming that she was a victim of sex discrimination and a violation of article 6.1 on access to justice and of art. 14 on non-discrimination. The US government claimed State immunity. The ECHR retained that the right of access to justice under art. 6.1 is not absolute and that the right of immunity of a State from jurisdiction of courts of another State pursued a legitimate aim of complying with international law purpose to promote comity and good relations between States.

In the case *US v. Tissino*[471], an Italian citizen sued the US government for damages arising out of the storage of nuclear weapons at an air force base, allegedly in violation of international law. The Italian Court of Cassation held that the US enjoy State immunity, noting that international practice since the Ferrini case favoured immunity even when States are accused of international crimes and that the Arrest Warrant of 11 April 2000[472] of ICJ makes clear that jus cogens violations alone do not provide the basis for lifting immunity.

In the case *Jones v. Ministry of Interior of the Kingdom of Saudi Arabia (*cited above*)*, Jones and three other applicants, all UK citizens, alleged that they were repeatedly tortured while in prison in Saudi Arabia and suffered psychological and physical harm as a result. They requested damages from Saudi Arabia and its officials. Saudi Arabia claimed immunity on its own behalf and for its officials. The task before the House of Lords was characterized from the beginning as that of considering the balance between "the condemnation of torture as an international crime

---

[471] Court of Cassation nr. 4461, 25 February 2009, in Oxford Report on International and Domestic Courts, 1282, 2009.
[472] Case R. D. Congo v. Belgium, ICJ Reports, 2000.

against humanity and the principle that States must treat each other as equals not to be subjected to each other's jurisdiction".

The House of Lords based its reasoning on that of the ECHR in the case Al-Adsani, concerning the question whether allowing State immunity as a procedural bar would be inconsistent with a peremptory norm of international law (the prohibition of torture), and the conclusion of the European Court according to which despite increasing recognition, it is not yet established in international law that States are not entitled to immunity in respect of civil claims for damages for alleged torture. It was underlined that the application of State immunity in such proceedings operates as a procedural bar, while the prohibition of torture is a substantive rule and that accepting State immunity does not mean justifying torture[473].

Analysts criticize the reasoning behind the decision in the Jones case for not taking into account the evolution in international law and mainly for extending the State immunity of jurisdiction to its officials in cases of violation of the prohibition of torture, as being in contradiction with the Statute of the International Criminal Tribunal for former Yugoslavia (art. 7) and with the Rome Statute of the International Criminal Court (art. 25, 27 and 28). They also consider the decision concerning the immunity of officials for committing acts of torture as being in contradiction with the Convention against Torture, because it is leaving no way to victims of torture to obtain civil redress for the suffering in a foreign country[474]. The case Jones was also submitted to the ECHR, against UK. The Court followed the decision of ICJ of 2012 and

---

[473] Case Adsani v. UK, cited above, p. 140.
[474] Case Democratic Republic of Congo v. Belgium, ICJ Report, 2000, p. 24.

said that this decision represented an authoritative statement on the contents of the norm of the immunity of jurisdiction of States. It excluded that the imperative character of the interdiction of torture has the effect of depriving of immunity the defending State[475].

Some cases were also considered by international or European bodies with regard to decisions taken by courts of Canada. The Committee Against Torture, created by the Convention on this subject of 1974 to monitor the application of the Convention, required in its observation to the decision of the *Ontario Court of Appeal of Ontario in the case Bouzari*, that the State party review its position in respect article 14 of the Convention which requires that States provide an effective remedy to victims of torture. The Court of Appeal of Ontario recognized State immunity to Iran in civil proceedings alleging torture. The Committee specifically asked how the State party implements article 14 of the Convention, remarking that there was no peremptory norm of international law that prevented States from withdrawing immunity of foreign States in cases of claims for liability for torture[476]. It seems that nobody claimed that such a peremptory norm of international law would exist; the question was whether the prohibition of torture, which is recognized as an imperative norm, excludes State immunity of jurisdiction in civil cases for damages when a crime of torture is alleged.

The State party should answer how it will implement article 14 of the Convention which requires to provide an effective

---

[475] Extensively presented by Elina Steinerte and R. M. M. Wallace, art. cit., pp. 906-908; applications 34356/06 and 40528/06, decision of 14 January 2014.

[476] Committee Against Torture, Summary Record, second part of the 646-th meeting, UN Doc. CAT/C/SR. 646/Add. 1, 2005, para. 67.

remedy to victims of torture and makes no exception to this requirement.

In the case *Kezemi v. Iran*[477], which was not submitted to other bodies, a Canadian citizen, photograph and journalist, visited Iran in 2003, was arrested, detained and interrogated, beaten and sexually assaulted, tortured, and lately died as a result of injuries sustained during the custody in Iran. Only one Iranian official was indicted, then acquitted. In 2006, a civil proceeding was opened in Quebec for damages against Iran and some officials. Iran opposed State immunity. The Quebec Supreme Court dismissed the action in respect of State immunity but found a statutory exception applicable to proceedings relating to personal injury and allowed the appeal. The Supreme Court of Canada dismissed the appeal, noting that the peremptory norm of jus cogens (the prohibition of torture) has not yet created an exception to State immunity from civil liability in cases of torture committed abroad.

Many analysts refer to cases treated by US courts considering cases of immunity of foreign States for serious violations of human rights either on the territory of US or in other States. The practice of the American courts on the basis of the Foreign Sovereignty Act (FSIA) is not uniform and does not offer a solid point of support for conclusions. Analysts noted that at some point in time it was uncertain exactly what the present US law of sovereign immunity was[478].

---

[477] Supreme Court of Canada, 2014 SCC 62(2014) 3 S. C. R.176, decision of 10 October 2014.
[478] Bruce Telles, Van Dordel v. USSR: Overcoming the Defense of Foreign Sovereignty Immunity in Cases under Alien Torts Act, in Boston College International and Comparative Law Review, vol. 10,

In the case *Letelier v. Chile*[479], applicants initiated a civil tort action before US courts against some individuals and against Chile for conspiracy, assault, reckless transportation of explosives, murder and violation of international law which led to the killing of the ambassador of Chile in the USA (an adversary of the president in function). The judgment had to be given in light of the Foreign Sovereignty Immunities Act (FSIA) of 1976. The applicants rejected the sovereign immunity of Chile in the tort action on the basis of FSIA. The USA courts refused immunity of jurisdiction of Chile but did not accept the execution of property of the State to respond to claims for damages.

Another interesting case considered by US courts is *Amerada Hess Shipping Corporation v. Argentina*, introduced in 1987 by this Liberian corporation which hired a ship Hercules to transport oil. The ship was attacked in 1983 by the Argentinian war planes in the context of the Falkland/Malvinas war and badly damaged. The District court dismissed the case, then the US Supreme Court granted review of the case and the Court of appeal found Argentina responsible for the attack. Then the US Supreme Court cancelled the decision, retaining that the act was not committed on the territory of USA and that the arguments invoked (mainly from the law of the sea) do not create an exception to the State immunity according to FSIA[480].

Issue 2, 1987. The author refers to cases Filartiga v. Paraguay, Forti v. Argentina, Siderman v. Argentina and Berkovitz v. Iran.

[479] US District Court for the District Court of Columbia, 488 F, Supp. 665(DDC)1980).

[480] US District Court 488 US 428, 109 S. Ct. 683; 1989 AMC 501(US January 23, 1989).

* * *

The cases which followed after the decision of the ICJ confirmed the immunity of jurisdiction of Germany, but did not offer to victims of the alleged violations any possible remedy, which leaves them in a situation of denial of justice, if one takes into account for instance the declared position of Germany with regard to Italians (not to recognize them the status of war prisoners and not to consider forced labour their work during the period of detention).

Other decisions taken by regional or by national courts reached the same conclusion, using mainly the same arguments; they accepted the imperative character of the norms invoked and the procedural nature of State immunity of jurisdiction before the courts of other States, but recognized that State immunity, including of officials of the State, can be invoked as an exception to the jurisdiction of other States concerning civil claims. No remedy was envisaged or offered to the victims of acts of torture or of crimes against humanity.

The situation in which the application of the rule of State immunity of jurisdiction leads to impunity and to denial of justice for the victims of serious violations of human rights is not acceptable and should not be accepted by States, courts, international organizations, by the legal profession as a whole. This is also not taking into account the evolution concerning the jurisdiction in cases of acts of torture, which should be universal according to the Convention of 1974 against torture and to the Rome Statute of the International Criminal Court, which includes in the jurisdiction of the Court crimes against humanity committed by individuals, including undoubtedly their civil aspects.

States should find a solution, in order to avoid leaving victims of serious human rights violations and their inheritors *in limbo*, without any remedy to protect their rights. Analysts say also that other ways should remain open and should be used in order to compensate at least partially for the prejudice suffered by the violation of individual rights. Some authors indicate the classical instrument of diplomatic protection, or to seize the ECHR if someone's own State committed the act violating his rights[481]. This seems, nevertheless, to leave it to the willingness of the State of the victims, while that State may be in a difficult position to protect the interests of its citizens. On the other side, one should not exclude the action by the individual if the State chooses not to act in such cases.

International organizations, international and national courts as well as States, in particular those directly involved in each situation, have to make efforts to find such solutions. It is not any more a question of recognizing culpability, sometimes after more than 70 years, but a question of protection of a fundamental human right, that of access to justice, as well as of credibility and responsibility towards victims of serious violations of their fundamental rights. Probably, as some analysts say, it would be impossible to open the way to millions of individual requests and to punish all the population and future generations of some States for the crimes committed by a governmental clique. But this does not mean that victims of such serious violations of human rights and of humanitarian law should not be protected. As an ad-hoc judge at the International Court of Justice affirmed in its dissident

---

[481] On this subject Christian Tomuschat, L'immunité des Etats en cas de violations graves des droits de l'homme, in RGDIP, 2005, I, p. 56, 70.

Opinion to the decision of the Court on the case Germany against Italy mentioned, „The fact that military activities may cause injuries on a large scale does not seem a good reason for depriving the many potential claimants of their judicial remedies. It may be that in practice the remedy will not be effective, but this applies more generally to all claims brought against foreign States, given the difficulty for successful claimants of enforcing any judgment that may be obtained"[482].

Some analysts made a distinction between positions of governments (of Italy and Greece mainly) and that of internal courts of these countries, which was noted by Germany before the ICJ. Analysts suggest that, considering that national courts' decisions generally represent powerful social forces and pressures, some of which executive branches may be hesitant to follow, there would be a merit to incorporate such judicial national decisions into the set of factors that determine the content of customary international law[483]. This does not seem to be a new idea; the jurisprudence of internal courts was usually taken into account in the evaluation of the international practice, to appreciate if a norm of customary law was formed; the difficulty remains to give the necessary weight to this jurisprudence in the context of other acts of international practice (international conventions, political and diplomatic unilateral or joint statements, decisions of international courts or arbitration bodies). But this is an issue pertaining to the formation of customary norms of international law, not to their application with regard to State immunity of jurisdiction in cases of

---

[482] Dissident Opinion of the ad-hoc judge Giorgio Gaia, ICJ, case Germany v. Italy, decision of 3 February 2012, p. 223.
[483] Opinion defended by Ingrid Wuerth, International Law in Domestic Courts and the Jurisdictional Immunity of States Cases, in Melbourne Journal of International Law, vol. 13, pp. 1-19.

civilian claims, which remains as an issue to which a satisfactory solution has still to be developed.

CONCLUSIONS

The developments analysed above show that there is not a uniform approach in Europe with regard to some institutions and norms and there are differences form the general norms of international law. Of course, this is not something new, but in Europe there are two systems of law and two courts of justice to which the same 28 member States are parties, forming the majority of the States on the continent. Probably the most salient aspects of this situation appeared with regard to the treatment of migrants and asylum seekers, in the context of the recent crisis determined by a massive flow of migrants towards Europe (identified usually as a problem of security for European States, which tends to separate it from its human aspects). Some approaches advanced and followed by the EU institutions and member States, mainly through the Dublin agreement and related secondary legislation, are different from those provided for in the 1951 Convention on the status of refugees and in the Covenants on human rights, as well as those promoted by the European Court of Human Rights on the basis of the European Convention of 1950 on human rights and fundamental freedoms to which all the 28 (still) member States of the Union are parties. The EU approach of excluding individuals from the examination of requests of asylum because they were previously condemned for crimes of war, crimes against humanity or acts of terrorism is not accepted by ECHR; the same with regard to the presumption that all member States of EU respect human rights and do not control each other's situation in this field; the absolute character of the right to life and of the interdiction of torture and inhuman and degrading treatment, emphasized by ECHR, is not always followed during the examination of requests of asylum by national courts of the EU member States.

Moreover, procedural norms concerning the protection of human rights in case of detention of asylum seekers (like access to an effective remedy, to a counsel, the duration of detention, the right to be heard and to be informed about the reasons of detention) were often not respected in EU countries and this led to reports of the UN Commissioner for Refugees and of other institutions, as well as to petitions before ECHR. The decisions of ECHR contained direct critical considerations of the functioning of the Dublin system and proposals of changes in order to make it compatible with human rights. ECHR formulated clearly the principle that the creation of international organizations or arrangements of cooperation in different fields does no exonerate States from their responsibility according to the European Convention of 1950 to observe human rights in the respective fields. Agreements concluded by EU institutions with Turkey concerning centers of detention of potential refugees to Europe and exchange of such refugees with Greece, at a rate of one to one, were heavily criticized by specialists for completely ignoring the rights of individuals and all procedural rights related to asylum.

European jurisdictions also gradually challenged internal acts of member States adopted in order to implement resolutions of the Security Council which decided that UN member States adopt measures to freeze assets of individuals related to Al-Qaeda and the Taliban's and other measures to restrict some of their human right (to travel, to work and others). The CJEU cancelled such acts of the EU institutions for being in contradiction with the EU fundamental rights of fair trial and defense and obliged the EU institutions to create their own mechanism to ensure the exercise of such rights in relation to the application of the respective sanctions. Although initially ECHR considered that it cannot control such internal acts because that would mean to control indirectly the validity of the Security Council's resolutions, then it stressed that national courts should control the compatibility of such internal acts with the human rights under the 1950 Convention. This may be considered a positive evolution, having in view that the application of the respective Security Council's resolutions was not accompanied at the level of UN by procedures ensuring access to an effective remedy and to defense (or by requests to national courts to resort to such procedures) in order to protect human rights.

On the occasion of the examination of a contestation of the validity of a regulation of the EU Council on this issue, CJEU formulated the conception that the legal order of the Union is independent, and that the validity of internal EU acts should not be considered according to norms of international law, but in conformity with the EU law. This conception was reaffirmed in other CJEU decisions. This places the EU as a subject of international law practicing a dualist system, according to which EU norms can depart from norms of general international law; such general norms can be introduced in the EU system of law only if they are explicitly adopted as EU law. The majority of EU member States adopted, historically, a monist system, considering that norms of general international law are part of the national corpus of law. Some EU member States follow the dualist system, but they added a kind of mechanism to ensure that internal law is not departing too much and for longtime from norms of international law (presumption of compatibility, interpretation so as to avoid conflict and finally the modification of the national law). It doesn't seem that CJEU has considered all the consequences of the dualist conception, in view of the position of EU as a subject of international law and of member States on this matter.

In the field of the protection of environment, where the European Union had always the initiative, some difficulties appeared with regard to the control by expert bodies created by international agreements of the conduct of EU as a party to these agreements (adopted with strong support of the EU). Recommendations of such bodies of experts, addressed to EU to ensure respect of some of the provisions of those agreements concerning access to an effective remedy (namely to justice) for alleged violations of the rights of the public (to receive information, to participate in decision making and to challenge activities affecting the environment), were not accepted by EU institutions; consequently, meetings of the parties which considered such recommendations were adjourned. This affects the independence and the integrity of the respective meetings of experts.

The same attitude can be seen regarding the accession of EU to the European Convention of 1950 on human rights and fundamental freedoms, to which EU committed itself through the Lisbon Treaty of 2007. Efforts to fulfill this commitment failed until now, despite negotiations with the Council of Europe which led to a draft agreement. The main reasons opposed by CJEU are that: States members of the EU could use some provisions of the 1950 Convention against some rules and practices of the EU concerning relations between member States; some provisions of the EU law would be interpreted by ECHR, without the advice of CJEU; the validity of acts adopted by EU institutions (in the field of the Foreign and Defense Common Policy) could be challenged by individuals before ECHR, while they cannot be challenged before CJEU; according to the 1950 Convention States parties can adopt legislation giving more protection to human rights than what is granted by the Convention. Essentially, such arguments relate to some action and interpretation by EU member States, which they can already exercise as parties to the 1950 Convention, to the autonomy of the EU law, and to the control by ECHR of some activities within the EU system, which is all the interest of EU accession to the 1950 Convention. No argument was submitted regarding the substance of human rights under the Convention of 1950 and the Charter of fundamental rights or about increased protection of human rights within both systems or by a better cooperation between them.

A separate chapter refers to European and other States' positions regarding the non-use of force and of threat to use force, considering that some European States are involved in such actions on the territories of other States. Moreover, the conception is advanced that there would be an evolution leading to changes in the application of this fundamental principle of international law, mainly meaning an extension of cases of legitimate use of force (to humanitarian cases) or of the right to self-defense in other situations than that of an armed attack (like in response to terrorist attacks). An analysis of the newest UN documents and of the position of the majority of States shows that such ideas are not accepted by the international community of States, which is not ready to give a place in international law to unilateral acts of use of force.

International criminal courts, regional and national courts in Europe recognize increasingly the existence of imperative norms of international law, refer to such norms and try to develop a motivation of their decisions accordingly. This represents a significant contribution to the development of international law.

There is also an interesting evolution with regard to immunity of jurisdiction of States before the courts of other States in civilian cases, when the violation of imperative norms of international law was invoked and such norms were not contested. Some national courts adopted decisions on retaining the responsibility of other States for facts committed during the Second World War or for other facts considered unlawful and attributed to other States, which were clear violations of some imperative norms and caused prejudice to individuals. Following the jurisprudence of the International Court of Justice, such decisions were not accepted by ECHR or by superior courts, which did not contest the imperative character of the norms invoked and did not take a stand on the responsibility of the States concerned, but considered that the State immunity is a general norm of international law which has to be respected. They accepted the use of the State immunity as an exception to the jurisdiction of other States, but they did not offer any remedy to victims of the harm inflicted to individuals, which risks to creating a situation of *de facto* impunity for the States concerned. This is a problem which remains to be solved in order to avoid the opposition of norms of the protection of sovereignty and equal rights of States to those of respect for human rights.

Another subject of interest is the jurisprudence of the two regional courts in cases concerning economic, social and cultural rights, although longtime considered non-justiceable. ECHR developed a consistent jurisprudence on the protection of these rights, although in connection with civil and political rights according to its Covenant. CJEU (which initially considered only cases concerning the freedom of circulation of labour and of discrimination) started more recently to extend its jurisprudence in these fields, based on the Charter of fundamental rights which sets forth also economic, social and cultural rights (along with civil and political). In this connection, it is interesting to see how EU institutions acted in a situation of economic and financial crisis affecting some member States (mainly Greece), by adopting decisions and positions which did not seem to take into account the protection of such human rights in the respective States in accordance with the Charter of fundamental rights of the Union.

With regard to the freedom of expression and opinion, international and regional regulations and the practice followed by the European Court of Human Rights show that the freedom of expression is not absolute. For the protection of some social and human values (interdiction of racist speech, of the exercise of expression meant to destroy the rights and freedoms of other persons, or of the denial of holocaust and of incitement to hatred and discrimination), the protection granted by international norms to the freedom of expression is completely refused by ECHR; in other cases, restrictions and limits are applied in order to protect reputation or other human rights or values that are considered important by the society or for national security or independence of the nations. The Court developed jurisprudence which recognized protection to publications as part of a debate, as well as protection of specific professions or public functions, like journalists, members of non-gouvernmental organizations, judges, counsels, members of parliament, although accepting that some of them may be more often subject to criticism.

The ECHR developed also jurisprudence with regard to defamation, clarifying the distinction between facts, which have to be proven and judgments of value which do not request a demonstration. The Court affirmed in a clear and constant way the conception according to which incitement to hatred, as a phenomenon which should not be admitted as exercise of the freedom of expression, does not suppose an appeal to acts of violence or to another offence.

To summarize, the Court defined some orientations, some basic directions, leaving open the possibility to differentiate in function of the context. This is why the practice of the European Court is not uniform, is marked by differences of evaluation of apparently similar facts and by an evolution in time, from a strict control to a more liberal approach towards the freedom of expression, which remains dominant.

The Human Rights Committee clarified, in its General Comments on the freedom of expression and opinion, the provisions of the Covenant on civil and political rights on this right, its limits and the responsibilities related to it, as well as its relationship with situations of emergency and the inadmissibility of reservations to or derogations from it.

The freedom of expression remains a ground of constant debate and a topical one within the European Court of Human Rights and other human rights bodies. There are nevertheless already areas of light which represent important points of departure in order to promote a solid application of the norms concerning the freedom of opinion and expression, taking into account all circumstances imposed by the respect for human rights as a global phenomenon.

The existence of two regional courts and two systems of norms and institutions, one within the Council of Europe, the other one within the European Union, offers not only different solutions of similar cases, but also different approaches, which leads to uncertainties and misunderstandings in some fields.

Of course, there are mostly common elements in the evolutions and approaches in Europe, as well as between evolutions in Europe and in other parts of the world with regard to institutions and norms of international law. They have the same basic sources-from Illuminists to the Charter of the United Nations, the Universal Declaration of Human Rights and the two Covenants on human rights, to which all European States and most other States are parties.

There is also no uniformity and coherence with regard to norms applied in Europe and there are aspects of departure from general norms of international law.

The book reflects both the common and different approaches and solutions, as well as efforts and trends to bring them closer and to ensure legal certainty.

Evolutions in Europe which are addressed in the chapters of this book should not be ignored, particularly when they affect human rights and freedoms. At the same time, they should not be exagerated, as there are already trends and efforts to bring the situation in line with principles and norms of international law promoted by the same European States. They are able to find the best solutions to respond to challenges, while remaining attached to principles of humanity, justice and cooperation.

www.ingramcontent.com/pod-product-compliance
Lightning Source LLC
Chambersburg PA
CBHW071018240526
45469CB00006BD/1969